BEYOND FRONTIERS

BEYOND
FRONTIERS

JASPER PARROTT
with
VLADIMIR ASHKENAZY

Atheneum *New York*
1985

Library of Congress Cataloging in Publication Data

Parrott, Jasper.
    Ashkenazy, beyond frontiers.

    1. Ashkenazy, Vladimir, 1937-   . 2. Pianists—
Biography. 3. Conductors (Music)—Biography. I. Title.
ML417.A83P4 1984   786.1′092′4 [B]   84-6211
ISBN 0-689-11505-9

To our parents, wives
and children

ILLUSTRATIONS

FOREWORD

It is strange how some important and difficult resolutions are made in the most unusual circumstances. The final decision that this book could and should be written was taken on a cable car half way up Mount Pilatus near Luzern on a fine late-summer day in 1980. The idea that my personal experiences could offer to an interested public some illumination of many issues of the greatest importance in the politically polarized world of the 1980s had taken considerably longer to formulate.

Jasper Parrott has worked closely with me as my manager and agent for over eighteen years. Our close and harmonious collaboration over this period has enabled us to spend a great deal of time talking about topics other than music and has given him a strong intuitive understanding of me from which to work. Inevitably, the events of my Soviet upbringing and the way that I have related them to my current evaluation of life in the West have been a most frequent subject of discussion between us. Jasper's own background – he is the son of a distinguished British ambassador who spent many years in Moscow and Prague – and his fairly extensive personal experience of life in the Soviet bloc did much to focus these conversations. This book, therefore, has had a much longer gestation than the three years actually taken to write it. The material itself was assembled in a series of taped conversations held at various times since September 1980 in all sorts of places around the world – in Amsterdam, Athens, Luzern, Vienna, New York, on a plane between Adelaide and Perth, and in a hotel lobby in Tokyo (here the tape has the melodious accompaniment of a party of Japanese ladies chatting over their morning tea).

The resulting material has been carefully reviewed and edited by us but inevitably represents only a stage in the continuous process of reappraisal which must be directed towards many of the difficult issues we have attempted to address. My life as an artist is, I hope, only at its half-way point. Enough time has passed, however, to enable me to see in some sort of perspective the contrasting natures of the systems which stand in confrontation across frontiers throughout the world. If we had let more time elapse, the resulting picture would probably not be materially different but my memories of my childhood and early manhood might well have begun to fade.

VLADIMIR ASHKENAZY

PREFACE

This book was begun in the summer of 1981, when Vladimir Ashkenazy had just turned forty-four. Despite his fame throughout the world, both as a pianist and as a conductor, he viewed with some dismay the prospect of contributing to his own biography, especially at a time when he hoped to be able to look forward to the same number of years again pursuing his life in music. And even at the end of his career he will doubtless view with little favour the idea that people should interest themselves much in anything about him apart from his music.

Books about musicians tend to fall into two different categories. In the first, the reader is regaled with details of the artist's rapid rise to fame and fortune, each stage embellished with charming anecdotes and descriptions of encounters with other famous people both inside and outside the musical profession. The second type of book is altogether more demanding, and aims to deal with questions of interpretation in musical performance, a hazardous field seldom covered convincingly even by the most discerning musical analysts.

Ashkenazy does not fit well into either of these categories. In any case he is probably too young a man to warrant an attempt at too definitive a portrait, not least because he prefers to be judged as an artist through the performances he gives in concerts or on recordings rather than through abstract, and necessarily imprecise, verbalizations.

He is an unpretentious man, constantly on the move, yet deeply absorbed in whatever he is doing or thinking. With apparently unlimited reserves of energy, he often gives the impression that time is always pressing, but this does not mean that he is austere or unapproachable. On the contrary, he is readily accessible and immediately friendly, especially towards music lovers. Those who know him well are impressed by his directness in dealing with people, regardless of their status. At times it is hard to believe that he is one of the best known, most widely admired and most committed of the luminaries of today's musical world.

He is, in fact, a very private man, devoted to his wife and five children and entirely uninterested in the aura of glamour which such celebrity inevitably imposes upon him. And yet he is idolized by thousands of fans and is constantly expected to give interviews for newspapers, television and radio, to make personal appearances in record shops and to sign hundreds of autographs after concerts. People want to know all about him, not just about his music but about what sort of person he is, and what his public and private lives are like. They want to know how many hours a day he practises, who his favourite composers are, what he does for recreation, whether he gives music lessons (he does not). They want to know how many children he has, what books he reads, what his political attitudes are. Many complete strangers write to him to express their admiration and appreciation for his concerts and recordings and, when he replies to thank them as he always tries to do, they write again to ask his advice or to pour out their troubles. This book attempts to satisfy some of this quite legitimate curiosity, even though its real themes are very different.

There are indeed special reasons for Ashkenazy's willingness to participate. His background is certainly unusual. Seeing himself partly as a free agent and partly a victim of circumstance, he has had the experience of seeing his work evolve in two totally conflicting social and political orders. Since his music provides the motivation and inspiration for his entire life, he sees his work as summing up all that he has learned, experienced and understood so far. For him, music is the noblest vehicle available to man with which to express his highest ideals and aspirations as he struggles to make a little sense out of a mysterious and unpredictable universe.

Ashkenazy's formative years in the Soviet Union were conditioned by life in a political and social system which, he is convinced, is inimical to all that is most valuable in man's spiritual and moral potential. His maturing and middle years spent in the West have been lived in circumstances which not only allow him the freedom of critical comparisons, occasionally not in the West's favour, but also the chance to seek out and hold on to a structure of values which he believes to have some permanence.

In the West there may be corruption, crime, the whole catalogue of human sins and frailties – all of which exist in the Soviet Union too – but the choice of living for higher ideals is there too if we can only remember to defend it. In the Soviet system there may be some areas where material benefits are less unequally distributed than in the West. But instead of encouragement of those characteristics which make man unique – his individuality, his spirituality, and his search for self-knowledge – Soviet man is confronted by a labyrinth of lies, an institutionalization of spiritual sterility and the suppression of his individuality. Ashkenazy knows these things from his own experience and would like them to be more generally understood. This, then, is both the theme and the purpose of this book.

I

VLADIMIR ASHKENAZY was born on 6 July 1937 in Gorky, a city
on the river Volga about 250 miles east of Moscow. His parents
David and Evstolia, whose maiden name had been Plotnova, had
been born in 1915 and 1916 respectively. The family name
Ashkenazy is, of course, inextricably connected with Jewish
history, in particular with that part of the Jewish nation which
settled in Eastern Europe, Russia and parts of Asia in the
centuries after the diaspora, while the Sephardic Jews spread over
North Africa, Spain and Portugal.

David Ashkenazy's father was by training a journeyman
mason but later worked as a book-keeper in a local soap factory.
He and his wife, a simple woman without any real education,
were deeply committed to the Jewish tradition and way of life,
even though they probably understood little of their historical
significance. David and his brother Mikhail went at first to
Jewish schools, but while they were still children their father died
and their uncle took over responsibility for them. He was a
convinced communist and moved them to the normal state
school; in any case most of the Jewish schools were closed during
the course of the early post-revolutionary years.

Anti-Semitism had been common enough in Russia throughout the centuries of Tsarist rule, but despite the active involvement of many Jews in the preparation and execution of the
Bolshevik revolution, Stalin's personal anti-Semitism led him to
sponsor their ever more implacable oppression. During much of
David Ashkenazy's life it has been difficult to be both Jewish and
patriotic; as a result he has always had ambivalent feelings about
his background, feeling, like so many Soviet Jews, at the same
time distinctly Jewish and intensely Russian.

Vladimir's uncle Mikhail showed some musical interest and
talent when he was in his early teens and was given the opportunity of taking piano lessons. David sat in on some of those lessons

and could not keep away from the piano when it was not in use. He quickly taught himself to play by ear and to improvise on tunes he had picked up and, by the time he was thirteen, his extraordinary aptitude for this enabled him to find jobs locally as the piano accompanist for silent films. When he was fifteen he had his first formal piano lessons and was able to make further progress with his music one year later when he entered the Gorky Technicum, a type of school where music, acting and the arts were taught alongside technical and engineering skills. Later he worked briefly as a metal worker.

Although he had obviously received some training in classical music, his amazing gift for improvisation and for popular and folk music quickly brought him to the attention of the local talent scouts for the Gorky branch of the Estrada, the nationwide concert organization for popular entertainment. The type of variety show it put on enjoyed considerable popularity throughout the Soviet Union and received practically unlimited official support in its guise as entertainment for the people, untainted by bourgeois intellectualism. The Estrada network provided entertainment for all sorts of audiences and occasions, from factory celebrations and Party gatherings to concerts for the armed forces and shows at official institutions.

These programmes would include a variety of different acts for which music was required primarily as an accompaniment. David Ashkenazy soon proved himself to be an exceptionally versatile pianist for this sort of show, and in a small place like Gorky the word spread fast that a useful new talent had appeared. While still a student at the Technicum he found himself in considerable demand. He was quick-witted, had a precocious flair for show business, and the local organizers and Estrada artists snapped him up.

The maternal side of Vladimir's family was, by contrast, pure Russian. His grandfather had been trained as a violinist and later served in the Military Band of a regiment of Hussars stationed in Warsaw, at a time when Poland was effectively a province of the Russian Empire. Later, on leaving the army, he became choirmaster of a local church in a small village called Puchesz in the Volga region. He had perfect pitch and was very concerned that his choir should sing with good intonation. He kept up his violin playing, too, and later taught at a local music school in the small town of Gorodetz, some thirty miles up-stream from Gorky on the Volga. He had ten children in all, but two died in their infancy. Of the eight remaining children, seven were girls; his son was killed tragically as a Soviet soldier in Berlin in May 1945, just one week before the German capitulation.

Vladimir's mother Evstolia was also a student at the Gorky Technicum, where she studied acting, and she seems to have met her future husband at one of his Estrada concerts. For him, indeed, a career in Estrada seemed the obvious choice, especially when economic pressures began to loom. A successful Estrada artist could earn very good money right from the start if he were in demand and there were plenty of other advantages from being in so popular a *métier*; not least being the many opportunities for making contacts at Party and bureaucratic levels. David and Evstolia got married sooner than might otherwise have been considered sensible at that time in Soviet Russia, but a child was already on the way.

Vladimir's birth did not prevent his father from getting caught up in his new career, which offered a very exciting life for a young man. He may have felt that his new family responsibilities were something of an encumbrance but he obviously decided that he was not going to let his wife and child clip his wings. During Vladimir's childhood, David was rarely at home and travelled constantly all over the Soviet Union; later, after the war, he also went on tours abroad. He was certainly much enamoured of this roving way of life, enjoying to the full the freedoms which his tours allowed him. He would disappear with a group of artists for weeks on end, doing much as he liked apart from giving concerts. These could be performed with the minimum of rehearsal once on the road, and in the meantime he could enjoy the unusual pleasures of mobility, very often free food and always free accommodation in a country otherwise inured to years of restrictions and austerities. Despite this agreeable vagrancy, he was nonetheless devoted to his family and made sure that they were well provided for financially; fortunately, he earned very good money by Soviet standards, and so this never posed a real problem.

Perhaps as a direct result of these long periods of separation from her husband, Vladimir's mother devoted herself all the more to her son, her only close companion and a child who, from a very early age, began to show quite extraordinary musical gifts. Unlike most Soviet married women, Evstolia did not go out to work; gradually and perhaps inevitably a sort of blind adoration for her son became all the more intense as his musical gifts revealed themselves. At the age of two or three he began to sing some of the numbers his father used to play and both his parents were struck by the excellence of his intonation. His mother was especially delighted because she sang beautifully herself and had a great love of and respect for music, presumably as a result of the important role it had played in her father's life. Her son's musicality must have seemed to her to be compensation for, even vindication of, all the sufferings and loneliness of those years when she felt half abandoned by her husband.

This later led to some difficulties for David since Evstolia was obliged to make most of the decisions not only regarding the family's domestic life – in this area it is almost unheard of for a Russian man to take any interest anyway – but later about Vladimir's musical education. Despite the recognition and success that his exceptional talent for the type of performances he gave brought him, David apparently felt some sense of inferiority later on as far as his son was concerned. Even though success in the Estrada could bring considerable status, it did not have quite the kudos associated with classical music. Certainly, Evstolia tended to look down on the things her husband did, which made it all the harder for David to contribute much to his son's up-bringing and education. Vladimir was in any case brought up in an entirely Russian and non-Jewish atmosphere. His father had himself had no real contact with Judaism and very little with Jewish traditions; his prolonged absences from home ensured that even the latter were not passed on to his son. Vladimir was baptized in an Orthodox church and only much later, as a schoolboy, realized with confusion that his name identified him as Jewish rather than Russian.

'Even though I am half Russian and half Jewish, I actually feel much more Russian. This may have something to do with genes but in fact it was my mother who brought me up; my father didn't participate at all in my growing up or education – he was always on tour. And even when he was at home in Moscow, he was at rehearsals or concerts. Very occasionally, he took me to a concert or to the public baths – we had no bath at home, and I couldn't really go to the baths with my mother once I had started to grow up. So my contact with my father was extremely limited. But even so, my father is not so Jewish; he considers himself very Russified and thinks of his home country as Russia.

'I myself do not feel that I am marked or affected in either a positive or negative sense as a performer or artist by the Jewish part of my background, primarily because I was brought up in a Russian environment surrounded by Russian literature and Russian music. I was even christened in an Orthodox church, and I feel close to Orthodox Christian ideas, at least in principle.

'Later on, at the Central School I had many Jewish friends, since Jews are generally very prominent in the musical world; there were many talented Jewish boys even though they never quite constituted the majority, presumably because the school authorities were afraid to have too many Jews. It really was not very advisable in the fifties, especially at the time of the campaign against the Doctors in 1952 which must have been partly inspired by Stalin's personal paranoia about Jews – he really was unbelievably anti-Semitic. I had Jewish friends who knew that my father was Jewish and so I tended to gravitate towards them, although at that time my father had for a while to perform under the name Ashkenazy-Plotnov. Actually my two best friends were not Jewish, but four or five other close friends were, with families to some extent devoted to some Jewish traditions and ideals. In their houses, I felt a sort of cultivated Jewishness and I remember that I did not particularly like being there; I didn't feel a part of it at all. And when their mothers and fathers said, "But your father is Jewish", I would reply, "Well, so what?"

'However when it comes to musical relations with Jewish artists, none of this background has any bearing on our collaboration; if I feel less close to some or grow apart from others, this is entirely a question of personality rather than of Jewishness. I don't care if they are Armenian or Jewish or Indian, provided that I get on well with them on a personal and musical level. Also, I don't feel that Jewish artists who know me well ever impose any sort of special expectations on me; people like Daniel Barenboim or Itzhak Perlman or Uri Segal think of me as a Russian, not as a Jew. If anyone ever said that I make music in a Jewish way, I would say that this was complete nonsense; firstly I don't and secondly, why should I? – there is no basis for it! And in any case, what is the Jewish way?

'I once told Itzhak Perlman that I thought that the Barmitzvah was the ritual of circumcision – and for him that was really the last straw!'

In 1940 the Ashkenazy family moved to Moscow but, following Hitler's surprise invasion of Russia in the summer of 1941, the family was evacuated from the capital. At first it was a wandering evacuation; a troupe of Estrada artists and their families lived and travelled together, sometimes staying in hotels but at other times living in the same railway car as they moved from city to city, stopping a few nights in each place before moving on again in another train. Ashkenazy remembers the car very well, although it was only much later that he could appreciate how squalid this way of life must have been, with so many families living together in a carriage with only the most basic sanitary facilities. They went east of the Volga, to the Urals and even as far as Siberia. Later, they stopped for some months in Tashkent where David left his family behind while he carried on with the rest of the troupe. That was a difficult time; relations between Vladimir's parents were not too good and the accommodation in Tashkent abominable. They lived in one room with another family and Evstolia went out to work to earn some extra money, when the funds sent back regularly by David were held up by the inevitable confusion of wartime communications. Vladimir remembers that cooking facilities were primitive in the extreme and that they had to share a kettle with several other families.

'We had to sleep on the floor because there was virtually no furniture except for one table in the kitchen area. Inevitably there were lots of quarrels and I remember that one particularly unpleasant woman got furious with my mother, probably because she tried to protect me in some way or another. She poured boiling water over my mother's leg, pretending afterwards that it had been an accident. My mother had to go to hospital for treatment.

'I also remember having to go to hospital myself for a hernia operation. Fortunately, it all went perfectly well, but my mother was in a complete panic. I suppose I was very lucky, really, because without proper hygiene and with that primitive equipment I could easily have died. I also remember how hot it was in Tashkent.'

Eventually they heard that David had gone on to Moscow and was working there, having been given the chance of something relatively regular through his Estrada contacts and his reputation for success. He seems to have been rather slow about arranging for his family to join him. A special permit has always been needed to live in Moscow and during the war this was even harder to get than usual. This was in the spring of 1943 and the German army was still rather close to Moscow, so Evstolia simply decided to take a chance and go. She sent her husband a cable to say that they were on their way and left it to him to arrange the permit as best he could.

'When we came to Moscow in 1943, it wasn't actually so badly damaged because the defence had apparently been very effective. Besides, it seems not to have been Hitler's policy to destroy Moscow as he tried to obliterate Leningrad. As a result there were undamaged hotels and thanks to my father's Estrada connections we lived in them for several weeks. We had to move on every so often because you couldn't stay in the same hotel for more than a few days at a time without some sort of formal police registration. For that you'd have to have the proper Moscow residence permit stamped in your internal passport but, since we had arrived relatively unexpectedly, we didn't have this and had to move on before each hotel passed on to the police details of our registration. I am sure that even a few days without the proper details were illegal, but during the war it was difficult to keep track on all the comings and goings of people arriving in or departing from Moscow. Later, in peacetime, the police became much more effective with all these sorts of controls and now, of course, they can use the latest computer technology, thanks to the help of the West.

'By this time my father was able to pull quite a few strings – you know, *blat* as it is called in Soviet Russia. Since artists of his kind were very much in demand at that time when there was so little entertainment of any kind available, they played all the time for government functions, or at embassies or for the allied military missions. This meant that they were in a very privileged position; they and the people involved in defence were always able to get the best supplies. My father also had enough money, so he could afford to pay for the hotels. I have no real way of judging what those hotels were like. At that age I saw that there was a bed and a table and a chair and after Tashkent that seemed more than enough.

'I remember that I caught all the usual childhood illnesses, measles and mumps and even scarlet fever which was at that time rather dangerous. Through his connections with the foreign embassies my father was able to get hold of a brand new medication from the West. This was simply not available in Russia and was indeed rather experimental in the West. Without it, it might really have been serious.'

As a further result of his excellent contacts, David managed to get allocated to them a room of eight square metres in a communal apartment. An aunt moved in with them and a small kitchen was shared with four other families; there was no bathroom, just a single toilet, again shared with the other families. Later, in 1949, the birth of Elena, Vladimir's sister, further added to the noise and overcrowding. All the washing for all four families had to be done in the kitchen. There were, inevitably, constant quarrels.

'My mother took great care of me, especially when I started to play the piano and when she realized that I was gifted. She treated me like crystal glass and because of this kept on getting into squabbles with the neighbours.

'Even so most of the time we had remarkably good relations with them, considering the conditions. As for the other families, well, they were straight from Gogol or from a Chekhov story. There was a widow with a grown son – he was eighteen or nineteen – and she was practically blind with glasses as thick as binoculars; she could hardly see at all. Despite this, she went to work every day, as a typist, and her son later went into the army. We were quite friendly with her. Then in the room next to us, the same size room as ours, there was an old widow or maybe a spinster; she was terribly quiet and gentle. The first widow often had the radio on at full blast and it was very difficult to sleep because the walls were just cardboard. In return, of course, when I practised she couldn't stand it but somehow despite all this we became friends and managed to balance things out. Then there were three very old ladies, all spinsters, sisters in fact; they weren't happy about having to live together and weren't happy about being spinsters. They were straight from old Russia – long dresses, always very heavy-looking, very heavy-thinking. And finally, the most important was a woman of between forty and fifty who was a real Baba-Yaga. She was just like a witch and she ruled the whole apartment. She was a heavy proletarian woman, terribly coarse, terribly loud and terribly difficult to get on with. She was always making problems in the kitchen, making things very uncomfortable everywhere. Everyone was afraid of her.'

In the Ashkenazys' room there was an upright piano on which David occasionally rehearsed on the rare occasions when he was not away on tour or working with Estrada groups in Moscow.

'His life really was extraordinary. As an accompanist he rarely knew until the last minute what was on the programme for any particular concert or who the other artists would be. When he arrived shortly before the concert, he would be told "Tonight you begin with the Italian-born artist who whistles, and then Boris comes on to play the harmonica. Your third number is a family of acrobats whose routine goes like this. You have to play this tune for about ten minutes but at this point when they start their big routine you have to do a big drum-roll on the piano to prepare for the climax . . ." He accompanied any and all sorts of people, from jugglers to opera singers to trick-cyclists. His ability to improvise was really astonishing and he could deal with any eventuality.

'I remember he told me once he came to a provincial place where there was a grand piano, a baby grand, but without legs or pedals! Fortunately there was a curtain, and so the curtain was opened just a slit and he played the whole concert, about forty-five minutes each half, with all these different people, you know, ballet and jugglers and I don't know what, lying down. And with those ballet people you have to watch, because you have to be together with them, so he watched through the slit. He said it was extremely difficult! And don't forget, it is one thing to play a slow melody, but in that type of variety show you would have a lot of very lively music, with the left hand going um-pah, um-pah, you know, and it's very difficult to do that sitting down, but to do it lying down, when you have no support – unbeliev-able! It really is a kind of wizardry!

'I wish that I could have some of his talent in this direction. Later I began to admire and appreciate him very much for what he could do, but as a child I tended to look down on it all, encouraged by my mother's attitude.

'I myself took very quickly and naturally to the piano and to music; once my first teacher explained to me how to read music, how the lines and dots worked, I began to read it very quickly, and soon could sight-read with unusual ease. This was when I was six. I learned so fast once I had started that it seemed as though it was something I already carried inside me and knew how to do without needing to be taught. This also happened with the theoretical side of music, including harmony, *solfège* etcetera. I only needed the very first clue to put me on the right road, then all the rest seemed like second nature.'

While the war lasted, piano lessons were hardly a priority; there was little energy or thought for anything but survival. In Tashkent in their one overcrowded room a piano would have been an impossibility, but once they settled in Moscow and the threat from the Germans receded, Ashkenazy's mother decided that a piano teacher had to be found for him. Contact was eventually made with a good teacher from a local district music school, and lessons commenced on a private basis in August 1943, soon after Ashkenazy's sixth birthday. Many musical children begin much earlier and he would probably have done so too but for the war and the conditions of their life as evacuees. Today, Ashkenazy feels that an earlier start would have been of no crucial significance since even with the most precocious of musical children, solid work can seldom be undertaken before they reach the age of eight or nine.

In each Moscow district – and the same system applies in some of the other large cities – there is a music school which takes children between the age of about seven and thirteen. The children attend as, so to speak, out-patients, having music lessons in addition to the curriculum of primary education taught in the normal elementary schools. However, children with exceptional musical gifts can be selected quite early for the Central Music School, which acts as a sort of junior school for the Moscow Conservatoire.

In Ashkenazy's case, after only a few months of private lessons with the teacher his mother had found, he had made such rapid progress that he was recommended for enrolment in the local district music school. There his future teacher, Anaida

Sumbatian, who taught both at that district music school and at the Central School, spotted him and decided that he should move on as quickly as possible to the Central School. This involved taking an examination while he was still only seven before a panel of teachers and professors. To pass, the children had to be up to a high level of proficiency – unless they happened to be the children of officials or people with important Party connections, in which case they might be judged just a little more leniently. But even then they had to be more than competent and, once inside the Central School – and this was certainly the same at élitist schools in other fields – everyone knew very well who the well-connected children were, especially those with less talent than influence. The classes numbered around fifteen; some class-mates had to be treated with care and, even at the age of eight or nine, it was natural for the children to differentiate between the élite and those who had no such affiliations.

2

THE CENTRAL MUSIC SCHOOLS are a Soviet invention, but the conservatoire system in Russia has its origins in Tsarist times with the two oldest institutions, those of St Petersburg and Moscow being founded in 1862 and 1866 respectively. The brothers Anton and Nikolai Rubinstein were the instigators and first directors, Anton in St Petersburg and Nikolai in Moscow, both enjoying the support and patronage of the Grand Duchess Elena Pavlovna. At the beginning the St Petersburg Conservatoire was the more illustrious, but gradually Moscow developed its own prestige, helped in part by the fact that Tchaikovsky had been engaged from the outset as teacher of harmony. The Rubinsteins were committed to a far-reaching programme of music education throughout Russia, their plan being that every major town would have its schools for music at elementary, intermediate and advanced levels.

By the time of the Revolution, some progress had been made along these lines and, as well as at least forty elementary music schools, conservatoires had been established in Kiev, Odessa and Saratov. However, it was only after the mid 1920s following far-reaching educational reforms introduced by Lunacharsky that the process which has produced a system of music education unique in its range and coverage really got under way. By the early 1970s there were twenty-four conservatoires in the Soviet Union, most of them with their own closely linked central music school. These in turn were affiliated with over two thousand children's elementary schools and some 190 intermediate level music schools. Although it is clear that there are wide divergencies in the quality of teaching in all these different schools and conservatoires, with those of Leningrad and Moscow tending to maintain their pre-eminence, the curricula are all unified and centrally controlled by the Ministry of Education. This provides extraordinary scope for the cohesive and uninterrupted training of musicians and teachers whereas by contrast music education in the West has always been haphazard and unco-ordinated, especially at the crucial elementary stages.

The pyramidic structure of Soviet music education has its base in the children's elementary music schools (*detskaya muzykalnaya shkola*) where children with an obvious aptitude for music begin at the age of seven or eight.

These schools are for music only and the children take all other subjects at a normal elementary school. This parallel system of schooling continues for five to eight years depending on the student, after which the child can graduate to a so-called technicum (*muzykalnoye uchilische*) where music, as well as other artistic subjects, can be taken alongside some other general studies. At the age of eighteen, the successful graduate will emerge with a diploma which allows entry as a teacher into the elementary school network. An exceptionally talented child can also have the chance of sitting an examination for entry into the conservatoire, but few succeed since competition is extremely keen for the few places available; most are taken up by graduates from the central music schools which provide an alternative 'fast lane' in the process of music education.

A child such as Ashkenazy who shows outstanding promise at the outset of his elementary schooling, may be encouraged to take the test for entry into the central school of music where music studies and instrumental teaching are integrated into the normal academic curriculum. This is partly to ensure that a musically talented child will not receive too one-sided a training and partly to enable children to opt out and move back into the normal school system without too much dislocation. Children remain at the central school for eleven years and, here too, those who graduate from it without going on to the conservatoire can teach in the elementary school system.

At the age of eighteen or so, students wishing to go on with their musical or instrumental studies take the difficult test for entry into the conservatoire; those who qualify, study for five more years before receiving their graduation diplomas. A few conservatoires offer a further post-graduate course called the Aspirantura, but this is available only to the most outstanding graduates.

The conservatoires have offered places to musicologists since the reforms of 1925 but despite this the emphasis has always been upon the training of performers, even if many of these subsequently become teachers. What is perhaps most impressive about the central school and conservatoire system is the consistency of the schooling available. In his excellent book *Music and Musical Life in Soviet Russia 1917 to 1970*,* Boris Schwarz points to the example of the violinist Viktor Tretyakov who won the first prize in the violin contest of the 1966 Tchaikovsky Competition. By that time, throughout his years at the Central Music School and the Conservatoire, he had had only one teacher, the outstanding pedagogue Professor Yuri Yankelevich. Although Ashkenazy's schooling involved two different teachers, their approach could be appropriately integrated because of the close affiliation of the Central School to the Conservatoire. This system may well help to account for the fact that so many Soviet performers are, at least in their technical and musical preparation, extraordinarily secure and self-confident. They may be weak in other areas – and for this the whole Soviet system may, as will be discussed extensively later, be responsible – but these talented children face up to the challenges and stimulus of conservatoire-level teaching with the sure foundation of a thorough and consistent preparation under expert guidance; in addition, they have lived in a truly musical environment from an early age with the obvious advantage of daily contact with other children of similar talent and motivation. Only in a very few and quite experimental cases has the West been able to offer anything remotely comparable.

On the negative side, however, there are indications that the intellectual environment at the conservatoires had tended to be conservative and restrictive in everything apart from music; even in music, curricula have not kept pace with changing international attitudes and there has always been an excessive concentration on Russian and Soviet music with a corresponding neglect of twentieth century non-Soviet music. Moreover, there seem to be continuing difficulties in coming to terms with some of the greatest composers, most notably Bach, Mozart and Beethoven. It is no coincidence that the majority of young and even mature Soviet performers seldom offer works by these composers in their programmes; when they do, the results are often thought to be unidiomatic and generally unconvincing.

* Barrie & Jenkins, 1972.

Non-musical subjects at the conservatoires appear to be treated routinely almost as a necessary duty rather than as an enlargement of the student's cultural and intellectual horizons. They are very much geared to Party-line education – as is, of course, all schooling at intermediary and graduate level in the Soviet Union – and required subjects include dialectical and historical materialism, Marxist-Leninist aesthetics, Marxist-Leninism itself and the history of the Communist Party. Ashkenazy remembers that these classes were endured by the students with a mixture of apathy, boredom and contempt; they could not be treated lightly, however, since the teachers responsible for these subjects were obviously not people to be trifled with. Indeed, Ashkenazy remembers that his main teacher for Marxist-Leninism was really impressive. He was a graduate of the highest Party school and an important KGB contact.

It is difficult for the average Western European or American accustomed to so many different stimuli and challenges to conceive of what it would have been like to grow up in Soviet Russia, especially during the 1940s and 1950s. Not only was daily life highly regimented with an almost total lack of freedom of choice in so many of the areas which are taken for granted in the West, but further burdens were added by the sheer difficulty and laboriousness of every aspect of day-to-day existence. Transportation, buying food or clothes, going to the doctor or dentist, getting shoes or other objects repaired, having leaks in the roof attended to – any and all of these matters could present the ordinary Soviet citizen with unbelievably time-consuming and demoralizing difficulties. Children became rapidly inured to this, and their expectations in the fields of recreation or entertainment were modest by Western standards. An intensely musical child, therefore, had one immediate and substantial compensation – an ever-absorbing occupation, even obsession, which could fill up each and every day, removing him from the arid and yet strenuous vacuity of Soviet life.

Ashkenazy remembers little of special interest to the Westerner about his life in Moscow as a child and adolescent. Although it might have appeared bleak to those brought up in the West, it seemed normal and eventful to him at the time. The highlights were visits with his father to football matches or to concerts, and summers spent in rented *dachas* in the country outside Moscow.

Other entertainments available to children included circuses, exhibitions, sporting events or perhaps Pioneer activities, but few of these impinged directly on him, in view of the rather special treatment he received as a musical prodigy for whom there were the highest expectations. He did join the national youth organizations which in practice are compulsory for all (although in theory voluntary), the Pioneers at the age of nine or ten and the Komsomols five or six years later, but he does not remember being involved in any special activity with either movement. Each and every day was filled up with his schooling, his musical activities and his homework. As for practising, he remembers that he always wanted to do as little as possible but was kept on the treadmill by the determined efforts of his mother.

'The problem was that I tended to learn the pieces I had to prepare for my lessons very fast, and so after that I didn't see why I had to do any more practising. I was far too immature to understand then that the more you work the better it could be. In the end my parents started buying me all sorts of operas and orchestral works in piano reductions so that I could be sufficiently motivated to sit at the piano, and it worked miraculously. Apart from broadening my general knowledge about all sorts of repertoire which I might otherwise never have studied, this did wonders for my sight-reading which eventually became exceptionally good. In the summers in our rented *dachas* there was always a piano, even though it was sometimes incredibly difficult to get hold of one to rent, not to mention all the problems concerned with having it transported. I didn't have any real understanding of what was involved at that age but I realize now how much my father must have wheeled and dealed to arrange these things. They could only be done by private arrangements involving bribery or barter or special connections.

'One summer when I must have been about fifteen and at the end of the Pioneer age-group, it turned out that an important Party leader, Voroshilov, began to take a rather public interest in music. A special concert was arranged for him at the Conservatoire and I and three other of the most gifted pupils at the Central School played for him. As a result, he arranged for all four of us to have a holiday in the most famous and élitist Pioneer summer camp in the Crimea called Artek. This was really reserved for the children of important Party people and the facilities were exceptionally good. It was the sort of place to which foreign visitors were taken to show off how much was done for youth in the Soviet Union. We had a very nice time with lots of swimming and activities of all sorts, all very disciplined. My friends and I did manage to find a piano so that we could do some practising, but it was a really horrible instrument.

'My parents sometimes took me to the Bolshoi, and that is where my love for the symphony orchestra began. I always liked to sit in a place where I could look over the orchestra pit; I was much more interested in what went on there than on the stage, which seemed to me to be very artificial and even ridiculous.

'I and some of my friends were voracious readers – whenever we could get hold of the books that interested us, that is. I remember that we read all the adventures of the Three Musketeers – all three books. We used to boast to each other about how one or other of us could remember the stories down to the finest details. But books were extremely scarce in the post-war years, so that even when something did come out, it was normally a very small edition which the ordinary person hardly had a hope of buying. You needed to be influential or have useful contacts to enable you to hear about an impending release and then get hold of a copy by fair means or foul before the book actually appeared at all.

'When I was about fourteen I heard that they were going to publish on subscription a fifteen-volume series of the works of Balzac. I decided that I wanted to get this but soon discovered that it was effectively unavailable before it even came on sale. However, I knew someone who had good connections in the black market and he said he could get it for me – at a greatly inflated price, of course. I asked my father to buy it for me and he could not understand why I wanted him to pay such a large sum of money for such an obscure series of books. I kept nagging him about it, however, until he finally gave in and went along with me to my black market contact. My father haggled like mad over the price and eventually we came away with the volumes. I felt so excited and read every volume from cover to cover – without really understanding much of what I read.

'As a child I don't think I missed much of what children usually do. I played football and was generally a very normal child, except that I didn't have much free time because of my music and other subjects I had to work on. But whenever I had an hour or two spare I would spend my time with other children and take part in whatever was going on. Still, there was a lot of resentment from other children in our housing block because I was rather gifted musically. In fact the children from the building where I lived were not friends of mine – they really seemed to resent me – even hated me, I think. I remember that it was as a child that I first realized that my name had special Jewish connotations; it was hard for me to understand what it was all about considering my very Russian upbringing when I found myself being called "Yid" by some of the children in our block.

'My friends were really all from the Central School; they were musically gifted, of course, and so I had lots in common with them and nothing I did seemed strange to them. Indeed, as I made progress and was obviously accepted as one of the most talented, I enjoyed a lot of respect from my school friends. It is, of course, wonderful to have a school where you can do all the normal subjects *and* music, to save time, and in Russia this is possible because there are schools like this in many of the main cities. In the West there are, by contrast, very few; I suppose the Menuhin school in England is a little like this but in general there seems to be insufficient initiative to set up such schools. It would have to come from governmental and municipal authorities and this always involves public money. In Europe, at least since the war, it would be politically very controversial to set up and maintain such avowedly élitist or specialist schools at public expense and so, of course, no one does anything about it.'

It is ironic that in the Soviet Union alone there should exist such abundant facilities for nurturing exceptionally talented children – the system of special musical schools is only one of a series of élitist institutions for children especially gifted in one field or another, as well as for the children of important Party members – and that this should have the effect of creating and maintaining a caste system of privileges which would be anathema to democratic socialists in the West. For Ashkenazy it is also one of the many inconsistencies and hypocrisies which permeate the whole of Soviet life. Even though he personally appreciates the benefit which this form of élitism bestowed upon him in terms of the development of his talent, he despises the way that it is dressed up as something quite different by official propaganda. It also infuriates him that most Western accounts of the system of musical education in the Soviet Union seem to take most of the propaganda at face value, but it no longer surprises him, given the generally superficial and uninformed attitude of Western commentators to almost everything in the Soviet Union.

3

'I FIRST MET Anaida Sumbatian in 1945, just at the end of the war in Russia. Things must have been very chaotic at that time, but oddly enough I don't remember this at all. I was still only seven then and everything seemed to me to be very ordered; I went to school regularly every morning for so many hours and did my practising and everything seemed to be quite normal.

'As one can see from her name, Sumbatian is Armenian by birth but she spent most of her life in Moscow; she was herself a pupil of a pupil of Yesipova, who was in her day a rather famous pianist. When I started taking lessons from her, she had in fact been teaching only for a few years. I owe her a very important debt.'

When he entered the Central School, Ashkenazy automatically became Sumbatian's pupil. It was soon very obvious that he was the sort of material that any successful teacher hopes to find, and she was certainly ambitious for him. But he has no doubt that she was also genuinely interested in him in artistic terms, wanting to help him to develop his talent in every way. She was especially effective as a teacher of young children and never went on to work with mature students. As a result, she did not enter the Conservatoire itself, although she could undoubtedly have done so if she had wished it.

'I believe that something inside her told her that she shouldn't – that it would not be right for her. But with young children, she was absolutely terrific. She inspired the imagination of her pupils with all sorts of associative ideas, something which works particularly well with children. She also had broad horizons as far as music was concerned. She encouraged me to go to orchestral concerts so that I would learn to think orchestrally at the piano. I remember as if it were yesterday her saying, "Look, in this piece, why don't you think of Bruno Walter conducting a fantastic orchestra – or perhaps Furtwängler . . ." Not that she needed to encourage me to go to orchestral concerts, since they were my great passion anyway. I spent all my pocket money on concert tickets but few of those were for piano recitals. I suppose that may well be the subliminal basis for my decision to take up conducting much later on.

'When it came to developing an artistic personality for a maturing or even adult student, she appreciated that a different approach was necessary. She had a very clear view of the proper priorities for her younger pupils and realized that for them some waters can be too deep. Very wisely and responsibly she left such areas of refinement to the professors and their teaching assistants at the Conservatoire. As far as the piano itself was concerned, I think it was she who knew how to bring out in me the real feeling of affinity for the instrument. This is partly a technical matter, if you consider sound production and everything to do with how the piano functions, but it was she who made sure that for me all of this became second nature.'

Even though Sumbatian did not teach at the Conservatoire itself, she had an important influence on the selection of the right professors for her pupils when the time came for them to move on. There is constant contact between the two institutions which are practically next door to each other, and the Central School is under the general supervision of the Conservatoire anyway. Teachers at the School often begin to get the professors from the Conservatoire to take an interest in the development of particularly gifted students long before they are ready to graduate, and some pupils are even officially registered in those professors' classes, so that they can be heard every month or so. In this way, Sumbatian arranged for Ashkenazy to be heard by Boris Zemlyansky, who was an Assistant to Professor Lev Oborin. She, therefore, played the crucial role in choosing the Oborin class for him and in establishing the contact with Zemlyansky, in the event a most perspicacious judgement on her part.

'In the last couple of years at the Central School, the teacher and pupil begin to think very seriously about the right professor at the Conservatoire. By the ninth or tenth grade one has often begun to develop likes and dislikes for certain professors; one might be attracted towards a certain type of teaching style or temperament. After all, the Conservatoire is only a few minutes walk from the School and is a sort of Mecca for the younger students.

'Oddly enough, even though I certainly knew about Zemlyansky and his teaching methods, I didn't really participate very much in the decision about who would take me on at the Conservatoire; for some reason, I didn't know so many people there. Sumbatian took the decision into her own hands and seems to have decided that it would be best for me not to go to the most obviously attractive and glamorous class, that of Heinrich Neuhaus. She may have been afraid that instead of devoting myself to hard work, I would be swept up into the wonderfully creative atmosphere of the Neuhaus class. There everything was rather easy-going with a lot of very heady talk – actually lots of wonderful ideas but not too much hard work. She knew that Neuhaus was the most attractive, the most irresistible force in the Conservatoire but she had a sort of sixth sense that I shouldn't go there.

'I am sure that she was right, too – I doubt if I would have survived there. There was so much admiration for him that he only had to say a few words to you and you would go home in a daze wondering how to interpret these great utterances. There was no hard-working assistant to balance the visionary aspects of Neuhaus's influence, and what I needed most of all at that age was very strong discipline. In any case that is where the process of self-discipline seems to have begun and, without it, I would have been lost later.

'Sumbatian may have imposed certain limitations on herself by working so much with children, but she provided a wonderful basis for my later development. Inevitably, and rightly for her rather young pupils, she was principally concerned with teaching them the piano and how to play not just naturally and attractively, but with imagination. This she achieved extremely well. It was Zemlyansky, I suppose, who really made music my life. For him it was always a matter of life and death. I don't remember specifically how much he expanded his lessons on a philosophical plane – although he certainly did so – but they were inspired and infused with the certainty that what one did, or at least tried to do, had a fundamental importance in an absolute sense.'

Ashkenazy remained at the Central School for ten years from the age of eight to nearly eighteen. He was still at the School when he was entered for the Chopin Competition in Warsaw* and, after winning the second prize there, went back to Moscow to take his final exams at the School as well as those for entry into the Conservatoire. This involved a five-year course with the further possibility of the post-graduate extension, the Aspirantura, to which very few actually progress; from about twenty-five graduates each year, probably only three or four are accepted. The Aspirantura course lasts about two and a half years, but Ashkenazy emigrated before completing the course. The Aspirantura is really a course of perfection for the graduate in his chosen instrument, although it is also possible to enter as a musicologist. Participating students have more time with the professors and have the right to give recitals at the Conservatoire. Later on, after completing the course, Aspirantura graduates have the right to teach music in a high school anywhere in Russia; the road may also be open to a professorship at a conservatoire. It may be a result of this particular system that many famous Soviet performers, including both instrumentalists and conductors such as Gilels or Kondrashin (Richter never taught) have tended to take an active role at professorial level in the Conservatoires of Moscow and Leningrad.

Graduate study at the highest level, therefore, as well as teaching itself, is clearly assumed to require the highest degree of accomplishment in performance. This may help to explain the consistently high level of preparation which has been achieved by several consecutive generations of Soviet performers; they have emerged from a system where successful public performance remains the principal objective of the training provided by the schools and conservatoires of music. In the West, with the exception of the Juilliard School in New York, and perhaps the Curtis Institute in Philadelphia, ambitions tend to be more modest. Too many teachers take up their teaching careers either because they have failed to develop successful activities as performers or because they never had such aspirations anyway. This makes it difficult for them to prepare their more promising pupils for a way of life and a level of commitment which they have never experienced themselves. There are of course, outstanding exceptions such as Rudolf Serkin, but as a general rule it is much easier

* cf. p. 45.

for a centralized state – and an all-powerful one – to call in the best and most illustrious artists to contribute to such institutions.

Nonetheless, Ashkenazy does not think that one should take these comparisons too far. He doubts whether the brilliant performing techniques of so many Soviet artists can be said to be the intentionally achieved result of a system concentrating exclusively on these objectives. He points out that in his own case his most admired teacher, Zemlyansky, was also a product of the Aspirantura, even though as a performer his achievements were limited. As a musician and teacher, however, he was quite outstanding and these were qualities which could also be recognized and fostered in the Aspirantura. Ashkenazy was in fact attached to Oborin's class, where Zemlyansky was only the Assistant. The contact with Oborin himself was less stimulating or fulfilling; they had little in common and there was no real personal rapport. Oborin also gave a lot of concerts and clearly preferred this to teaching. His lessons tended to be formal and routine; perfectly pleasant but not very inspiring. His heart never really seemed to be in his teaching, whereas Zemlyansky had an exceptional gift for finding the right way of working with each particular student and of releasing the best and most creative impulses in widely differing personalities.

Apart from Zemlyansky and Oborin, Ashkenazy had little direct contact with other teachers at the Conservatoire, although he did once play for Heinrich Neuhaus, whose former students had included Svyatoslav Richter and Emil Gilels.

'He was a powerful and remarkable personality and, because he had heard and liked my playing, he asked me to play for him again once or twice, just to see what I had to offer, I suppose. I attended his classes a few times and played second piano for one of his pupils. He was very encouraging and it was certainly a great experience to see him teach.

'He was no conductor but when a student played for him he would still conduct the music in such a way that you could not fail to understand what he wanted. It was so inspiring; I'll never forget those few occasions. He was revered to an almost exaggerated degree; girl students, in particular, would become besotted with him – it was almost a kind of hysteria. This was when he was in his sixties and seventies – I remember his seventieth birthday very well; he played a concert in the large hall of the Conservatoire. He died when he was about seventy-five, after I had left Russia.

'There were other influences, of course, since I went to a great many concerts, particularly orchestral concerts, but to some piano recitals too. Among the pianists I particularly admired Richter, of course. That devotion started from a very early age. I liked other pianists, too, but to a much lesser extent. Richter magnetized me, like he did so many others, and I wouldn't have missed his concerts for anything.

'I think that he communicated more than anyone else complete devotion and sincerity to his art. When I look back, this was what attracted me most to him then, and continues to do so today. I now understand that the strongest element in his magnetic appeal to audiences is his conviction that what he does is absolutely right at that particular moment. It comes from the fact that he has created his own inner world, absolutely complete in his mind, and if you argue with him about anything it's almost no use. He might say "Yes, perhaps you're right, but I just don't feel that way. This is what I feel and this is the way I play." And that's it. I often don't agree with him after the performance, but during it I can see that everything fits together and is completely sincere and devoted, and that wins me over. I'm sure that many people feel exactly the same but, in my case, since I am a practising musician, the fact that I am won over at the time of the performance is extraordinary. In almost all other cases I disagree right there and then at the moment when a performance is taking place!

'In addition to his many other wonderful qualities Richter is for me the greatest interpreter of Debussy; his playing really has three or four dimensions. It's not just beautiful sounds and beautiful sonorities; I find the imagination behind the sonorities unmatchable. There is a fantastic feeling of spontaneity and of "creating at this moment". In fact, everything is worked out before, but at the same time he always creates "at this moment", and this feeling is marvellous.

'He is, of course, in every way a great individual; maybe his legendary unpredictability is partly a defence against the negative impact of Soviet uniformity. There are many wonderful anecdotes about him and I remember one delightful occasion myself.

'Sometime in 1961 or 1962 I called on Richter to play

39

something to him, since he had kindly taken an interest in me. His wife opened the door when I rang and explained that although he would see me, he was in a terrible depression and was lying in bed reading *Moby Dick*. I went into his room and he greeted me lugubriously; it turned out that the reason for his despondency was the fact that he was trying to prepare the Shostakovich Preludes and Fugues but could not get through the G sharp minor Fugue without stopping. When I expressed some surprise at this, he got out of bed, went to the piano, started the fugue in question and duly came to a halt somewhere in the middle. "There you are, just as I told you," he said, climbing back onto his bed. Before he could immerse himself again in *Moby Dick* and his depression, I went to the piano myself and played the music I wanted him to hear, and he made some helpful and perspicacious comments. Then, since it seemed the right thing to do, I said "Why don't you try the Fugue again? I am sure you will get through this time." Reluctantly he went back to the piano and this time sailed past the difficulty triumphantly. He was very pleased, too, as though he was Ahab who had just succeeded in despatching Moby Dick.

'When I was at the Central School, I played hardly any concerts except for school concerts. But in the context of that particular set-up, those school concerts were and are very important because we always played in the Conservatoire. There are two halls there, the Big Hall, which isn't actually very big but is famous for all the best recitals and for orchestral concerts, and the Small Hall which is tiny. At the end of each year while we were still at the Central School, we had around twelve concerts per year in the Small Hall and one in the Big Hall. Naturally, it was a particular honour to be chosen for the Big Hall concert which would include a number of different pupils, each playing a five- or ten-minute piece depending on the repertoire they were preparing at that time. I was invariably chosen whenever I auditioned for the Small Hall concerts and there was a lot of competition even for the auditions. I was also chosen for the concert in the Big Hall whenever I was ready to play something. All of these concerts were very exposed because all the students and many of the professors from the Conservatoire went, particularly when the word got about that there was someone interesting coming up. This was one way that the professors and the whole musical world in Moscow would keep informed, and they would always come and listen if they heard that there was a new talent at the Central School. The general public could also have free admission to these concerts, and if there was a whisper about a new prodigy, more people would come and the word would spread further.

'As a result of this sort of reputation, I was often asked to play at events put together by the local Moscow organizations for concerts, including even Mosestrada, or the Moscow Estrada. There might be a seventy-fifth anniversary celebration for something like the Moscow Arts Theatre and for this they would invite perhaps a famous singer to perform an aria and a well-known pair of ballet dancers to do a number from the Nutcracker – in addition they might bring along someone like me who was known on the grapevine as a child prodigy.

'These concerts or celebrations would take place in all sorts of different venues ranging from the Arts Theatre itself to an Institute of Technology. From the age of ten or eleven I played six or seven times a year for occasions of this kind. It was, of course, very good exposure even though the concerts were completely unpaid. It was an honour to be invited to play and you never knew who might be in the audience and who might take an interest in you. There were many of these concerts – I played in the Institutes of Mathematics, Technology, Literature etcetera. I even played at the KGB Club in Moscow, but that was just before the Tchaikovsky Competition by which time I was really rather well-known. Obviously the KGB thought it was not worth wasting their precious efforts gathering information about child prodigies and decided they could wait for the finished product – either that or the musical grapevine didn't extend as far as the KGB. Perhaps they felt they should reserve their talent scouts for other types of investigation!

'I also played at a secret defence establishment. This was outside Moscow and I remember that we were all taken in a bus without being told the destination or the directions or anything. There was a big audience when we got there – very warm and interested – and I played a Chopin Ballade and something else. Then we were taken straight back to Moscow and were told that we had been to a secret establishment and that that was all we were going to be told about it. This, too, was when I was at the

41

Conservatoire but as a boy at the Central School I had played for many of these things, as well as quite often at other schools.

'This sort of opportunity was invaluable for young performers in giving them concert experience, but only a few in each year ever got the chance to participate. The initiative always came from outside as a result of the grapevine; you would have thought that the Central School and the Conservatoire would have tried to establish these openings themselves by making contact with the various institutions. For some reason, however, they never did, so all the opportunities went to a handful of students – those who had already established some sort of reputation for being exceptional.

'Otherwise, there was no machinery for organizing concerts for students in the provinces. For a while the Moscow Philharmonic had a series of Sunday morning concerts for children and they tended to engage students to play, but there could not have been more than five or six concerts per year and they inevitably tried to get only the most talented pupils from the music schools. They engaged me to play Beethoven Piano Concerto No. 1, I remember, but by then I was already fourteen. Kabalevsky apparently heard me play at this concert at a time when he was completing his Third Piano Concerto, which is called the "Youth Concerto". He came to the Central School to bring me the score and engaged me to play it at his Author's Concert with the Moscow Philharmonic, which he conducted himself. Apart from this concert in Moscow, I also played it twice with him with the second Leningrad Orchestra and again in Tallinn. This was in 1953 when I was still fifteen. The performances were successful, but he then asked Gilels to record it with him, which I thought was rather mean after our four concerts. Stupid too, because if it is supposed to be a "Youth Concerto" and it is being performed reasonably well by a young boy, why not have him for the recording as well? In fact, I know that Gilels really did not want to waste his time on it, but could not refuse because he and Kabalevsky were friends.

'Later, in 1955, when I won my second prize in the Chopin Competition in Warsaw, Kabalevsky quickly got hold of me again because he saw that I had become much more famous. He asked me to play the piece with him in Sochi and, in order not to offend him, I ended up by having to play it four more times that summer. It was very tiresome to have to prepare the piece again –

42

it really is trivial stuff – when I wanted to get on with the opportunity of playing real music in the concerts I was asked to play after the competition. When I won the first prize in the Brussels Competition in 1956, Kabalevsky started pressing me yet again to play his concerto, both in Moscow and Leningrad. I'm afraid I refused, saying that although I had been happy to play the piece as a boy, by now I had a lot of other music to play and I didn't really feel right any more for a "Youth Concerto".

'Nevertheless, I don't really like offending people, so when I won the Tchaikovsky Competition in 1962, which obviously put me on the highest level of public recognition in Russia, I asked Kabalevsky, who had been on the jury, whether he would like me to play the new version he had recently made of his Second Concerto – a real concerto, not a piece for youth. He was quite taken aback but he said that it was nice of me to offer and he would think about it. In fact, I emigrated a few months later.

'I feel that the whole story illustrates rather well how things happen in Russia. It was certainly very Soviet of him to get Gilels to record his piece without worrying about my feelings – prestige really tends to obliterate other considerations – but perhaps less Soviet of me to make peace when I was in a position to ignore him. I suppose that was why he was so taken aback!

'Of course, after the various prizes I won, the Chopin Competition, Brussels and finally the Tchaikovsky, it became progressively easier for me to play as many real concerts as I wanted and to a certain extent I could decide where and when I wanted to appear. However I don't remember very clearly how it all worked, what the procedures were. At that age when everything suddenly opens up for you, you just tend to take whatever is offered. It was exciting but very nerve-racking because it involved a sort of exposure which I wasn't used to. With the passing of time I became much more choosy and took more initiative in deciding what I would or would not do.

'I also began to play more often with orchestras in the provinces and at that time they were pretty awful. Or it may have been that the conductors were terrible but I couldn't tell and thought it was the orchestras' fault. We really did not have much basis for comparing orchestras in Russia at that time, and we were all used to the fact that they all played more-or-less out of tune all the time and with terrible ensemble. This may at least have contributed to my learning how to get on with conductors, however bad they were. My basic attitude then was that I had to play as well as I could and that it didn't matter too much what happened with the orchestra and conductor. My attitude is quite different now, of course, but at least it taught me how to make the best of bad circumstances.

'In the last fifteen or twenty years, the level of orchestral playing in the Soviet Union has improved considerably, even dramatically. This is partly due to the fact they started to buy foreign instruments and partly because people became aware of different standards in the West once the isolation of the 1940s and 1950s was broken down during the Khrushchev period and afterwards. By now, out-of-tune playing is a fairly grave crime but in my day it was the norm. We couldn't stand it, but we had to get used to it. At every concert we went to, even with supposedly the best orchestras, there would be continuous brass cracks, untuned woodwind chords and so on. We just knew that there was nothing that could be done about it. Then in 1955 the Boston Symphony came – the first foreign orchestra to visit since the war – and we all heard what an orchestra really could and should sound like. It was not just a matter of virtuosity or interpretation but basic ensemble and intonation. It was a sensation for us all, it really opened our eyes. Later, other foreign orchestras began to come, including the London Philharmonic and we continued to be very impressed, not only because of musical or artistic revelations but because the orchestral playing was on so significantly a higher plane than anything we were used to in Russia.'

4

ASHKENAZY ENTERED his first foreign piano competition in 1955 at the age of seventeen when he was chosen to represent the Soviet Union in the fifth International Chopin Competition in Warsaw. This competition was inaugurated in 1927, when it was won by Lev Oborin, and since then it has taken place approximately every five years, with an interruption between the third and fourth competition of twelve years because of the war and the German occupation. At that time musical life came to an almost complete standstill and Polish music including Chopin was banned. The competition has always enjoyed singular prestige and has attracted not only brilliantly talented young contestants but also, especially in earlier post-war competitions, distinguished international jurors. First-prize winners during more recent competitions have included such famous artists as Maurizio Pollini, Martha Argerich and Krystian Zimerman, the last, of course, being a Pole. The competition is held in the concert hall of the National Philharmonic Society in Warsaw and attracts the widest following and enthusiasm, particularly among young music lovers.

Despite Ashkenazy's age, he was the leading figure in the Russian contingent selected through a series of internal competitions involving over seventy candidates from all over the Soviet Union. Ashkenazy had come out first by a large margin in these preliminary contests and headed a team of five other Soviet pianists. He had had little say himself on being entered. It was not even a particularly logical move because he had never thought of himself as a Chopin specialist; indeed, he had to prepare quite a lot of the repertoire just for the competition. However, he was considered to be sufficiently outstanding to be able to carry off an important prize and that was the prime objective. He feels that he hardly had a mind of his own at that age.

All the same, he enjoyed the competition very much,

especially the early stages. He did not have any particular expectations and was happy to have the chance to go abroad. In the competition he was placed first at every stage until the final, when he knows that he did not play very well. 'I had to play first at the final stage which was rather unsettling, and the Queen of the Belgians was there, so it was even more of an event than usual. As a result, I felt terribly exposed and didn't do well. I ended up with the second prize because the distribution of prizes was based on the finals. I was told that points from the earlier rounds were not carried over, although naturally the members of the jury make their own notes for the final placing based in part on their impression of each participant throughout the competition. If true, this is rather an odd system, considering that the bulk of the repertoire is performed in the preliminary rounds whereas the final involves only one or other of the two concertos – not, after all, perhaps the most representative works of Chopin. The jury must have remembered that I was good in the earlier rounds, so at least I got the second prize; it could easily have been worse, I suppose. I remember that Michelangeli, who was a member of the jury, refused to sign our prize diplomas because he thought it was unfair that I got only the second prize. When I heard about this, silly boy that I was and not realizing that one doesn't do such things, I took my diploma to him in his hotel room and asked him to sign just mine. He replied, "No, I can't sign yours because you shouldn't have had this prize in any case, and if I sign one I might just as well sign all the others."'

One year later, when still only eighteen, Ashkenazy was entered for the Queen Elisabeth of the Belgians Piano Competition in Brussels. This was his first visit to the West and he remembers it as a stimulating and thoroughly enjoyable experience.

'It is very interesting to note that although we were used to hearing many fairy tales about the West in Russia – and they seem like fairy tales because one cannot see anything for oneself – that first feeling of being free is quite incredible. In the West we all take so many freedoms for granted and so it is hard to imagine what it is like to cross the border for the first time from a communist country into the West and feel that suddenly one is an individual and can do with oneself whatever one likes without having to ask anybody about anything. It's very hard to describe this feeling unless one is talking to someone who has lived in a cage before.

'Oddly enough, when I was in Belgium for the competition, no "guardian angel" was sent by the Ministry of Culture to look after the Soviet competitors. I don't know why – maybe they thought that Gilels, who was a member of the jury and was in Brussels together with another person from the Ministry of Culture, would somehow guard our delegation. In any case, they did not send anyone with clear orders to take care of us and so we were fairly free. Since one of the conditions of the competition is that members of the jury are not supposed to have any contact with the participants, even Gilels could see us only rather furtively, if at all. The other person, who was actually the Deputy Minister of Culture, was much too high up to keep an eye on us; he had really come along in order to enjoy himself since at that time even comparatively senior officials travelled very seldom to the West. Then, as now, Belgium was rather famous for its food and drink.

'In fact there was only one other Soviet competitor, Lazar Berman, and we were not particularly good friends, so we went our own ways. I made some good friends amongst some of the other pianists; a few of them have remained quite close ever since.'

This time Ashkenazy won the first prize unanimously and the word began to spread not only in Europe but in America that a really major young artist had appeared on the scene. Invitations for concert tours began to pour in and he returned to Moscow with greatly enhanced prestige and with a brilliant future at his feet.

Ashkenazy remembers that already as a child he sensed the fundamental falseness permeating daily life in Soviet Russia; now he can identify clearly the causes for this but then he could do little more than feel a growing unease about so many obviously contradictory or unexplained factors surrounding him. He remembers the air of indifference, the lack of motivation, the general purposelessness which characterized the lives of most people he knew. Even in organizations such as the Pioneers where the teachers and Party representatives tried hard to instil in the children a sense of awe at being a part of this great union of communist-minded people, he remembers how hollow it all seemed to him. He could not take it seriously. The Pioneer movement, after all, was more than just a Soviet type of Boy Scouting – great efforts were made to invest the whole movement with a kind of mystical significance. And yet, even though there were things about Pioneering that were obviously appealing to a growing boy, he remembers quite distinctly how he rejected the larger framework. He feels sure that this had nothing to do with the fact that he was already rather single-minded about his devotion to music and the piano. He felt intuitively that this was something to which he could not belong because he knew it was all false.

At that stage, however, it had to remain on the intuitive level; he had no way of making comparisons with how things were outside the Soviet Union because he had no contact with foreigners until he joined the Conservatoire. Until the late 1950s, the country was still almost completely isolated and virtually no information about the West was available except that served up in the crudest propaganda. Furthermore his mother, always the dominant influence in the family circle while he was growing up, was what he describes as 'a good Soviet'.

'She was simply an unthinking product of the Soviet system. Her Sovietism was of the kind: "Look, every country has its own ways, and these are ours." She also knew that if you do not go along with things, you get into trouble, and she wanted to protect us from this. She obviously thought, "This is the way we operate, this is the way we think, this is the way the country is run, so just conform, don't think too much. Life is hard enough, so don't make it worse." Later, when she had visited us in the West, her critical faculties were gradually awakened. She discovered things about Russia which she couldn't even have suspected before. At first she found it very difficult to admit to this and to risk losing face, but she soon began to face up to some of it.'

Ashkenazy doubts whether as a child he had any real understanding of the political purges which continued in the post-war years right up to the death of Stalin. 'I don't remember being afraid of the KGB or of knocks on the door in the middle of the night. Of course, I heard of arrests and camps and exiles but, in the mind's eye of a young boy, all of this tends to be seen as part of normal life – at least until one personally experiences something terrible. You hear that someone's father has been arrested but you don't pay very much attention. Since your schooling is full of heroic workers fighting capitalists and warmongers and since you constantly hear about the need to beware of traitors, you think that is just how the world is and you have no real conception of anything else. You may even automatically assume that anyone who has been arrested must have done something wrong and deserves to be locked up.

'In fact, the process did once come very close to home, when the singer who had worked regularly with my father for many years was arrested not long after the war for talking too much on one occasion. He was popular and sociable and he made some harmless but unwise remark about somebody in power. In those days you could be arrested for anything – even for wrapping your shopping in a newspaper with a picture of Stalin on it. And as for making a joke about the fact that the Generalissimo's moustaches were too long, well, if someone who didn't like you heard you and reported you, the next day they would arrest you. So this singer was picked up by the KGB for something trivial like a joke about Stalin and sent to the terrible camp at Magadan in Eastern Siberia. My father was called to the KGB headquarters in Moscow and stayed there for several days and nights while they questioned him about the singer. Of course my mother was in a complete panic but I remember that I wasn't – it seemed to me that either he would come back or he wouldn't. In the end he did, and everything went back to normal. He told me recently that they were in fact very good to him, very polite and not too threatening; they made it clear that they had nothing against him and didn't expect to find anything wrong with him but they simply wanted as much information about this singer and his private life and friends – he was apparently a homosexual – as they could get.'

Later Zemlyansky also fell foul of the system because of accusations that he had had a homosexual liaison with a professor when he was much younger. This was brought out in the early 1960s when there was a campaign against homosexuals and Zemlyansky fell into the net even though what he was denounced for had happened many years before. Homosexuality is strictly prohibited under Soviet law but, as with so many other similar purges, the investigation was almost certainly an excuse for a security round-up. Under Stalin it was convenient to concentrate from time to time on different categories of malefactors; on one occasion it would be 'embezzlers', on another 'anti-Soviet para-sites and wreckers'. The purges following the discovery of the 'Doctors' plot' were typical. Vague and seemingly hysterical accusations against a group of eminent doctors who were charged with attempting to poison members of the Politburo provided a convenient cloak for a vicious campaign against Jewish professional people and academics. In the 1960s, cam-paigns against swindlers and racketeers became the order of the day, whereas in the 1970s, with the explosion of public dissent amongst writers, artists and scientists, charges of anti-Soviet activities took over as the catch-all for the security organs.

In the Soviet Union concepts of justice are travestied; whereas traditional jurisprudence is concerned with specific charges based on provable evidence relating exclusively to relevant areas of investigation, in Soviet Russia any individual can be pre-judged by the security organs as someone who must be isolated from society. Once the victim is selected, any and every conceiv-able charge may be brought against him in order to ensure that the courts can convict him without difficulty. If he is deemed worthy of only a relatively minor punishment, perhaps as much as anything else as a form of warning to ensure good behaviour in the future, he will be accused of some minor offence or some trivial irregularity in his documentation. If the KGB decide that the person under investigation poses a more substantial threat, then a more serious charge will be cobbled together. It should be understood that all of this is remarkably easy in the Soviet Union because the entire society can only function by breaking rules to a greater or lesser degree. Everyone cheats and steals, whether on the massive scale found in factories or collective farms as de-scribed by Vladimir Bukovsky or on the level to which Ashke-nazy himself confesses, of stealing the occasional volume of music from the Central School library* because it proved abso-

---

* Ashkenazy remembers that he would never have dreamed of taking any-thing from the Conservatoire library: there the scores and music were too precious and in many cases unobtainable elsewhere. It would have been a crime against his fellow students to handicap them by removing something they might desperately need. In the Central School, on the other hand, the demand for some music was nil and Ashkenazy remembers reasoning that if no one ever asked for certain volumes which he desperately wanted it seemed only sensible to appropriate them before they fell into less appreciative hands, or simply disintegrated on the shelves.

lutely impossible to get hold of it in any other way, certainly not in shops, as the number of copies printed was ridiculously small. Since everyone in the Soviet Union is guilty at least of some peccadillo at one time or other, it is the easiest thing in the world for the KGB to find a charge appropriate to the type of punishment they wish to see imposed. Poor Zemlyansky, therefore, was almost certainly swept up in a campaign which was labelled anti-homosexual only because it enabled the KGB to pull in a lot of people they were interested in eliminating from normal society for quite different reasons. Even those who fell into the net without being of any real significance to the main theme of their investigations could help to spread the impact of the terror.

Zemlyansky spent nine months in prison and was eventually released before he had completed his full term. Some years later he was allowed to teach once more in the Conservatoire. He died in 1976, the rumour being that he committed suicide.

Even though the pressure was overwhelming to be swept along on the tide of dogma, banner-waving, the interminable glorification of Soviet achievements and corresponding vilification of the West, a seed of scepticism took root somewhere within Ashkenazy's mind. But only a seed, because life had to go on, examinations had to be passed, the Marxist-Leninist catechism had to be swallowed as the basis for the whole educational process. If he was treated in one way as a privileged student because of the élitist structure of the Central School, in other areas of life he and his family enjoyed no special advantages, and in his general schooling he had to go through the same process of indoctrination as anyone else. At the Central School there was no specific Marxist-Leninist instruction, since these courses become part of the curriculum only at high school level, but the humanities and even the sciences were and are so permeated with Marxist-Leninist dogma and interpretation that the basic indoctrination was complete. School books of all kinds were saturated with the appropriate ideological conditioning and in the Conservatoire itself there was formal teaching not only in Marxist-Leninist principles but also in its 'aesthetics'.

'You soon begin to laugh at this, with all its socialist realism, as you go on writing essays in which you have to write exactly what the teacher tells you without the freedom to examine any work of literature or its characters. It all has to fall in with the Party line . . . It's quite different from religious instruction in the West where religious teaching tends to be kept separate from the rest of the educational process. For us, whether it is history or literature or any other subject, the Party's attitude to man's entire intellectual and spiritual life is dogmatic and doctrinaire. Even such a thing as Pushkin's great poem *Eugene Onegin* is presented to you only in a particular interpretation. At the time you don't fully realize this, because you have no means of comparison and because you may like or respect your teachers and feel naturally well-disposed to whatever they tell you. But what they tell you even about *Eugene Onegin* is and must be the Party line, so it gets into your system without you noticing it.

'It is difficult to estimate how fundamentally one's environment and background form one's views. How can one separate the development of one's own spiritual self from the influence of people around you? To say, for instance, that the suffocating intellectual, spiritual, and aesthetic climate of the Soviet Union inevitably destroys people is clearly wrong; because we can see some instances of individuals who can develop, in spite of everything, an inner world of their own and an understanding of what is happening of significance in the world outside. Nonetheless, it is certainly true that this environment must have an important effect, and a largely limiting and depressing effect, on even the strongest minds and personalities.'

As far as music is concerned, Ashkenazy does not think that Party manipulation is central to the differing aesthetic responses to be found in Russia and the West, although it certainly plays a role.

'I don't think that it has very much to do with the Party line; it seems to me to be more a matter of the make-up of the Russian character and of Russian values which are essentially very different from those of the West. It is difficult to generalize, of course, and if we were to say that the Russian is *always* passionate and emotional whereas the Westerner is more intellectual, this would clearly be foolish and a travesty. But people in the west picture the average Russian as someone rather effusive, warm, hospitable, extrovert, often not very intelligent, and generally unpractical – in other words, not terribly bright but certainly interesting. Having by now spent many years out of Russia, I am convinced that what is particularly cultivated in Russia is the emotional aspect of your attitudes to life and everything around you. This has much less to do with the Party than with national consciousness, although the Party certainly knows how to make good use of it. The practical, pragmatic side of a person's make-up is simply neither cultivated nor appreciated; indeed, if someone is practical and efficient, methodical or even exceptionally rational, these characteristics tend to be viewed with suspicion. Among artistic people, the very reverse of these qualities are cultivated, as though unpredictable and unworldly behaviour – generally manifested in a disordered, unpractical, even irresponsible life-style – is a necessary part of the artistic temperament. I suppose this does not apply to Soviet scientists; if it did they would probably never have been able to develop those rockets!

'As an example of my general contention, I telephoned my old teacher Sumbatian a couple of years ago – and she, although an Armenian, is very much a Russian, having lived so many years in Moscow and Leningrad – and we talked about my children. She asked whether I was teaching them Russian and I replied that I wasn't, since the little time I do have for my children I would prefer to spend in other ways than in lessons which would not be appreciated; in any case, they would have very little use for Russian, or for the little that I could teach them, and so the most they would learn from me would be odd words or phrases – not enough to read the great Russian writers in the original, even if they could communicate a little. There seemed to be so little point, I said, since they would never live in Russia or in a Russian-speaking community.

'At this point she interrupted me. "But what an expression you use about Russian – 'It has so little point' – I didn't expect that from you." She automatically expected that I as a Russian and as a product of Russia would want my children to try to learn and speak Russian regardless of whether there might be any reason for it or not. Well, I am against that sort of attitude to life. Of course, I often like emotional people very much indeed, and appreciate a very direct and natural expression of emotions, but when they are allowed to overwhelm the rational in us, that is something I don't approve of.

'Perhaps, in that sense, I am not a typical product of Russia. I have the strange characteristic that I don't want to be the same as

53

the people I see around me. This may be a reaction to the excessively conformist society in which I grew up, but something inside me always protested against certain things in Russia – the excessive emphasis on the emotional, the refusal to think rather than just to feel. In musical terms this carries over into my work. With Mozart, for instance, a composer with whom many Russians have a lot of difficulties, there is his impeccable sense of form which one could describe as the practical gift of putting your material in an ideally communicative shape – the very thing which is probably most foreign to a chaotic, emotional Russian. So even with a Russian who does not wear his heart so much on his sleeve and who tries to use his mind as much as he can I am not so sure that there are initially too many points of contact between Mozart's essentially well-organized presentation of material and the Russian's instinctive approach. In my own case, I hardly played any Mozart while I was still in the Soviet Union – maybe at most one or two sonatas – and I'm sure that I didn't understand a note of what I was playing. Now, of course, Mozart is a central part of my repertoire.

'The Party is an anonymous mass of people who know very little about music – they just demand a collective victory. As a result the professional people who are subordinate to this Party hierarchy develop a particular attitude based on the achievements and success they can lay claim to. In other words, if you are a performer and win prizes at competitions, that is your way of showing the top Party people that you are successful in the collective cause. In order to win, you have to be extremely proficient technically and so you try to develop a brilliant style of playing. The fact that there have been so many brilliant Soviet performers has, of course, something to do with the Soviet way of life and its technique of discovering potential talent, just as in other fields including sport. In effect, the system is such that if you can do something extraordinary, you will be allowed to develop that gift for the good of the state. But when it comes to expressing something transcendental on a spiritual rather than a material level, then the state cannot do anything for you – on the contrary, it will try to suppress any individualistic thought and development.

'The system is weighted to produce formidably trained and technically brilliant performers, but at the same time it works against the nurturing of specially creative artistic qualities in those same performers.

'However, one should not ignore the fact that talent of a more substantial kind can still be recognized and cultivated and that certain compromises may be made in the short term without necessarily affecting the longer outcome. In other words, if you write a cantata called "Glory to Lenin" and your colleague composers including those who are members of the Union of Soviet Composers find the music perfectly horrible, then no one will ever ask you to write a more substantial and personal work later. On the other hand, if you are talented and people around you see your potential even in a work of the type "Glory to Lenin", then perhaps the next time they will ask or rather allow you to write a symphony – not just a symphony for Lenin, but a truly personal work. This even happened with someone as celebrated as Shostakovich, although in his case the process seems to have worked in reverse, at least in the beginning. In the early post-revolutionary years there was still a lot of scope for individualism in the arts and in the early twenties there was a lot of enthusiasm for a new type of "revolutionary" art and music. Shostakovich's Second and Third Symphonies were really very "Soviet" and voluntarily so. The trouble began with the Fourth Symphony, which was never performed and the opera *Katerina Ismailova* which Stalin saw part of and heartily disliked. After that, when Shostakovich was really in peril of his life, not just of his livelihood, he had to win space for himself, first with the Fifth Symphony, the "Answer to Just Criticism" and then with all sorts of meaningless music for Party occasions.

'Thereafter, and especially after the Zhdanov decree of 1948 against "formalism", Shostakovich seems to have seen the necessity of composing on two levels, one for the purposes of the state and one for his own. Being a great composer, it was never entirely clear where the second category took over from the first. The Eleventh and Twelfth Symphonies, for instance, were seen almost as acceptance of the concept of socialist realism in music; he also became a member of the Party, although we now know how painful a decision this was for him. Indeed, someone who knew him very well told me that he saw Shostakovich weep only twice in his life; the first time on the death of his first wife and the second time when he joined the Party. He seems to have felt this to be a humiliation. These "socialist" works were followed by the controversial Thirteenth Symphony based on Yevtushenko's poem *Babi Yar* and still later by such a work as the "Songs after Poems of Michelangelo" which referred quite clearly to Solzhenitsyn.

'In any case, there are indications that the Party decided some years ago that it wasn't worth the trouble to tamper too much with music, provided that no potentially subversive or controversial texts were involved. The new policy was that you could write and even perform almost anything – within certain limits, of course. Even if you wrote only serial or aleatoric pieces which would not be accessible to the masses, your works might still be performed, but inevitably very seldom. The authorities had probably decided that most of this sort of music is likely to be self-condemning and will be heard by only a tiny minority anyway. After all, music is only sounds, or so they think, not words or books or poems with potentially inflammatory content.

'Music therefore, which rarely trespasses into forbidden territories, can be allowed to flourish more than any other art form. The irony is that when it does trespass, as was the case with many of Shostakovich's greatest works, it is not easy for the watchdogs to decide whether it has done so or not. In the end, despite his much publicized submission to the official line, it is clear now that Shostakovich in his later symphonies simply continued with his own, highly personal critique of the system which he so profoundly despised. It is almost as though, threatened with the direst penalties for the way he used his mother tongue, Shostakovich developed another, deceptively orthodox style which proved in the end to be still more damning for being so much more accessible.

'The ultimate justification of success in the Soviet system is the furtherance of the interests and prestige of the state and decisions are made on this basis alone, whereas at the Juilliard School and other advanced conservatoires in the West, the final arbiter is the individual participant. The priority of state interests is seen most clearly in the way in which the destinies of individual artists are manipulated after they have achieved the very status and prestige which their training has brought about. With cynical disregard for contracts and agreements, let alone for the desires and needs of the artists themselves, the state grants or withholds the licence to perform abroad according to the political climate of the day. Even artists of the calibre of Richter, Oistrakh or Rostropovich have been subject to these vagaries. As we know from Khrushchev's memoirs, Richter was first allowed to travel abroad only because Khrushchev himself overruled the view of his officials that he was "unreliable" on account of his German origins. In its dealings with foreign agencies and institutions Goskoncert* makes no effort to pretend that its decisions reflect what is best for an artist's creative development. Prestige, hard currency, and adherence to the Soviet foreign policy of the day are the dominant considerations at all times.

'Other factors are important too. When Soviet performers go abroad they are generally expected to offer Russian works in their programmes with particular emphasis on Tchaikovsky, Rachmaninov, Prokofiev and Shostakovich. If they want to be successful, they have to try to make sure that they are asked back for further tours since this will greatly enhance their standing within official circles in the Soviet Union. There is little incentive, therefore, to espouse music which might be controversial or unpopular, or even unexpected. It is only fair, however, to say that some of these considerations apply in the West too – it is just that Western musical establishments have different vested interests to support – for example, the music departments of radio stations are often run by composers or would-be composers – and artists feel that they have to offer controversial contemporary music in order to get their foot through the door. In other cases, they may feel that they have to go along with the wishes of a recording company even when this is in conflict with their own most natural inclinations. Even if motivations in the East and the West can be similar – the desire to get on, to make a career, to be re-engaged – the options in the West are numerous. In Russia you must conform. If you don't you have no chance at all.

'Another feature of the subjugation of everything to the interests of the state is the almost manic pursuit of international prizes. This is an obsession which has dominated the activities of

---

* Goskoncert is the Soviet State Agency which deals with all engagements for Soviet artists abroad and for foreign artists performing in Russia. It is subject to the Ministry of Culture and all negotiations have to be channelled exclusively through its offices. It is notoriously inefficient and ill-informed artistically.

schools and conservatoires alike, particularly in the 1960s and 1970s. As a result, the total number of prize winners in the Soviet Union is so great that the value of a major first prize has been devalued; the impact on lesser prize winners has been correspondingly greater.

'There has always been a rule that if you win an international prize you are automatically entitled to give recitals and concerts in the principal cities of the Soviet Union. But there are now so many first-prize winners that there are no longer nearly enough concerts of the right quality to go around. This may have added to the incentives for talented younger artists to think of emigration, and yet the system has gone on producing more and more prize winners in the full knowledge that when they return home with their prizes there will be nothing appropriate for them to do. Yet they go after still more prizes because of the superficial prestige involved. If they cared about the prize winners as individuals or about their potential as artists, or if they saw that the system produces such grave consequences, they would try to modify it.'

The goal of prestige for the state carries with it more tangible benefits for successful international artists, however, so the incentive is still there. Acceptance within the top echelons of society can bring enormous material benefits including better housing, more valuable connections in all areas of life – and in the Soviet Union contacts are everything – perhaps even the possibility of acquiring or building a country house, that combination of dream and status symbol so beloved of all pre- and post-Revolution Russians. Successful artists used to be able to import cars, and although this has been prohibited for many years now, they can still find ways round the ban because of contacts and *blat*. They can also get hold of all sorts of Western electronic and luxury goods which make them the envy of their peers and occasionally – and more dangerously – of senior Party officials. Significantly, they have never had access to the whole network of special shops and services which are reserved for the Party hierarchy, although the similarly exclusive hospitals and clinics can sometimes be used by artists of public standing. The Party must always retain certain areas of exclusive privilege but the occasional glimpse of Canaan can be a potent reminder of the rules of the game. Ashkenazy recently approached a Soviet

Embassy abroad asking for permission to buy for his father a Russian car to be paid for in hard currency but for delivery in Moscow, but without success. Such benefits as remain are still powerful incentives and were all the more keenly desired in Ashkenazy's day when the differences between Russia and the West on a consumer level were even more glaring than they are today.

Achievement in the performing arts can, therefore, bring incalculable benefits, not just to the performer but to his whole family and circle of acquaintances. It is tempting for parents and teachers to take advantage of the access to privilege which the success of a talented child may open up. Even so, the absence of a truly commercial base for the performance system in the Soviet Union probably provides, at least initially, a more healthy environment for gifted young musicians. In the West, an infant or child 'prodigy' can be exposed from the earliest age to continuous and most damaging exploitation if his parents are irresponsible enough to permit it; fame and financial reward can be irresistible to those blind to the dangers of premature over-exposure.

Not that Ashkenazy believes that talented children should be over-protected as far as performance is concerned. Exposure to the public may be demanding, but it is also an essential part of the process of maturation. What he feels to be crucial is a careful balance between exposure and good, hard work. The implementation of such a balanced attitude depends very much on parents and teachers, both in the West and in Russia; if they are often insufficiently mature or wise, this is not a fault typical of either system and there are, fortunately, plenty of cases where gifted children have survived the worst kind of irresponsibility from those who should know better. Others, however, have suffered; Ashkenazy points to the example of a talented contemporary of his, the pianist Nasedkin. As a child this boy was written about in the Soviet press as 'our Mozart' since he played the piano and composed with great precocity from the earliest age. Perhaps because he was the son of a worker rather than of an intellectual, he received enormous publicity as a child. Even though his parents were not much in favour of all this, his teacher was extremely pushy, and exploited the campaign to the hilt. Later on, after winning one of the lesser prizes in the 1962 Tchaikovsky Competition, Nasedkin seemed to fade from view.

As for the immediate benefits of having a talented child in the family, parents might conceivably get access to someone in the government and thus find a way of jumping the queue for an apartment on the grounds that their child's gifts required better circumstances within which to develop, but there could be no question of the parents building up wealth and position on the backs of their children as happens so depressingly often in the West.

'There is a story which illustrates perfectly not only how this system of privileges and of patronage works in the Soviet Union, but also how inventive people become when it comes to seeking out ways of finding access to it. Before the war there emerged in Moscow a brilliant child prodigy violinist called Boris Goldstein; for a while, he was very much in vogue in musical circles, much abetted by a particularly pushy and ambitious mother. Unfortunately, as so often happens, he never quite realized these brilliant expectations when he came to maturity. It seems that the boy was invited to play at some sort of high-level party function where many of the top leadership were present. After he had played, and while people were milling around with drinks in their hands, the boy's mother took him aside and said, pointing to Molotov,* "Go over to Molotov and ask him to come to our home to have dinner with us." The boy was rather taken aback and began to protest that they could hardly ask so important a minister to have dinner with them in their one room in a communal flat with a shared kitchen and toilet, but she shut him up and told him to do as she asked. The boy then approached Molotov but the moment he diffidently uttered his invitation, his mother interrupted him and said, "But Boris, what are you thinking of? How can we invite Comrade Molotov when we live in only one room and have nowhere for you to practise properly let alone put a big enough table for people to sit down to dinner?" Not long afterwards, they got their own apartment!

'In our own case, my parents got their two-room apartment – for us an incredible dream of luxury – as a reward for my winning the first prize in Brussels. We were able to move in at the end of that year, in 1956. If you have something like that to write about

* Another version of the story has it that the minister in question was Kaganovich, who was Jewish, and perhaps a more obvious target for Mrs Goldstein.

in your letters to top Party functionaries, complaining that you do not have adequate facilities for your work, you stick out from the thousands and thousands of other people who are using any sort of contact or lever they can think of in order to improve their material situation. By pointing out that one has done something which was of use to the State and by implying that more could follow if only the conditions of work were improved, one stands some chance of success. This worked in 1962 after the Tchaikovsky Competition when I wrote to both Khrushchev and to Furtseva, the Minister of Culture, telling them that I was married and that having won the competition, I needed more room so that I could prepare myself for the important tours and concerts that I now had to do.

'It may seem bizarre that in so highly bureaucratized a system, one still has to write to the head of Government to get something done, almost as though one was appealing for patronage to an oriental pasha, but it is all connected to the pyramidic structure of power; only when there is endorsement from the top will people take the risk of making decisions which are out of the ordinary. So, the more privileged you are, the more you can have access to the people who have the power to draw you still further into the élite. In the end, of course, the true Party élite is almost totally isolated from the sort of life which the rest of the population has to live; they live in a state within the state depending upon a different kind of economy and social order. Ultimately, it's also a sort of trap; once you are inside the charmed circle, life is so incomparably easier that you want to do anything and everything not to jeopardize your position within it – indeed, you want to continue your way up the ladder, since the further you go, the more benefits of a material kind are open to you. They talk grandly of the dictatorship of the proletariat, and the funny thing is that it is precisely that, only the emphasis on the word "of" is quite different; it is the Party and the leadership who exercise the dictatorship over the proletariat.'

*   *   *

In the West – and in much of the developing world – young people in their teens tend to be greatly involved with matters of principle, with ideals and aspirations which extend far beyond their own immediate ambitions. In the Soviet Union there is virtually no scope for these expressions of developing intelligence and personality. Only the very few who embrace the ultimately hopeless cause of dissent believe in the possibility of real choice in moral or social behaviour; for the rest, the options are perceived to be exclusively materialistic, in so far as they concern jobs, housing, privileges, even the avoidance of trouble. Such humble aspirations might seem to provide little stimulus for creative minds and indeed it is tempting to make a connection between these factors and the remarkable concentration on the external aspects of performance – the cultivation of technique and musical panache rather than of more introspective qualities – among the most recent generation of Soviet artists. But Ashkenazy obviously does not feel that his education was bereft of finer influences; Zemlyansky, for instance, very much encouraged a high idealism in the thinking of his best pupils and tried to nurture the loftiest aspirations as part of the basic psychological equipment of the artist. Neuhaus, too, was vitally concerned with wider philosophical dimensions and even Sumbatian, teaching at a much less mature level, was aware of these elusive goals. One could say that the élitism of the whole special school system with its objective of cultivating excellence as both a weapon and advertisement for the state contains a fundamental contradiction. By providing scope for teachers of extraordinary dedication and efficacy – they themselves products of the Aspirantura – to arouse and develop the highest aspirations among their best pupils, the regime is also contributing towards the gradual undermining of the very uniformities upon which it so much depends. Even in other fields it has not been uncommon for the children of the most committed and privileged of Party functionaries to emerge from those special schools which are designed to create the next generation of Party rulers with their critical faculties attuned to question rather than to accept the structure of dogma their fathers expect them to maintain.

Ashkenazy admits that if he was aware of these contradictions at all, it was at most subconsciously, since he was still emotionally and intellectually immature when he left the Soviet Union. But even if his own thinking had only just begun to develop along these lines, he feels sure that many more mature artists including, as became clear later, such 'establishment' figures as Shostakovich and Kondrashin, had long held both the

Soviet way of life and the workings of its system in the deepest contempt. There were even rumours that David Oistrakh, in public an uncontroversial figurehead for the musical community, was in private equally critical. But when Ashkenazy tries to recall what he and his contemporaries used to think about or discuss amongst themselves, he can remember little or no preoccupation with universal issues. In theory it would be reasonable to expect that Soviet youth would be as anxious for reform as their counterparts in the West, but he remembers that the dominating concern was not so much to establish what was right and what was wrong as to try to distinguish between propaganda and truth. Idealism could have a relevance only on a very personal level, since the state had an absolute monopoly on all the answers as far as the outside world was concerned. In exceptional cases in the arts and humanities or in the movement for human rights, those energies which in the West seem so easily to be dissipated in an unfocused search for questions rather than for answers, are distilled in the Soviet Union into a more personal search for a fundamental scheme of values.

Music, as we have seen, has seldom been viewed as a potential hot-bed of independent thought, since the degree to which a musician dissents from the values of the system can seldom be discerned from the way he performs. Ashkenazy himself never claimed that he had the makings of a dissident. 'I can't pretend that I wanted to be a dissident or anything similar; this is something you become only if you decide upon such a course of behaviour in almost specifically political terms. As such you bank everything on your devotion to what you believe in and you are willing to go to prison or the camps – there really is no other way. You may end up like Solzhenitsyn expelled from your country, or like Bukovsky who suffered in psychiatric prisons and in the camps for so many years only to be expelled as well. You have to become a martyr quite deliberately over many years, or all your life; very few people are ready to suffer so much.'

So the choice available to thinking people is really dramatic, even desperate. Ashkenazy goes on, 'What happens is that any-one with any degree of active intelligence in Russia knows that what is happening there is a disaster. They must decide, there-fore, whether they will go along with it, somehow making everyday life bearable by trying not to think too much about what they should or could be doing about it since they know that even though they really *should* do something it would only bring disastrous consequences to themselves, to their families and to those closest to them. But if you decide that for these reasons you really can't do anything, you are already making a big compromise with your conscience, and that can begin to destroy a person. Conversely, those few people who do decide to do something are choosing a life of such incredible difficulty that they are perhaps destroying parts of themselves in another way. The horrible irony is that when the KGB confine dissidents to psychiatric asylums on the grounds that they are not sane, there is a certain weird logic. In a way you really have to be mad, really crazy to do what dissidents do because it is tantamount to suicide. You are condemning yourself to unbelievable suffering, both physical and mental, since you will spend half of your life in camps or prisons or asylums – which adds up to a form of suicide. The KGB and the Party élite cannot understand how anyone sane can condemn himself to all this voluntarily. So the authorities simply decree that those who put themselves outside the bounds of normal society – as defined by them – are abnormal and therefore mad. To a degree most societies and certainly all proscriptive ones do this, but in the Soviet Union the proscriptions are incredibly broad, encompassing all those who express opinions different from the officially promulgated dogma of the Party and the state.'

One of the difficulties facing the Western observer interested in understanding the workings of the Soviet system is its very inconsistency. Even Soviet citizens themselves have a most imperfect comprehension of what their rights are, at least on paper, and what legitimate resources are open to them to defend themselves against the officiousness of the state bureaucracy or to avail themselves of its protection. It is an important part of state propaganda that the Soviet citizen is protected by a comprehensive written constitution guaranteeing him his rights and establishing his duties. As in other countries laws are promulgated, and lawyers and judges are trained to interpret them both on behalf of the citizen and the state. However, since everyone knows that this constitution and its laws have been flouted since their first adoption, and since it is accepted in the Soviet Union that power and repression combined with corruption and a system of privileges are the things that really matter, no one bothers to examine these notional rights or to attempt to live by them. Since the 1920s, it was enough that an instruction, even a rumour of an instruction, descend from a higher level for it to be carried out. Procedures covering every conceivable aspect of life are laboriously established, and even more mindlessly complied with, but every stage can be dispensed with from time to time provided that such a step is perceived to have been taken by 'authority'. The citizen's rights, therefore, are only those things that he can get away with; authority is whatever is imposed from above.

But this is only part of the story. In the 1960s and early 1970s many of the brave and determined activists in the dissident movement decided that the only realistic way of pressing for reforms within the Soviet Union was to act as though there really were for the ordinary citizen a system of laws and rights guaranteed by the constitution. They decided to take the propaganda about Soviet Man being the freest on earth at face value. Whenever they came in contact with state organs or bureaucracy, they insisted on the strictest respect for the law and for official procedures, responding to any breach of these with a flood of written complaints both to higher authorities and to contacts in the West. This ensured that the issues were properly reported in the foreign press or broadcast back to the Soviet Union by the BBC, the Voice of America or Radio Free Europe. Vladimir Bukovsky has described how this procedure could be successfully adopted even from within the labour camps. On occasions the whole administration of the prison camp system could be undermined because of the constant stream of complaints and representations that were sent out to every kind of authority about abuses or irregularities suffered by prisoners within the camps. In the end, of course, the system always finds a way of dealing with this sort of initiative and re-imposes total control but it is significant that for a time it can be thrown out of step.

To understand this bizarre state of affairs better, one must remember that a mechanism as comprehensively repressive as that of the Soviet Union makes everyone involved in administering the system dependant upon it. A complaint about someone on one level of the bureaucracy can reflect badly on the standing of his immediate superiors; this in turn could have an adverse effect on the career of an aspiring middle-level Party official. He will certainly be most anxious not to lose the special privileges and contacts he has worked so assiduously to secure, and will do everything possible to avoid being used as the scapegoat when a case which is within his area of responsibility becomes a pawn in some complex power struggle.

A perfect example of these delicately balanced relationships came out recently as a result of a Soviet–Swiss trade deal over a process patented by the Swiss for preserving milk. The Soviet Milk Board acquired the licence to manufacture the equipment required and duly paid the agreed royalties on the Swiss patent by regular banker's order. After some months, it was discovered that the whole process was really unnecessary given the different climatic conditions applying, and the machinery was modified in such a way as to make the patent inapplicable. The Swiss lawyers responsible for the deal duly acknowledged that no further royalties had to be paid, but to their surprise, despite repeated reminders, the payments continued. Many months afterwards, one of the lawyers found himself in Moscow and had occasion to speak personally to the official responsible for making the payments. He pointed out that these were no longer necessary and that notice had been given to that effect. The official wrung his hands and begged him not to concern himself with the matter further. He pointed out that it was his job only to make the payments; this he did on the authority of a superior. Since something had obviously gone badly wrong with the chain of command, he could not possibly stop the payments now, since this would bring under scrutiny the whole process by which the decision had been made in the first place. Even if such a review might have a much more serious effect on those of his superiors who had made the original decisions, he too might suffer some repercussions. He was terrified that he might lose his job and said that the best way of preserving it would be to leave things as they were, even if this meant that funds continued to trickle out to Switzerland unnecessarily.

Seen as a whole, a few brief signs of attempts to respect the law, therefore, are mere spasms in an otherwise dead organism. The overwhelming mass of the population has never believed in the existence of an effective structure of laws and rights and any departure from the normal process of manipulations, coercions, *blat*, and special incentives adds yet another imponderable to an already unbelievably complicated situation, but one with which they have at least learned to live. Only a tiny handful of the most intrepid idealists will want to have anything to do with it, and in the West such efforts are seen to be heroic but ultimately hopeless. Indeed, it becomes just that, as the KGB reinforce their powers to disregard a totally ineffective legal code by means of detention in psychiatric prisons, labour camps or expulsion abroad.* Meanwhile, as the decades roll by – and three generations have now grown up under the system – the mindlessness imposed by the state Leviathan corrodes ever more deeply the last vestiges of Soviet Man's belief in the possibility of a free mind or the pursuit of individual aspirations.

The novelist and dissident philosopher Alexander Zinoviev who was expelled from the Soviet Union in 1976 and now lives in Munich has developed this theme cogently and comprehensively. In a recent interview in *The Times* he said, 'It is the general belief that the Soviet Union is comprised of a wicked government and a down-trodden people – the government oppressing the people, the people hating the government. But you can't divide the Soviet Union into the leadership and the people like that. There are perhaps sixty million people involved somewhere in the ruling system. Every individual has a piece of power. That provides a cohesive system, not a fragile one.'

Dissidents, therefore, encounter not only the full force of state repression, but also far-reaching hostility and rejection by the population as a whole. Since the only way of making a

* As a macabre symbol of the West's failure to understand the price of freedom, it turns out, as Bukovsky has reported, that the KGB import handcuffs from the United States because the quality and choice are so much better than in the Soviet Union; they particularly favour the kind which tighten automatically if the prisoner struggles or resists. These handcuffs are paid for with currency earned from the sale of Russian raw materials such as natural gas, or industrial diamonds, to the West. Another part of the bitter equation is that cheap grain exported to Russia by America to satisfy the political needs of Republican Senators from the mid-West or cheap butter sold by the EEC, facilitate the purchase of every kind of superior piece of technology, including those handcuffs. It is ironic that prisoners serving out years of the harshest deprivation in Soviet labour camps understand perfectly how this sort of trade allows for a corresponding increase in the Soviet capability to invest in armaments or to pay for the war in Afghanistan. The apparent refusal of Western leaders and opinion formers to see the logic in all of this leads many Russian commentators to fear that the self-tightening handcuffs will end up on our own wrists.

tolerable life in the Soviet Union is by conforming to the perverted set of rules which control its special scale of values, the ordinary citizen unavoidably becomes a co-conspirator and deeply resents the disturbances caused by those who obstinately insist on modelling their lives on more absolute standards.

The Soviet authorities eventually realized that expulsion was by far the most effective way of dealing with even the most publicized and implacable dissidents. Not only did the Western media tend to lose interest in these austere, almost Old Testament figures once they could no longer be treated as lone voices crying heroically in the wildernesses, but they also removed a source of irritation and frustration from amongst ordinary people who would on the whole prefer not to have their consciences raked over in such an unsettling way. As the 1970s were followed by the early 1980s, it became clear that Soviet official policy had shifted. Instead of concentrating all the attention of the KGB and the courts on the most prominent figures among the dissidents or among the monitors of the Helsinki agreements, they put increasing pressure on the smaller people who surrounded the spokesmen and provided sympathetic support but little visibility or influence in their own right. Most of these were easy to silence or eliminate and by doing so the authorities made it difficult for the leaders to function with any effectiveness or impact. Without this infrastructure of support, the dissident movement of the 1970s seems largely, but probably temporarily, neutralized.

5

IN 1957, immediately after his success in the Brussels Competition, Ashkenazy was engaged by the famous impresario Sol Hurok for a tour of the United States, to take place during a period of around eight weeks between mid-October and mid-December 1958. Hurok, already a legendary figure in the twenties and thirties when he made and lost several fortunes in his presentations of all sorts of exotic stars from the ballet, opera and concert world, always seems to have managed to keep his fingers on the pulse of what the American public wanted. He had been quick to see the opportunities offered by the opening up of the Soviet Union after the death of Stalin; his flamboyant and forceful style of negotiation mesmerized the officials at the Ministry of Culture, who were suddenly faced with a flood of invitations from the West for prominent Soviet artists and ensembles. Hurok not only took the lead in arranging tours for such mature artists as Richter, Gilels, Oistrakh and Rostropovich, but also kept his eye on a few of the younger performers beginning to make names for themselves both in the Soviet Union and also abroad in competitions. Ashkenazy, with his somewhat controversial second prize in Warsaw already behind him and now a brilliant and undisputed first prize in Brussels, was snapped up without delay.

That 1958 tour was not, unfortunately, a happy experience for Ashkenazy, despite its artistic success. The problems began even before the tour started. The Ministry of Culture could not itself apply for visas for artists with contracts abroad until the Central Committee of the Party had approved the details of each particular tour. However, the Central Committee had and has no sense of urgency when it comes to the details of a predetermined concert itinerary. The fact that a visa had to be secured by a certain date so that concerts scheduled for particular days could go ahead was of little interest to them; the Central Committee and its officials have their own highly developed sense of self-importance and would simply expect dates on such a tour to be changed in order to fit in with bureaucratic procedures in exactly the same way as would happen in the Soviet Union.

As a result the approval from the Exit Commission of the Central Committee often came through to the Ministry of Culture at the very last minute, or even after the tour should actually have commenced. The inevitable and all too familiar consequence was that Soviet artists often could not live up to the commitments made for them by Goskoncert, which is itself an agency under the direction and control of the Ministry of Culture and the KGB. In those days, at least, when the Ministry did finally get the green light for a tour from the Central Committee, visa applications still had to be lodged with the consular offices of the countries to be visited. This could produce additional delays because consular relations with the Soviet Union tend to be at best strictly formal and are often managed on a reciprocal basis. This would mean that if a visa application by an American to visit the USSR took, say, four weeks, then the Americans imposed a similar time-lag on all Soviet applications to visit the United States.

When Soviet artists toured in the West, there was the further complication that a 'companion' was automatically and compulsorily assigned by the Ministry of Culture to travel with the artist. These agents, for such they of course were, were supposed to act as interpreters and travelling managers, their expenses being covered in most cases by the impresario or organization engaging the artist. Their role was to spy on the artists and to check up on their contacts abroad, or to discourage too much fraternization. They were also supposed to line up their own contacts with people who could be helpful to the Soviet Union and garner any useful information for the KGB's dossiers at home. Given these 'companions'' highly dubious and unattractive standing, their visa applications when submitted together with those of the artists could produce additional delays.

In Ashkenazy's own case, following no doubt frantic interventions at the American end from Sol Hurok's office, he was finally given his passport and tickets only on the morning of the day before his first concert in Washington.

'Even without all of this I did not feel psychologically well prepared for the tour and felt burdened down with the pressure and the responsibility. I worried that if I did not have success, I'd be back at the beginning again and everyone would look down on me. Also, I did not know what to expect going to a country so very different from Russia. When I had gone to Western Europe, I hadn't felt too bad, but I was really intimidated about going to America with its skyscrapers and unashamed, dynamic commercialism without being able to look to anyone I knew or could trust for moral support. Then, as it turned out because of a mess in the preparatory arrangements, I was able to arrive only the day before my first concert. Imagine having to face such an important debut in a totally new and alien world after all that flying and eight hours time change – and the very next day the rehearsal and concert in a huge hall, far larger than any I had been accustomed to in Russia.

'At the rehearsal my fingers felt like cotton wool. I played the Chopin F minor Concerto and it turned out to be very successful – why, I still can't understand because I thought that I had not played well at all. I felt terribly sleepy and could not concentrate. I then had two recitals before my Carnegie Hall recital, one in Chicago and one in Toronto. Fortunately Claudia Cassidy* was sick and didn't come to my concert; if she had, she would probably have destroyed me. Even so, the reviews were not very encouraging. When I asked Shelly Gold,† who was at that time one of the booking representatives for the Hurok office, about the reviews, he replied that they were "not very good, not very bad". But I went on feeling absolutely terrible; just imagine, a young boy under so much pressure, feeling lost in such completely foreign surroundings, but knowing instinctively that this world was much tougher than Europe, altogether more alienating. At that time, this was just a sort of gut feeling but I was sure that I was right. And now, of course, I know that I was right. In the event, the Carnegie Hall recital was very successful, really terrific, but I still felt so unhappy that I asked whether I could go home early.

* Claudia Cassidy was the ferocious critic of the *Chicago Tribune* who was responsible for some notorious critical assassinations.

† Shelly Gold later headed the Hurok organization after Sol Hurok's death and then went on to form the ICM Classical Management which has represented Ashkenazy in North America from the mid 1970s.

'I explained this to my companion who then cabled the Ministry of Culture. They were obviously perplexed by my request and replied that it was out of the question and that I simply had to go on with the tour. But oddly enough they appear originally to have had permission from the Central Committee only for one month, although they had never told me this, so at the end of the first month, which was exactly half-way through the tour, there was a great panic and I received a cable from the Ministry that I had to go back immediately. I suspect that my companion had also started to send back some alarming signals that I was not too reliable and that I had too much of a free mind.'

On this tour Ashkenazy was very isolated. He had virtually no contact with the people working in the Hurok office and admits that it never really occurred to him to try to get to know them. He also took little interest in the general organization of the tour. He was put in third class hotels and was obliged to share a room with his 'companion' throughout the tour, partly to save money for Hurok and partly to ensure that no unauthorized contacts could be made. He never thought that he had any say in these arrangements.

In the middle of the tour there was a gap of some two weeks which he spent in New York. It seems that one or two of the concerts originally included in the itinerary were in areas prohibited to Soviet citizens in retaliation for similar restrictions on Americans in the Soviet Union, and these had to be cancelled when Hurok could not get clearance for them. There were also continuing doubts as to whether Ashkenazy would indeed be recalled early by the Ministry of Culture, so Hurok decided to cancel one more concert on the West coast while he waited for the second half of the tour to be approved. He did not want to incur the expense of sending Ashkenazy – and the 'companion' – all the way across the continent only to find that he would have to fly him back again to New York at the last moment.

Ashkenazy practised most of every day during these two weeks but he also spent a lot of time in record shops which seemed to him like unbelievable treasure houses. He also gave a lengthy interview to Harold Schonberg, who later became the highly influential critic of the *New York Times*. Ashkenazy remembers that Schonberg was extremely nice to him and very attentive, and played him some records of the legendary virtuoso

Hofmann, one of his particular enthusiasms. Unfortunately, Ashkenazy was not a great admirer of Hofmann's playing and said so. Partly to make amends, he felt that he ought to be as polite as possible about the United States in the interview; he said that he was enjoying the tour very much and liked the country and the people, despite the fact that he had been miserable for most of the time. These diplomatic untruths were later used as evidence against him by his 'companion' to demonstrate his un-Soviet and irresponsible behaviour during the tour.

On this first American tour Ashkenazy was paid approximately what he would have received per concert in Russia; this amounted to about $114 per concert, or around £45 at that time. Out of this he had to pay for his meals and all personal expenses; only his travel and hotels were paid for by Hurok – hence the third class hotels on this debut tour. Hurok knew how to be generous at the most auspicious moments, but he also knew how to save money on those who were not yet accustomed to a better standard of life. Since he was obliged by contract to pay for the travel and hotel expenses of the 'companion' as well, he wanted to keep the combined charges as moderate as possible.

'For my first tour Hurok paid Goskoncert between $800 and $1000 (£285 and £360) per concert. For the second tour in 1962 he must have paid a little more but sold me to the local sponsors for $2000 (or £700) per concert. I received a little more than on the first occasion, something like $145 (£50) per concert because my official fee in the Soviet Union had also gone up and this was the equivalent sum to my Soviet fee converted at the official rate of exchange. The rest went to Goskoncert. Mind you, Hurok also paid the same basic fee for my recitals in New York where he promoted the concerts himself. He must have made a lot of money on those concerts, because even my first Carnegie Hall recital was financially very successful. And when I also got good reviews he quickly arranged a second recital at the end of the tour. Fortunately, I had prepared two programmes for the tour so I was able to take this on. Hurok was a very gifted businessman and impresario and he used to keep certain dates at Carnegie Hall on a speculative basis so that he could follow up a success with the New York press and public. At the end of the tour he gave me a couple of hundred dollars extra in cash, just as a gift. He usually did this with Russian artists who were successful; I suppose he wanted us to understand the principle of rewards and incentives as quickly as possible! I spent all the dollars I earned, mostly on gramophone records. Since I played around twenty-five concerts, I earned between $2,000 (£700) and $2,500 (£900).

'Interestingly enough, I happened to be one of the first Soviet artists to whom they applied this system of payment. Until that year or perhaps even just before my tour, artists used to get half of what the foreign impresario had agreed to pay to Goskoncert. Since the hotels and travel were paid for by the impresario, this was a fantastic deal for the artists. People like Oistrakh and Gilels would receive fees of $3,000 or $4,000 (£1,250 to £1,425) per concert, so they would come back with large sums of money after a long tour, and with wonderful things like cars and furniture which put them effectively above anyone in the Soviet Union and caused a lot of offence. People like Oistrakh, Gilels and Rostropovich first made tours to America in 1951 or 1952 and regularly thereafter. Of course, when the Ministry changed the system those established artists were upset, but what could they do?

'I had benefited from the old system myself in 1957 when I played some concerts in West Germany the year after the Brussels Competition. Since I had done very well out of the arrangement then, we thought at first that there must be some mistake when we were told about the new financial arrangement for the American tour. My father even asked about it at the Ministry of Culture while I was still on tour and was simply told that this was the new deal and that was all there was to be said. My father complained that this made things very difficult for me: "The boy can hardly eat properly; he can't even afford to order a steak when he wants to. And now he will have nothing left at the end, when he wanted to buy a piano to bring back with him; after all, you can't buy a good piano in Russia." They got furious and accused him of interfering in Ministry of Culture affairs and of poisoning my mind with anti-Soviet ideas by encouraging me to think that I was badly treated whereas I should be proud that I had been trusted with such a great opportunity and responsibility. My father suffered from this whole affair – they never let him perform abroad again. Previously he had been almost everywhere – all over Europe, to Africa and to the Arab world where the Russians were busy establishing important links. But after

74

this incident they just cut him dead, almost as though our whole family was infected with some sort of cancer.'

In retrospect, Ashkenazy seems to have developed less negative feelings about that first tour; after all, it had been successful and the psychological pressures it had imposed were soon forgotten. Moreover, towards the end of the tour he started to get a little more accustomed to the country and the way of life, even to enjoy its vitality and energy. Once back in Russia, he felt some nostalgic appreciation of the total freedom that had surrounded him, and had a strong desire to experience this feeling again – though it never crossed his mind that he might want to live abroad. The materialistic advantages were of less interest; he had already seen what the West had to offer in Belgium in 1956 and in West Germany in 1957.

From a musical point of view there had been few encounters of lasting importance to him; he played the Prokofiev Second Concerto with Leonard Bernstein and the New York Philharmonic but this proved less enjoyable than he had expected. Somehow Ashkenazy did not find the musical rapport he had hoped for. The only other orchestras of importance on the tour were the San Francisco and Washington National Symphonies, but the conductors were not artists with whom he felt any special compatibility. The emphasis on recitals was presumably a business decision as far as Hurok was concerned; major orchestral engagements in the United States customarily involve two, three or even four subscription concerts with the programme repeated. The fee for the repeats used to be very heavily discounted, so that the artist or in this case Hurok would end up with perhaps only one and a half or two fees for as many as four performances. Hurok would still have had to pay to Goskoncert a fee per concert, so it was in his interests to avoid too many orchestral dates. Also, recitals do not involve extra days of rehearsals and so more could be fitted into each week.

Instead of making any rational evaluation of the general musical level he experienced in America compared with that to which he was accustomed in the Soviet Union, Ashkenazy feels that he was a typical victim of the traditional Russian ambiguity about the West. On the one hand the Slavophiles feel that Russia has its own largely self-sufficient, cultural idiom which is inherently superior to that of the West but still vulnerable to adulteration if not properly isolated and protected; on the other hand, the Westerners have tended to argue that everything of real value in Russian life has been imported from the West and then re-fashioned to suit Russia's particular needs. Much of his thinking about all this was incoherent at that stage and his English was much too limited to enable him to get much benefit from Western books and newspapers.

'My "companion" spoke English and used to read the newspapers, and every now and then would translate for me what was in the news, though very selectively. There was one incident, however, which he could not hide and that was the Pasternak affair. He had won the Nobel prize and *Dr Zhivago* had just been published in the West. This made things very difficult for me because every journalist who wanted an interview with me immediately asked me about Pasternak through my interpreter. Obviously I had to be careful, but the fact that I had not had the chance to read the book at that stage gave me at least a valid excuse for not making any comments. Later on in New York, just before we left the country we got hold of a copy of *Dr Zhivago* in Russian. We had to stop over in Amsterdam for the night and I remember that both of us read the book, one after the other, during the thirty-six hours or so available to us on the journey because we could not bring it into the USSR. Back in Moscow, my "companion" wrote in his very negative report on me that I had read *Dr Zhivago*, omitting to mention the fact that he had read it just as voraciously as I and with just as much interest. I pointed this out, but it made no difference. I suppose he was entitled to do such things in order to know the enemy, whereas I was not!

'I don't remember finding the book particularly anti-Soviet. I thought that it was a touching book, very warm and human, and I suppose I didn't see the significance behind it all. Maybe I read it so fast, gulping it down, that I couldn't digest it properly.'

6

ALEXANDER ZINOVIEV'S REMINDER that a great part of the adult population of the Soviet Union becomes actively involved in the process of repression and demoralization is admirably illustrated by Ashkenazy's own experiences with the KGB.

'It must have started in the winter of 1956 or the spring of 1957. I was called to what they call the Otdel Kadrov or the Personnel Supervisor's office of the Conservatoire. In the Soviet Union, every organization has such a department which deals not only with those people who are employed or who are students or members – naturally enough they keep files on everyone – but is also directly controlled by and answerable to both the KGB and the Ministry of Internal Affairs. There are always two parallel channels to satisfy the need for information for the different purposes of the KGB and the Ministry. So, whenever the KGB wants to recruit someone it is normally done through these offices, although of course it can be done in many different ways.

'When I was called to the office I found a man waiting for me all alone. He was rather grim, introduced himself as a KGB officer and gave his name. It could have been a false name; I realized that it did not mean much anyway. He then said, "We know that you have a very high standing here as a pianist and as an artist and that you are highly regarded by the few foreign students who are studying at the Conservatoire as part of the International Exchange programmes. You will certainly come into contact with them sooner or later and we would like to know as much about them as possible, especially anything unusual about their private activities. You know, of course, that the KGB –" and then he made one of those routine little speeches we all became so accustomed to – "is for the ordinary people of this country. You as a loyal Soviet citizen will certainly appreciate and understand this and we expect you as a patriot to cooperate fully in your reports. You are free to agree or not to. If you agree, you must sign this paper confirming that you will keep all of this confidential and that you will not reveal it to anyone."

'I agreed and signed because I was scared out of my wits; I had never been confronted with such a situation in my life and I thought that probably everyone who was approached did this sort of thing. I imagined that if I refused, something bad would certainly happen to me.'

Ashkenazy was instructed to choose a code name and decided upon Mitya, one of the diminutives for Dmitri. He chose this because he had a close friend called Dmitri Sakharov, an excellent pianist and musician.

'I had a liaison person whom I called Vasily Ivanovitch. He gave me a telephone number where I could reach him at any time, but I remember using it only a very few times. He contacted me once every two or three months, took me to a hotel room – each time a different hotel – and asked me what I knew about various people at the Conservatoire including, for instance, a French pianist there and another foreigner, a girl student. I felt that this was all terribly unsavoury and remember only that I didn't write anything negative about them; anyway, I hardly knew them, but I decided firmly that I would never say anything that could be interpreted or used against them.

'When I returned from America in 1958 they called me and asked me to tell them whom I had met. I remember that I wrote something about Malcolm Frager, something very nice about his being a very good colleague and a very good pianist. They asked questions like, "Does he smoke? Does he drink?" – you know, they wanted leads on anything, especially the sort of character vices which they could make use of later. I always answered "No" to this sort of question. Either because I was still very unsophisticated or maybe because I didn't feel that I wanted to promote myself with them, I didn't feel that because of my implicitly threatened position I had to tell them anything that would be of real interest to them. And eventually I was fired.'

This seems to have been for a combination of reasons; certainly, he was not proving to be a very useful contact but perhaps more important was the fact that his 'companion' on the first American tour wrote such a negative report about his behaviour and attitudes. He remembers having been absurdly open with the man as they travelled together.

'I would say such things to him as "Well, you can see this country is doing well. Do you really think that there will be a revolution here?" Then I'd go on to remind him that Lenin had said that not everywhere would there be a socialist revolution and that some countries would go to communism in different ways. Unfortunately, the idiot hadn't even studied his Leninism well enough, because in his report he said that I falsified Lenin's teachings by saying that there would not be socialist revolutions in many countries. Poor fellow, he was just an average hack who didn't know his Marxist-Leninism; I was, in fact, perfectly right, but when I tried to explain this to the officials at the mock court set up by the Ministry to investigate these charges against me, they wouldn't listen to me. He had to be right and I wrong.'

The court consisted of about five people from the Ministry plus the head of the Komsomol cell at the Conservatoire; no one from the KGB was directly involved but Ashkenazy remembers the experience as both frightening and threatening. The 'companion's' report was read out to him and he was asked to explain his behaviour. Needless to say, there was no question of having anyone to defend him.

'I replied that most of the report was completely untrue since my "companion" did not know what he was talking about as far as his ideological accusations were concerned. Maybe there was some truth in my having reputedly said that I liked some modern music or even some aspects of American life, but why did he say that I was not proud to be a Soviet citizen? Firstly, I never said that I wasn't and secondly, how was I supposed to express this pride anyway?'

Then followed the charge that Ashkenazy had claimed that he would never again set foot in the Ministry of Culture. He did not deny that he had said something of the sort, but only prompted by extreme exasperation at the poor arrangements that had been made. He described in detail all the things that had gone wrong and agreed that he had expressed disgust about all of this to his 'companion' and had said that he did not want to have anything more to do with the Ministry of Culture if they could not handle properly the arrangements for a simple foreign tour.

Ashkenazy went on to argue that all of these accusations were so unbelievably trivial that they certainly could not justify this sort of interrogation, as though he were some sort of criminal.

The court ruled, nonetheless, that whatever his excuses and even if there were only a grain of truth in the report, it would be quite enough to find him guilty. Ashkenazy was so distressed about this mistreatment that he went straight to the nearest telephone to speak to his KGB contact Vasily Ivanovitch; if there were to be any redress against this "conviction", it would have to come from the KGB. By that time, however, the KGB had apparently lost interest in him; they took no action and would do nothing to alter the decision of the Ministry of Culture "court". He was, therefore, banned from going abroad with immediate effect and a few months later the KGB dispensed with his services altogether, perhaps because another example of his apparent disinclination to cooperate had come to their attention.

Ashkenazy had a friend at the Conservatoire, let us call him Jan S., who came from Bulgaria but was really Russian, the son of an Orthodox priest. They became friendly because he liked Ashkenazy's playing and helped him a little with French, which he spoke very well and which Ashkenazy was studying. He had also been recruited by the KGB earlier on and had told Ashkenazy this, despite the fact that he was supposed to keep this fact entirely to himself.

'I don't know why he told me – maybe the KGB asked him to do so in order to make me put my confidence in him. The fact that he told me certainly made me trust him, and when I was recruited I told him too. The KGB obviously knew that we had admitted our connection to each other; later I discovered that he had told them this. Anyway, because he spoke French so well, in 1957 they assigned him to a French pianist who had turned out to be a homosexual. The KGB clearly intended to arrange a combination of circumstances so that they could catch the Frenchman in a compromising act and then blackmail him.'

Since neither Ashkenazy nor Jan S. were homosexuals, the KGB could not make use of them directly but there was another student, a Russian, with whom this Frenchman was friendly and who the KGB plainly thought was homosexual too. As it happened, they were wrong but he was a naïve, friendly person who was interested in the Frenchman both as a musician and as a foreigner from a country with which he was fascinated.

One day Vasily Ivanovitch telephoned Ashkenazy to arrange a meeting, this time not in a hotel room but out in the open air, in fact in a street near the Kursky railway station. He explained that they had a plan involving the Frenchman and his Russian friend and that they wanted Ashkenazy to help in arranging it since both pianists greatly admired his playing and would certainly trust him. They wanted Ashkenazy to suggest that they should join him on a tourist trip to Leningrad, or alternatively to invite them to go with him when he next had a concert there. It could then be arranged that they stayed in the same hotel and the KGB could take care of the rest.

'I remember telling him that this simply wouldn't ring true, that people don't do things in such a way. I pointed out that the Frenchman and my Russian friend would think it very odd if I suddenly invited them to go with me to Leningrad. And anyway, what was the point of all this? Vasily Ivanovitch then explained that since the Frenchman was homosexual and was interested in my friend, they could arrange to have him filmed in a compromising situation in a hotel. This could be useful because the Frenchman was also friendly with someone in the French Embassy and in this way the KGB could penetrate the embassy. "This is very valuable to us and you as a true patriot should help us to achieve it," he added.

'I replied that honestly I had no time for this sort of game; I was too busy with my concert career. At this Vasily Ivanovitch expressed astonishment that I should have no time for "Soviet power" – a standard cliché. (In Russian it is *Sovietskaya vlast* which really has no adequate translation.) But by this time I had become just a little more sophisticated and replied, "Well, of course, for Soviet power I am ready to give my life but I think that the time I spend on this project would be less well spent in the interests of Soviet power than if I continue to devote myself to preparing for the Tchaikovsky Competition. After all, there I might win the first prize which would bring much more prestige to Soviet power." He didn't like that answer very much but was at least temporarily nonplussed and could not insist further.'

Ashkenazy's teacher Zemlyansky also felt responsible for this Russian friend and became very concerned about the risks he was running in spending so much time with the Frenchman. Zemlyansky obviously knew he was homosexual and was afraid that the Russian pianist might become embroiled in something unpleasant or dangerous; in any case it was generally inadvisable

81

for any Soviet student to become too close to a foreigner. Zemlyansky took Ashkenazy and Jan S. aside and suggested that since they were both friends of the Russian pianist, they should warn him to keep his distance from the Frenchman and not risk his whole future.

'Jan and I had in any case decided that summer (1958) that there was absolutely no reason for this French pianist and his friend to get caught up in this sort of trap; after all, he was a nice fellow who had come to Moscow because he wanted to study music. Why should he end up by getting himself blackmailed after being caught in some nasty KGB spider's web? So we decided to warn him. Imagine being recruited by the KGB to spy for them and to help them blackmail people and then warning the victim instead! I don't remember who first suggested the idea, whether it was Zemlyansky or Jan (I certainly remember that it was not I) but eventually it was decided that Jan would actually tip him off, partly because he could do so in French and could ensure that the message would really be understood. We all arranged to go for a walk together and Jan gave him the warning as we had agreed. I actually said nothing at all.

'Later that year and during the winter, Vasily Ivanovitch called me up for a few more rather inconsequential meetings and, as usual, I had nothing useful to give him. Then in spring 1959 a campaign against homosexuals suddenly started within the Conservatoire, and a few highly placed teachers were arrested. Zemlyansky was one of those pulled in even though his involvement with homosexuality was long in the past and he had by then been "straight" for many years. Three or four weeks after his arrest, Vasily Ivanovitch called me to yet another hotel room and dismissed me on the spot from the service of the KGB. He reminded me that I had refused to go to Leningrad with the Frenchman and then told me that Zemlyansky had "given evidence in prison that I had been planning to find an opportunity of warning the Frenchman and had indeed succeeded in doing so." I knew for sure that Zemlyansky never said anything of the kind either at his trial or at the preliminary investigations, because he was a man of absolutely crystal integrity, and was completely devoted to me as a person and as a musician. So it must have been Jan who betrayed me, presumably saying that it was my idea to warn the Frenchman and that it was I in the end who did so. I for

my part was very careful not to incriminate either Jan or Zemlyansky, but simply affirmed that I did not believe that my teacher
had said anything against me, especially since it wasn't true
anyway.

'In the end, I suppose that I was a convenient scapegoat since
Vasily Ivanovitch had failed in his plan with the Frenchman and I
had an unsatisfactory background in the form of the bad report
after the American tour; I had also proved to be useless as a
source of incriminating information about the people I was
supposed to be covering in my reports. So I was dismissed and
made to sign a paper that I was no longer in the service of the KGB
and that I promised never to tell anyone that I ever had been. I
signed all this still using my code name Mitya – and that was the
last I ever saw of anyone from the KGB. Vasily Ivanovitch was
very threatening and hostile – he shouted at me, banged his fist on
the table and even said "Do you want to go to prison?" I was
dreadfully afraid and even cried, I was so scared.'

Happily there were no further repercussions, perhaps because Ashkenazy was known to be a potential winner of the
Tchaikovsky Competition and therefore had some protection
from the relevant forces within the Ministry of Culture. Later on,
victory itself in the Competition in 1962 made him too valuable
an asset not to be made use of – indeed, owing to the considerable
international interest in him thereafter, it would have been
counter-productive for him to have been seen to be the victim of
any official displeasure or embargo.

Interestingly enough, when Ashkenazy was interviewed by
the British secret services six years later, after he had decided to
stay in London, he talked very little about his relationship with
the KGB. He only felt absolved from his original promise of
silence many years later when the Soviet authorities decided to
manipulate him shamelessly and untruthfully at the time of the
Kuznetsov defection.* Even then, he felt free to speak only
because he knew that the story as described above would be
entirely valueless in that the information provided would by then
be long out of date.

Ashkenazy adds a brief postscript to the events of this period:

* The Russian writer Anatoly Kuznetsov, author of the novel *Babi Yar*
among other titles, defected to the West in 1969. His outspoken attacks on the
Soviet system attracted enormous media interest.

'It turned out that the "companion" who caused me so much trouble after my first American tour had a sad fate. His daughter married a foreigner and then emigrated. Apparently he died soon after this shattering experience, and probably as a direct consequence. He was very much a Party man and his daughter's actions would probably have brought about his downfall within the Party; in any case, such a state of affairs within his own family with its inevitable effect not only on his own prospects but on that whole network of people who would have depended upon him, must have been more than he could cope with.'

———•••———

7

VAN CLIBURN'S sensational victory in the first International Tchaikovsky Competition in Moscow in 1958 dealt a heavy blow to Soviet prestige; in America, it was heralded as some compensation for recent humiliations suffered at the hands of the Russians in the field of space technology. In looking forward to the next competition, it was thought essential, not only by the Soviet musical establishment but also by the Ministry of Culture and the Party leadership, that the very competition which had been designed as an international showcase for the superiority of Soviet achievement in music should not turn out to be quite the reverse. Since there had been no question about Van Cliburn's pre-eminence in 1958, the strongest possible team of Soviet pianists had to be selected and trained to carry the day for Soviet art in 1962.

The process of selection commenced in 1959, the year after Van Cliburn's victory and three full years before the next competition. By the end of the year, the basic team had been chosen and Ashkenazy and the other successful candidates found themselves summoned to the Ministry of Culture to hear a speech full of fine clichés about their duties as patriots to their fatherland, to the Revolution and to Soviet power.

Ashkenazy had tried to avoid being selected and had ended up as the Soviet Union's best hope very much under duress. 'I told them that I did not want to enter, largely because it was not my sort of music. They replied "What do you mean? How can you say that Tchaikovsky, our great Russian composer, is not your kind of music?" So in the end I had to swallow my words – there was simply no way of making them understand that one artist may be more suited to play, say, Beethoven, than Tchaikovsky. It wasn't so much that I was afraid to enter because I might not win; it was much more that I had never tried to play much Tchaikovsky. Even when I had sight-read the B flat minor Concerto (which is unavoidable in the finals if you get that far), I hadn't liked it too much. Besides, my real objection was that I had already won the Brussels Competition, not to mention the second prize in Warsaw, so why should I have to go through yet another contest? There were even comments in the American press later that these competitions were surely not intended for artists with established careers. Even though it was made clear that if I entered, and even more if I won, the official cloud might be removed from over my head, I was not too impressed. I had mixed feelings about going abroad again after the American tour in 1958; even though it had been very successful and I had in retrospect got over some of the worst feelings of insecurity, I still remembered how miserable and alienated I had felt much of the time. In the end, however, the pressure from all sides was just too much. I was told officially that unless I agreed to participate, my whole future career would be in jeopardy, not just abroad but also in the Soviet Union. This was my first explicit experience of blackmail from the authorities, if one does not count my recruitment by the KGB when at least nominally I was under no direct compulsion. The second occasion, as will be described more fully later, was when my wife was blackmailed into taking up Soviet citizenship by exactly the same threat to my career.

'All in all, I was still very young and accustomed to accept that in the Soviet Union you do not resist pressure from above for too long if you do not want your life blighted in all sorts of ways. Finally, as so much was expected of me it was difficult not to take up the challenge, even though I knew it was not really the right competition for me to show my best work.

'I think that the 1962 Tchaikovsky Competition achieved a high standard. Eliso Virsaladze won one of the lower prizes and another prize winner was Susan Starr who has had a rather successful career in America. Also Yin Chen Tsun, the Chinese pianist who recorded the "Yellow River Concerto" with Ormandy. Another excellent pianist who got into the finals was Alexei Nasedkin, although he has not been allowed out to play in the West much.

'Even though I did not enjoy the Competition because of all the artificial as well as musical pressures, once I had heard most of the other competitors I did feel that I had more to say, though whether I could win the first prize was another matter. That, after all, depends so much on how you play on that particular day, and with attention centring on the Tchaikovsky B flat minor in the last round the outcome was particularly uncertain. To play all that bravura, which I actually detest, you have to believe in it passionately as well as having all the equipment. And that type of octave equipment was really not my thing – that was really for John Ogdon, Van Cliburn or Horowitz.

'When the first prize was eventually divided between John Ogdon and me, there were many people in Moscow who thought that he should have had it all by himself. His natural gift for the piano as well as the brilliance of his performances made a great impact on the public; in addition he cut a rather exotic figure and there tended to be a tremendous admiration for and fascination with foreigners, who performed with a type of charisma that we were not used to.

'Whatever the reasons were for dividing the first prize, the importance of it for me was incalculable. Now, of course, when information is published by the Russians about earlier Tchaikovsky Competitions, my name is never mentioned. It is almost as though I never took part at all. Still, I suppose I am in distinguished company among the countless non-persons removed from Soviet "history"; even Trotsky, who after Lenin must be considered as the most important architect of the Revolution, was erased from all Soviet encyclopaedias not long after he fell from power. These disappearing tricks must be a real headache for editors and archivists in the Soviet Union; after all, someone might end up being rehabilitated later. I suppose the purchase of a few good Western word-processors might help.'

In the first Tchaikovsky Competition in 1958, one of the competitors was a nineteen-year-old Icelandic girl called Thorunn Johannsdottir,* a student of Harold Craxton at the Royal Academy of Music in London. Her own childhood had been unusual. She was born in Reykjavik in Iceland where her father Johann Tryggvason was a pianist, choir master and music teacher. In 1945 he left Iceland to study music in London at the Royal Academy and was joined two years later by his wife Klara and their three children, the oldest being Thorunn (Dody).

* In Iceland, the patronymic is used as the family name. However, while living in England, she was obliged to use her father's name, Tryggvason, under which she also entered the Competition.

Johann's family seem to have all been musical, in that his sister and three brothers all played or sang and one of his brothers, Jakob, also came to London to study music, returning later to be organist and music teacher in Akureyri, in the north of Iceland.

During the first few years in London, the family moved around from one accommodation to another; there was very little money and times were hard but Dody remembers that they always seemed to be warm, comfortable and well fed. A small Icelandic community tended to congregate around them, so the most could be made of the food rations of the time.

Dody had already shown the most extraordinary musical precocity in Iceland, having started to play the piano at the age of two. At four, she had learned to read music and had started to compose her own pieces. In her own words, she became quite a little Icelandic monument and had given quite a few concerts as well as radio broadcasts by the time that she left for England at the age of seven. Later on, she returned to Iceland every year or so to give a concert tour, which helped to supplement the family income.

In London she was enrolled immediately at the Junior School of the Academy but her father taught her the normal Icelandic school syllabus at home until she was eleven. As a result, even though the family language has always been Icelandic, she alone speaks it correctly; her two brothers and three sisters only learned the language orally. Since they all went straight to local schools, to a certain extent their Icelandic suffered compared with English. At the age of eleven, Dody went to King Alfred's School in Golders Green where in fact she spent little time, apart from attending her normal school lessons. She was always more involved with her musical studies at the Academy or at the Craxtons' home, where she had her piano lessons and spent most of her time. She also played concerts in England from time to time; at the age of seven she played a concerto by Alec Rowley, first at the Academy and then one year later with the London Symphony Orchestra at the Central Hall in Westminster. When she was eleven she played a Mozart concerto with the Hallé under Sir John Barbirolli, a memory she cherishes. She also continued with her compositions during her teens but she now dismisses all these experiments as being of no importance.

Dody is rather unclear as to why it was decided that she should go in for the Tchaikovsky Competition or who first suggested the idea; she thinks that it was just that the literature and application forms were on display in the Academy, and she remembers large envelopes arriving covered in imposing-looking red stamps, containing all the documentation. She admits now that she was quite unprepared for such a venture, not least because the required repertoire was new to her and included few of the works she had been playing since her childhood. Her main reason for wanting to go was her hero-worship of Richter and Gilels, and admiration for some of the other Russian pianists whose records were beginning to filter through to the West.

Once in Moscow, she was accommodated with the other foreigners in hotels, which seemed to her rather a luxury. Everyone seemed to do their best to make the visitors comfortable. Still, she found the Competition a strange experience, as though she had suddenly landed on another planet. She remembers liking Van Cliburn both as a person and as the obviously pre-eminent pianist in the Competition. They used to eat together with some of the other Western contestants, and she used to give him her share of the caviar with which they were liberally served. She also met quite a lot of Russian musicians, including Vladimir Ashkenazy who was then very much a star in the ascendant. Apart from Van Cliburn himself, she was greatly impressed by how incredibly secure the Russian contestants were in their schooling and in their pianistic preparation. It seemed to her that the Russian method of teaching, especially as far as technical perfection was concerned, was simply the best in the world and she decided that she would like to return to Moscow to study at the Conservatoire. This would in fact have been beyond her family's means, but an old friend and benefactor, Mrs Bibby, who had known Dody since she was a small child, very generously provided funds to make it possible for her to go.

When she returned to Moscow in 1960, she lived in a hostel for students in which three rooms, a kitchen and bathroom were shared by nine girls; she and an older Venezuelan student had the smallest rooms. Fortunately, no one spoke English, and so they all had to use whatever Russian they could pick up with the help of two Russian students who lived in their little group. Dody was able to learn quite a lot and this proved helpful later on.

'Although I first met Dody at the 1958 Tchaikovsky Competition, she was not successful so she left after only a few days. We saw each other once or twice, but there was no hint of romance at that stage. She then came back in autumn 1960 to study in Oborin's class at the Conservatoire. Naturally, there was a lot of interest in her arrival because she was considered to be very attractive and all the boys looked forward to meeting her. I remember first seeing her at one of the classes of Oborin's assistant Voskrysensky who was quite a good pianist in his own right. She never worked with Zemlyansky.

'I started going out with her almost immediately and it became rather serious pretty well straight away. There was a very strong attraction, not only because of her looks, but because of her whole personality. Obviously, she was also rather exotic, being a foreigner, and since she spoke no Russian at the beginning I had the opportunity of exercising my very rudimentary English picked up from my American tour in 1958. So there was the added incentive that she taught me how to speak better English and how to enlarge my vocabulary. Later, she learned to speak Russian but we never really spoke it together because I had a head start over her in my English; since then we have always spoken English as our family language.

'I was certainly aware of the fact that it wasn't exactly wise to go out with a foreigner but by that time things had eased up a little and there were a few other foreigners at the Conservatoire so we weren't the only ones who were seen together. The general atmosphere was better than it had been before Stalin died and with Khrushchev in power the feeling in the country as a whole was that you could be a little more individual, although no one knew exactly how far you could go. I suppose, being near the top of the pile because of the Chopin Competition and Brussels, I was in a rather more privileged position than most and could always claim that she was interested in my piano playing and in me as a musician.

'In any case, it was much better if you did things quite openly rather than trying to hide and be surreptitious. Then, if someone wanted to warn you off, they could do it straight away. In fact, some attempts were made – I was summoned to see the head of the Komsomol who expressed his disapproval, and later the Director of the Conservatoire contacted my mother to suggest that she should intervene. When we started to see each other every day, my mother got very worried and said "Look, you got a reprimand after the American tour, and now you're doing this. You really must take care not to get yourself into worse trouble." But I didn't hesitate. I thought, if it's really serious, I won't pay any attention to what anyone says or thinks – and it was. Any sort of pressure always produces a very strong reaction in me and I felt all the more that I should do as I wanted. So we finally got married.'

As soon as it became clear that her relationship with Ashkenazy was developing into something serious, the atmosphere began to change for Dody too, as though she had somehow become a different person. In the summer of 1960 a friend of Ashkenazy's in the local Komsomol organization warned him that his relationship with Dody was frowned upon and advised him to stop seeing her and that steps were being taken for her stay at the Conservatoire to be terminated. As a result of this, Dody took the precaution of going to the Icelandic Embassy to ask them to apply for her visa to be extended for a further year, even though her current one was valid for quite a few more months. The extension was given by the Ministry of Foreign Affairs whose decision unwittingly overruled the wishes of the Ministry of Culture.

Despite these ill omens, once Dody had fallen in love with Ashkenazy and they had decided to get married, she felt completely reconciled to the idea of making her life in Russia. She had no particular qualms about living under the Soviet system and was indeed largely innocent of any political attitudes one way or the other as far as communism was concerned. Consequently, when it was made abundantly plain to her shortly after their marriage by an official called Stepanov, then head of the foreign department of the Ministry of Culture that her continuing with her Icelandic nationality would terminate her new husband's prospects of playing abroad, she did not hesitate to take on Soviet citizenship and hand back her Icelandic passport. It may have been that this step did not seem so grave at the time, despite the extraordinary pressure brought upon her to make her do it, because she had friends amongst the Icelandic diplomatic staff in Moscow; she still felt Icelandic and assumed she could count on help if she should ever need it. But once the exchange of citizenship had actually been made, she began to feel immediately how different things were going to be. In some ways she was worse off than any ordinary Soviet citizen; she had none of the special rights of a foreign national and yet was unable to fall back upon those long-practised Soviet attitudes and responses which help people to survive there.

Two incidents stick vividly in her mind. On one occasion she went with her husband to a concert wearing round her neck a small gold cross which had been given to her by her grandmother. A few days later Ashkenazy was rebuked by the Director of the Philharmonia* and told that his wife, now that she was a Soviet citizen, should not be seen wearing a cross in public. A little later, they were visited a few times by two Icelandic students who were living in Moscow and who happened to be convinced communists. After a few such visits, Ashkenazy received another summons and was told that he should not be receiving foreigners in his apartment; the fact that the foreigners in question were both Icelandic and communists, as Ashkenazy vainly pointed out, did nothing to lessen the rebuke.

Even as far as hospital care was concerned, Dody was able to discover during her first pregnancy the difference in treatment when she threatened to miscarry, once before and once after her change of citizenship. On the second visit, conditions were infinitely less satisfactory; visitors including her husband were not allowed and the treatment as a whole was callous and offhand. Fortunately, by the time that the baby was actually due, Dody was in fact accepted at the hospital she had originally visited as a foreigner six months earlier. The head of the department kept to a promise made to her at that time that she would be delivered at his hospital, but even then Ashkenazy was prohibited from attending the birth, or even from visiting her. In fact, he set eyes on his first child, Vovka, for the very first time nine full days after the birth.†

Years later she had cause to remember this when their third

* The organizations responsible for providing all types of concerts including orchestral concerts and solo recitals are the so called 'Philharmonias' which exist in most major towns of the Soviet Union. They are, of course, under direct governmental control and almost every aspect of a professional musician's life is regulated by them.

† Vladimir Stefan. Vovka is the diminutive his parents have always used for him.

child Dimitri (Dimka) was delivered in a New York hospital. On one of his rounds the American doctor in charge remarked that the Russians had been pioneers in encouraging the presence of husbands during childbirth. Dody was quick to correct this particular piece of misinformation – or more probably disinformation since it is the sort of 'human interest' detail the Soviet publicity machine spews out to mislead the unwary – from her own personal experience.

'Our early life together was not made easier by other factors. Until the very end of 1962, we lived with my parents in one room of their two-room apartment. Of course, we had to share everything and although this was not so strange for me, having been used to it all my life, you can imagine that for Dody it was hardly an easy or romantic beginning to married life.

'When her Soviet passport was eventually issued, it came with a speech delivered by the official in charge welcoming her as a citizen of the "freest country of the World". How free she was, she learned very rapidly, but at the time she really gave Soviet life a fair trial; I suppose she only turned against it eventually because of the stupid and to her incomprehensible way in which we were treated. Dody was entirely apolitical and had gone to Moscow with the highest admiration for the level of music and musical education there. At that stage, while she was still young, inexperienced and full of good will, it would not have been difficult to keep her relatively content. But the whole society and system of life cannot cope with independent spirits who at first fail to understand and then refuse to conform to the inherently dishonest and overbearingly insensitive nature of authority and power in the Soviet Union.

'What really opened her eyes was when she decided that she would like to take Vovka to London to visit her parents. In the end it took five months for our application to be answered, and I'll never forget the occasion, two or three months after making our application, when we inquired whether a decision had been made. The officials, annoyed because we had telephoned a few times, said "Why is it that you are disturbing us? There is no decision yet, and in any case we don't know whether it will be negative or positive" – implying that Dody could very well be refused permission entirely to visit her parents. Well, that wasn't very encouraging, but we Soviets born and bred would expect all this; Dody, however, as a foreigner, who was not accustomed to such treatment, was profoundly shocked.

'This sense of outrage and shock was compounded when she decided to try to save time by applying for her British visa before her Soviet permission had come through, thinking that otherwise she might lose a few more precious weeks while her visa was processed. She decided to go to the British Embassy to make the application in person.

' "They'll only stop you at the gate," I told her.

' "Oh no, they won't do that. Why on earth should they?"

'Well, she went to the Embassy and was promptly stopped by the KGB militia man at the gate who took her immediately into an office in another building next door to the Embassy. He asked her if she was a Soviet citizen and she replied that she was but that although she was still waiting for her foreign passport to be issued, she wanted to apply for her British visa immediately, for a visit to her parents in England. Despite this, the KGB officer told her that he could not let her onto the territory of the British Embassy. She couldn't understand it then and indeed still cannot.'*

In the end Dody's permission did come through and she went to London with Vovka in August 1962. By this time Ashkenazy had already won the Gold Medal of the Tchaikovsky Competition and had had his travel ban removed. He had done his bit for the greater glory of Soviet power.

---

* Rudolf Barshai, the distinguished émigré conductor and founder of the Moscow Chamber Orchestra, had similar experiences with his Japanese wife. She could never understand that he could not travel to Japan with her whenever she wanted to go back home to visit her family. In the end, she thought it was because he did not want to go with her: she could not believe that the authorities would impede him from travelling with his own wife to visit her country.

8

As SOON AS it became known that Ashkenazy was once again available, a contract was signed with Goskoncert by Sol Hurok for a second tour of the United States in the autumn of 1962; by now Ashkenazy was an even greater attraction for the American touring circuit, given the ever-increasing fascination in the West for top-ranking Soviet artists.

There was also immense interest in the next Tchaikovsky Competition winner after Van Cliburn, who had become a household name throughout the States. When it was confirmed that Ashkenazy would be allowed to take up the tour, he applied for permission for Dody, who was still in London, to accompany him. She, by now increasingly aware of the need to make the most of the fact that she was already outside the Soviet Union, suggested that Ashkenazy should fly first to London so that they could go on to America together. The Ministry of Culture, however, insisted that she had to return to Moscow before a decision could be taken as to whether she would be allowed to go to the States or not. It is possible that they were concerned that if Ashkenazy were allowed to join her in London with their child already out of their clutches, he might be tempted to stay in the West. Also, given the complexity of Soviet bureaucracy, Dody had to have a different type of passport for the American tour, since the one she was using for her visit to London was the type issued only for visits to family abroad.

Ashkenazy tried to explain all of this on the telephone from Moscow when she called to find out the results of his investigations. In the end she agreed to return and a few days later they did receive the necessary permissions to leave together. However, the authorization came through only at the very last moment, once again obliging Ashkenazy to travel to Washington the day before his first concert. As on the occasion of his first tour, there was no consideration as to how this might affect the success of what was obviously a critically important return visit. It was only a few days before the Cuban missile crisis erupted.

On this occasion, though, there was one unlikely recompense. Despite the fact that the visas had obviously been applied for too late, those for the Ashkenazys were rushed through at the American end, no doubt as a result of all sorts of pressure from the Hurok office. However, the visa for the 'companion' from the Ministry of Culture was processed normally, with the customary delay of four to six weeks, since the Americans saw no justification in extending any favours to someone who was effectively a KGB agent. Unusually, a woman had been selected by the Ministry but, when she finally got her visa half-way through Ashkenazy's tour, the Soviets decided that it would be pointless to send her at all. As a result, Dody's expenses were in the end covered by the Hurok office, since they were supposed to pay for the 'companion' anyway.

Perhaps the impending Cuban crisis also played its role. In this most elaborate poker game of the decade, both the Americans and the Soviets may have wished to maintain the fiction that everything was going on as normal, and that any aberrations which might tilt the balance would be entirely the responsibility of the other side. Oddly enough, the Cuban crisis erupted in the middle of one of the most hectic periods of cultural agreement and exchange between the Soviet Union and the United States. While the Soviet missile ships were steaming towards Cuba, the New York City Ballet was performing to rapturous audiences in Moscow; they even danced before six thousand people in the Kremlin Hall. At the same time, the Leningrad Philharmonic made its American debut in New York under Mravinsky to much critical and public acclaim. This concert took place on 21 October 1962, only five days after Ashkenazy's first concert in Washington. It is tempting to think that Khrushchev may have calculated that the warmth and enthusiasm with which the cultural exchange programme was being received might have weighted the scales just a little more in his favour when Kennedy had to decide whether or not to turn a blind eye to the progressive infiltration of Soviet rockets into Cuba. Perhaps it is too fanciful to read into Khrushchev's famous diatribe against modern art at the Manège exhibition in Moscow in December a sign of his frustration and anger that his great throw of the dice had failed, but it is interesting to note how rapidly the halcyon days of international exchange were followed by a new crack-down on 'formalist' tendencies in the arts. This was carried out by the newly constituted ideological committee responsible to the Party's Central Committee. But the clock could not be put back too far; in the face of manifest official disapproval, that same December saw the Moscow première of Shostakovich's Thirteenth Symphony 'Babi Yar' with its controversial poems by Yevtushenko. This important work, as well as the revival of the same composer's *Katerina Ismailova* for the first time since its condemnation by Stalin in 1936, were virtually ignored in the press but warmly received by the public. The fact that they were allowed to be performed at all proved how much times had changed.

* * *

Even today, with the benefit of Concorde, Ashkenazy would not dream of travelling to Washington from London, let alone from Moscow, the day before an important concert; in 1962 there was no direct service from Moscow at all and so he and Dody had to change planes, and airports, in Paris. The people in Goskoncert had given no thought to the fact that this would involve not only extra stress and time but that the journey between Le Bourget and Orly meant that the Ashkenazys needed transit visas.

Fortunately, Hurok had arranged for them to be met on their arrival in Paris, and for the visas to be taken care of, and he even up-graded them to first-class for the transatlantic portion of the journey. He certainly did not have to do this by contract, and one could put this down to an act of generosity on Hurok's part. On the other hand, ever the shrewd businessman, he certainly understood how much was at stake at the outset of this important second tour. If such a gesture meant that Ashkenazy would arrive that little bit more rested thus improving the chances of a successful start to the tour, Hurok was just the man to make that sort of clear-sighted judgement. It is interesting to compare the Ashkenazys' somewhat cavalier treatment at the hands of Goskoncert – an organization dedicated to the promotion of Soviet prestige abroad through the arts – with the care and foresight shown by their sponsor in the West.

This second tour was altogether more enjoyable for Ashkenazy. First and foremost, he had Dody with him, and her constant companionship on future tours was to provide him with invaluable and irreplaceable support as well as a critical objectivity which he continues to find essential to this day. Dody, an exceptionally gifted pianist and musician herself, has the truest of ears. She is also committed to the truth in a way seldom found amongst the wives or husbands of famous and successful artists. Even when it may be painful, Ashkenazy has always been able to rely on her for a true impression of what actually happened rather than of what might have appeared to be the case in the passion of the moment or amidst the adulation of admirers. She also has the gift of detecting the false in the motivations of those who have sometimes appeared initially very beguiling to her husband. Like many Russians, Ashkenazy tends to be both enormously trusting when he is drawn to people and very suspicious when he finds their attitudes unappealing. In the early years after his emigration, these conflicting responses were particularly confusing as he struggled to find his way in the West; he always states that without Dody's clarity of vision and true instinct, he might have been absolutely lost. Her contribution has not always been quite so well appreciated by others. Although by nature shy, and by choice not involving herself in business discussions concerning her husband's career, Dody can be very direct when she detects something wrong or phoney.

As the years have passed, her musical contribution has become equally indispensable. Even though she stopped playing the piano when they married, her knowledge of most of the piano and much of the orchestral repertoire has been invaluable, especially since she is possessed of a truly extraordinary musical ear. André Previn, himself one of the most naturally gifted of today's musicians, likes to tell the story of how Dody heard a performance of the Walton First Symphony in Israel for the very first time; she then went to the piano and played absolutely correctly the rather complex brass chording in the last movement without ever having seen the score.

Over the years Dody's constant presence at concerts, rehearsals and recordings, and her unfailing and unfussy smoothing of the path for Ashkenazy both at home and on tour, has made it possible for him to build his life and career on the surest of foundations. Ashkenazy has the greatest confidence in her artistic objectivity and relies upon her as a touchstone in many moments of doubt and uncertainty.

A further factor in Ashkenazy's feeling of liberation on this second American tour was his greatly improved English. Even though Dody had learned to speak fluent Russian, English was the family language and over the next few years Ashkenazy was to develop a rich vocabulary and a remarkable facility with the language. He is inclined to be a little self-conscious about the fact that his idioms and pronunciation still betray his Russian origins but he is capable of writing expressively and stylishly in English.

In 1962, he could already read the American newspapers freely and could communicate without difficulty with the people he met on the tour. He remembers that this feeling of freedom and access to information was extraordinarily heady; he suddenly realized how stifling it had been not to have had the opportunity of informing himself about what was going on in the world around him.

He was also able to follow the development of the Cuban missile crisis with a new understanding of the true implications of what was being said on both sides. He watched the developments on television and heard the Soviet representatives denying publicly that rockets had been deployed on Cuba. This time he did not just have to rely on his intuition to decide that the Russians were lying; now he had concrete evidence to go on, including the high-altitude pictures taken by American surveillance planes. He remembers feeling rather pro-American about the whole affair but was surprised how seriously the ordinary man in the street took the threat of nuclear war. He later surmised that this was probably because the American public was infinitely better informed about the developing crisis than would ever have been possible in the Soviet Union. In retrospect, now that he understands the American mentality better, he sees the national *angst* of the time as being characteristic of the American passion for hyperbole and drama in any unusual situation, whether in politics or the arts.

Everything out of the ordinary has to be blown up into a crisis or a sensation, a tendency which he deplores when applied, as it so often is, to music and the arts. To be interesting in the United States, and most especially in New York, every important artist must be reported to have the biggest technique in living memory or must be billed as the last in a direct line of pianists stretching back to Brahms or Liszt. Everyone has to be legitimized by reference to some previously hallowed myth or legend; only rarely is something judged or appreciated for its intrinsic qualities alone. It is for this reason that publicity and press exposure are so central to the public's perceptions about artists and their performances. It is almost as though the arts remain insubstantial and inchoate until they have been written about and categorized in the reassuringly concrete form of newsprint.

In this respect, Ashkenazy is himself something of an anomaly. Until recently he avoided all forms of publicity and gave very few interviews. Indeed, he sees himself as being just a little too reliable and unsensational to provide the sort of exotic fare which is sought by the excitement-starved New York audiences. And yet despite his reticence, he has one of the biggest followings of any artist, with sold-out houses year after year for his New York recitals. What is more, in a country where an artist can be a household name in Chicago and unknown in Los Angeles, he is one of a tiny handful of soloists who can be relied upon to pull in the public right across the country.

Ashkenazy believes that the breadth and depth of his following must partly be ascribed to the fact that he was in 1958 the first young Russian pianist to appear on the American scene after the incredible impression made by Richter and Gilels. American interest in Russian artists may also have been heightened in 1958 by the nation-wide swell of pride in Van Cliburn's victory in the Tchaikovsky competition. Somewhat self-disparagingly, he also admits that his playing on the first two tours was extremely virtuosic and must have seemed very exciting. Since both tours were long and covered a large number of different cities, he now appreciates that the very best basis was laid for a lifetime's career in the United States.

This second tour was again enormously successful and right at the end a message came through from the Ministry of Culture telling him that he was to stop over in Iceland for a couple of concerts before going on to London. This must have been a political decision of one kind or another, putting to good use Dody's Icelandic origins. It was obviously thought to be highly expedient to cash in on the human interest that such a visit would undoubtedly arouse. The Soviets – and, for that matter, the

Americans – have always appreciated Iceland's important strategic location, an interest the Icelanders have managed astutely for their economic advantage. Ashkenazy surmises that something of importance was going on behind the scenes; a short notice about his first concert in Reykjavik even appeared in *Pravda*, which would never have happened unless there was some political significance to the timing of his visit. In any case, they were both delighted at this unexpected opportunity to visit Dody's country together, and Ashkenazy immediately felt at home there. It seemed a real haven of peace and quiet after the intense pressures of the American tour.

After this happy Icelandic interlude, they went on to London to spend Christmas with Dody's family. They arrived in London on 24 December 1962 and left again for Moscow on 2 January 1963.

'This was only a private visit without any concerts, but an interview was arranged with William Mann of *The Times*, which I felt I could not escape because my first British concert tour was to follow three months later. It was a very nice interview, in the end, very positive and very friendly. I was much impressed by the contrast with the few American interviews I had reluctantly had to give. All in all, I fell in love with London and the way of life I saw there, particularly with Hampstead and the little bit of Hendon where Dody's parents lived. I felt absolutely at home in London, infinitely more so than in America despite my enjoyment of the recent tour. I had already sensed that there was so much emphasis in America on business and money and show, whereas in Europe the attitude to these things seemed much healthier. I still feel this and now, of course, I can support my views with concrete arguments, whereas then I just had intuitive reactions. Even so, I was later able to put these impressions into better perspective; whatever my criticisms of America may have been, I could also appreciate how many wonderful people of the greatest integrity and real culture one can find there. Still, at the time the superficial differences were particularly striking when seen in such sharp and close contrast.

'When we finally had to return to Moscow after those happy days in London, I felt terribly low, as though prison gates were closing behind us. I had no idea whether I could ever leave again and even, were I to be allowed to travel again, whether Dody would be able to accompany me. I was so depressed that I told Dody the very day after our return that if we ever should get the chance again, should we not think of staying abroad, particularly in London?

'She didn't take it seriously at first, but I kept nagging her, saying that I really meant it. Her own intuition was probably that despite the fact that she dearly wanted to stay in the West, the whole proposition was quite unrealistic in practice and that even if I was saying then that I wanted to stay in the West, something deep down within me would reject this and would at the last moment make me retreat. And she was right because when it came to it, I very nearly did retreat.'

The next tour abroad was planned for England in March 1963 but in the meantime there was a little time to enjoy a momentous change in their living conditions. After the Tchaikovsky Competition, Ashkenazy had written both to Khrushchev and to the Minister of Culture, Ekaterina Furtseva, appealing for an apartment of their own, on the grounds that better working conditions were indispensable given the added pressures of his developing international career. Up to that time, they had continued to live in his parents' apartment and since the birth of their son Vovka in November 1961, living and working in such cramped circumstances had been very difficult. Perhaps fortunately, Dody's own parents in London had brought up their six children on very little money and in cramped housing; since her father was a piano teacher, and she had had to learn how to practise the piano in an overcrowded home, Dody was probably a great deal more adaptable than many Westerners might have been. As it was, when they finally moved into their very own two-room apartment at the beginning of January 1963, their new home seemed almost luxurious. In fact, the whole apartment with its two small rooms, diminutive kitchen and tiny bathroom measured thirty-five square metres in all, but it was in a relatively well-favoured building in Smolenskaya Street, overlooking one of the routes used by the government to get out of Moscow and only a few minutes from the Ministry of Foreign Affairs. Furnishing the apartment was no great problem; by the time that a bed, a table and a few chairs had been added to the baby grand piano there was room for virtually nothing else. Ashkenazy had bought the piano, a Steinway, with his entire savings from the recent American tour – in fact, he even had to borrow $500 extra from his friend Malcolm Frager.

Oddly enough, even after his emigration, the apartment remained in his legal possession for several years. At first it was probably felt in official circles that it would have to be kept for his use on the assumption that he would return sooner or later. Then, perhaps because of some administrative oversight, it seems to have been forgotten and eventually Ashkenazy's sister Elena moved in. It would have been risky for her to have lived there without official registration, however, given the anomalous standing of her brother abroad. Normally such transfers can only be made with the help of some well-connected contact within the Party and fortunately David Ashkenazy must have found someone to help them to ensure that Elena's occupation was formalized without too much trouble; in any case the authorities may have wanted at that stage to avoid accusations abroad that the Ashkenazy family was being victimized.

In such cases a hearing in a district court is required and Ashkenazy recently heard from a friend who is now also in the West how these things can sometimes be arranged. His friend's father knew one of the deputy judges serving the district court circuit and he secured her interest in his case by the promise of a foreign-made refrigerator which the lady deputy judge was most desirous of owning and which he was able to acquire through another contact. However, even after securing her support, all was not plain sailing. Apparently, if the normal circuit judge had taken on that particular case, he would have certainly ruled against the applicant and so it was essential that the case should come up when he was away on holiday. This was successfully arranged and the lady deputy duly sat in his place; she also managed such other complex stratagems as were necessary to ensure that the case could not be reviewed later, as it normally could be if anyone raised an objection. All went well: the lady judge got her refrigerator and the new occupant of the apartment was officially registered.

Another bizarre state of affairs centred around Ashkenazy's military service obligations. In the Soviet Union one of the most essential documents is the certificate confirming that you have either done your service or, in very special circumstances, that you have been exempted. In his case, given his status in the

Conservatoire and his international prizes, there was no problem about arranging the dispensation, but when it came to the actual document confirming the release, this somehow went astray. For a while he managed without it, what with the build-up to the Tchaikovsky Competition and the flurry of events in the months afterwards. But when the new apartment was authorized, it was absolutely necessary to de-register with the military office of the district he was leaving and then to register with the new district. He went along to the head office of his local military district and explained the whole problem to the senior officer in charge. This man, a major at least, received him very cheerily and complimented him on his great victory in the Competition. When he heard that Ashkenazy had no exemption certificate he replied equally breezily, 'Well, you should go to prison for that. But let's see what we can do. What do you say if we make you a reserve lieutenant? Will that do? That should take care of things.' Such a comic-opera scene being played out by an official within a ruthlessly coercive system hardly seems probable, but Ashkenazy assumes that such a solution could be possible only because the major had already covered himself by referring things to his superiors; no one would risk his whole future by dealing with so serious a matter with such frivolity.

Once settled in the new apartment, the Ashkenazys began to think seriously about the practical arrangements for the British tour coming up in March.

'As always, I had to apply for permission for Dody to accompany me to England and I included Vovka in the application saying that since it would only be a short tour and confined to one place it would be appropriate for us to take the child with us to London. There he could be with his grandparents as well as with us, rather than staying alone with my parents in Moscow, as had happened during the American tour. So, the people at the Ministry of Culture had to make a decision about this and they obviously wanted to try to talk me out of it. The point is that they had to apply in turn to the Central Committee, to the so-called Exit Commission there, and an important Ministry of Culture official would have to be the guarantor of the application in order to take the responsibility in case anything happened. In the end Stepanov, the very same official who staged the kangaroo court for me after my first American tour, and the one who put pressure on Dody to take Soviet citizenship, was the one to whom I had to apply and who, I assume, eventually became my guarantor. Strange that in the end he should have staked his career on such an issue. Probably at some point he felt ashamed of what he did to me, so, who knows, maybe he had something human in him.

'They called me to the Ministry roughly two weeks before my supposed date of departure for London. It was at the end of February and I had 'flu, so I said that I couldn't come. It was very cold and I was afraid that if I went out I might end up by having to cancel part of the tour. The next thing I knew was that they told me that someone would visit me. This proved to be Supagin who was a subordinate of Stepanov, the head of the department. Supagin had been my "companion" when I went to West Germany in 1957, so they must have decided to send him because they knew that we got on well and they hoped I might trust him.

'His task was to try to talk me out of my application but it is a mystery to me why they thought they should try to get me to withdraw the application when Stepanov could have told me from the start, "Don't do it."

'So Supagin said, "We have been thinking about your application and although there is nothing wrong with the idea of your wife going with you, she has just been on the American tour and to London and we feel that if we allow one artist to take his wife along too frequently, we'll be in a difficult position with other artists. After all, we can't let artists' wives go too often because it costs a lot of money; even though you are buying her ticket, it is still with convertible roubles."

'In retrospect I have never been able to understand this, since Soviet artists are always obliged to use Aeroflot wherever possible. Since my flights to London and back could be easily booked on Aeroflot connections, no hard currency or convertible roubles would have been involved. I suppose it was just bluff; he had no real argument with which to oppose my request, so he had to fabricate one which he thought would sound convincing.

'I replied that I saw their problem and didn't want to make difficulties but asked them to judge for themselves whether this wasn't a rather special trip since it was to England where Dody had lived for a long time, and where her parents and brothers and sisters lived. I also pointed out that it would be diplomatically wrong for me to play my first concert tour in England without bringing Dody and my son with me. I went on to say that they could cancel the whole tour if they preferred, since I didn't mind if I went or not. Then, if the tour were set up again in a year or so, they would perhaps feel better after an interval about my wife and child going too. I pointed out that I had 'flu and they could easily use this as an excuse for cancelling the tour. But Supagin said, "No, absolutely not, we can't do that, that's out of the question." Incidentally, Supagin later became the Director of Goskoncert for some years during the seventies.

'Why they didn't initially just prohibit me from taking them is still a complete mystery. All I can think is that within even such a rigid system as the Soviet state, certain attitudes or judgements of individuals can sometimes play an influential role, particularly at a time when the traditional policies had been somewhat undermined as was the case during the Khrushchev period. At that time the general attitude of the top echelons of the Central Committee became for a while less uncompromising about certain more personal or individualistic aspects of life, including things like foreign travel. Khrushchev himself, for example, took the decision to let Richter go abroad for concert tours, although previously this had been considered impossible because of his German connections. But even though a new flexibility might be discerned among the top party leaders, partly perhaps because no one wanted to be left behind in what seemed to be a new trend, it would still require an important official in the Ministry of Culture to give a personal guarantee before permission to travel abroad could be granted. Khrushchev's intervention in the case of Richter was necessary because the case was so controversial that in all probability no single official could have taken upon himself such a responsibility, and yet the interest in Richter from abroad was so intense that the matter simply could not be shelved. As a result it must have passed higher and higher up the chain until Khrushchev himself became involved.

'Stepanov, who had presided over the mock "trial" four years earlier felt that they had been too hard on me at that time – I know that for sure. Now that is a human response – and even within the system one cannot discount the effect of simple human feelings. I know he felt that way because in the intervening years I met several people who had seen Stepanov and told him that they knew I wasn't as bad as I had been made out to be, and was certainly not anti-Soviet. Stepanov seems to have been increasingly on the defensive, yet in general his reputation was not so bad; he used to go to concerts which was very unusual for a senior official in the Ministry of Culture, and he seemed to be genuinely interested in music. I was always very correct but cool with him because I wanted him to know that I felt that I had been most unfairly treated. I am sure that he sensed this and indeed seems to have taken a personal interest in promoting the idea that I should play in France and Czechoslovakia about a year before the Tchaikovsky Competition, just after we had got married.

'He called me in to see him and I told him then that there seemed little point in even discussing it because I was sure that they would never let me go, both because of the past and now all the more so because I had married a foreigner. But he kept on insisting that it was time for me to go abroad again. In the end, I was proved right because I was not allowed to go, but it went quite far with official invitations issued and even specific concerts arranged.

'This was in April 1961, two months after our marriage. In fact I was supposed to have gone off on this tour on my own despite my recent marriage, which may have encouraged Stepanov to support the idea. In the end, perhaps the reason why it all fell through was because he did not give the sort of personal guarantee which the Exit Commission of the Central Committee would have required. As a result the usual nonsense went on; I had to get my tickets and passport from Goskoncert but whenever I called to find out if they were ready, nothing had come through. Finally, on the day of what should have been my first concert in Czechoslovakia I called Goskoncert again but, when they still had no information to give me, I gave up chasing them and heard absolutely nothing at all for the next ten days, while the dates of my various concerts passed by one by one. Finally Stepanov telephoned but asked for my mother. He said that, what I really needed to do was to prepare myself for the Tchaikovsky Competition and not be distracted by other things, so it would be better for me not to go abroad just then. He was obviously too embarrassed to have to say all of this to me, especially in view of the fact that the tour had been his idea in the first place and I had told him from the start that I did not believe that I would be allowed to go.

'Anyway, to come back to 1963, following my conversation with Supagin, they eventually called me to the Exit Commission in the Central Committee Building. This is one of the most security-minded places in the Soviet Union with all sorts of paraphernalia of entry permits, questions as to whether one is carrying weapons and so on. After all this, you go into an office to face two stern-looking officials who say, "You seem to be very nervous. Why should you be nervous? You are at home here, among friends." The hypocrisy is really unbelievable. They are there to test you, find out what is in your mind and yet you are supposed to feel at home.

'Anyway, they seemed to be pleased with what I said. I behaved entirely naturally and didn't hide anything. I just repeated what I had said to Supagin about my not caring whether I went on tour to England then or a year later but that it was diplomatically important to have my wife and child with me. They seemed impressed by this and said, "Well, if you want to go with your wife, you should certainly do so."

'I went straight from there to the Ministry of Culture and was given my passport and even the tickets. But as for the rest, unfortunately and perhaps predictably, the combined passport for Dody and Vovka wasn't ready yet. The official told me, "You can go as planned tomorrow and they will be able to follow you in a day or two."

'There was no reason to disbelieve them after all that had gone on before so I just had to accept this situation and go alone. When I got to London, I telephoned Dody who had already gone to the Ministry but had been told that the papers were still not ready and that she would have to come back again the next day. When she went again the next day and the papers were not there I decided that the Ministry was either being evasive or was actually trying to cheat us. Dody told me on the telephone that if they didn't give her the passport and tickets that same day so that she could leave on the next, she would go straight to the Icelandic Embassy, and she said exactly the same to the officials in the Ministry. "If they try to stop me, I'll phone my friends there and ask them for help. I'll make it public that they are not letting me go to join my husband and to see my parents." That very same day she got the passport and tickets.

'Obviously she made them realize that she was a force to be

reckoned with and they decided they did not want her to create an enormous fuss. I tend to believe that they had decided not to let her go and that they expected that she would react as Soviet citizens normally do in such situations when officials begin to lie; in other words, that she would just accept the situation and not do anything objectionable. After all, most Soviet citizens have learned from their childhood how to avoid trouble by not rocking the boat. They realize that they have everything to lose and very little to gain by confronting an uncooperative or mendacious official. It is always impossible to know whether any particular response is due to the attitude of the official himself or whether he is just passing on the wishes of the official above him. As for Dody, they certainly did not expect her to speak her mind and since we will never find out whether or not permission had been given by the Exit Commission, it is impossible now to reconstruct the goings on those last few days before Dody's departure.

'There must have been quite a traffic between the Ministry and the Exit Commission and in the end they probably decided to avoid an international incident and let her go.

'When Dody finally arrived in London, she told me that she wasn't going to go back after this latest experience. So, after a couple of weeks by which time I had played my first concerts, we went to the Home Office on the advice of a very good friend in the Foreign Office, who set up the initial contacts for us. We explained everything, also to someone from the security services who attended our interview. He gave us a number which we could call at any time for assistance or advice, just like in a detective story. We used the number many times in the coming weeks and when we decided that it was time to break the news to the Soviets, we called the Soviet Embassy and arranged to meet the Cultural Attaché who was my contact there. His name was Jarotsky and like most Cultural Attachés must have been either a KGB man himself or at least worked closely with the many KGB officers on the Embassy staff. This was, after all, long before the mass expulsion of "Soviet officials" by the Home government and at that time the Soviet Embassy contained a small army of agents.

'Having set up our meeting, we called our special number and told our contact about the meeting with Jarotsky so that it could be put under surveillance. They arranged for our meeting to be covered but Jarotsky noticed immediately. He said, "It's that couple over there – I've seen them a thousand times – they are always watching us." I suppose they attach very little importance to such low-grade surveillance; it becomes a normal feature of their daily life, just as in Moscow Western diplomats get used to the fact that their every move is followed by the ubiquitous KGB agents.

'We met in the Cumberland Hotel, near Marble Arch, and I told Jarotsky in the middle of lunch that we had decided to stay. He replied in consternation, "What do you mean, you are staying? How can you stay?"

'We told him, "Well, we've already been to the Home Office and we have residents' permits stamped in our passports." He couldn't believe his ears and hardly finished his lunch before he was on his way to the Embassy to report to Moscow.

'Then – and by this time it was the end of March – a great saga started with everyone alerted and my parents in a panic and the Embassy trying to get us to go there to talk things over. But we didn't feel like going there; there was really nothing to talk about and anyway, why go to the Embassy when we could meet anywhere we liked? We did eventually go there, however.'

Then a new development arose, one in which Ashkenazy feels sure Victor Hochhauser had a part. At that time and for many years afterwards, Hochhauser was the principal trading partner for the Russians in the field of music and other attractions such as the various folk ensembles which were very popular in the West at that time. His successful business was absolutely dependant on good relations with the Soviet authorities and he continued to be the main outlet for Soviet musicians until, in the 1970s, public opinion began to move against this sort of trade, especially within Jewish circles which were important to the Hochhausers.

Ashkenazy feels sure that Hochhauser intensely despised the Soviet Union and was quintessentially a man of the West in his personal devotion to free enterprise, being therefore sympathetic to the idea that one could do so much more for oneself in the West. But he had too much to lose in his business with the Russians if he were to be seen to offer the Ashkenazys overt support or assistance. At one stage in a private conversation with

Hochhauser, Ashkenazy told him that he was naturally very unhappy about the reaction of his parents and that perhaps the only solution would be for him to have unlimited freedom to travel to and from the Soviet Union for an indefinite period of time – in short, for him to get some sort of multiple exit and re-entry visa which would remove any fear that once he returned he might never be able to get out again. A few days later Jarotsky suddenly contacted Ashkenazy to say that the authorities in Moscow had decided to provide him and Dody with exactly such a multiple visa valid for six months. He pointed out that this was absolutely without precedent but they felt that this would give Ashkenazy the opportunity to go back home without any sense of restraint to talk things over with his parents and friends; he could then make a decision calmly and without pressure. If he and Dody still felt that they wanted to come back to London, they would be free to do so, although Jarotsky hoped and felt confident that they would see things in a different light and would decide to stay in the Soviet Union.

Ashkenazy told Hochhauser about this without asking him directly whether the initiative for this plan had come from him; Hochhauser remarked that the Soviet Ambassador had told him that they were going to offer this solution, and that it was a new departure, something they had never done before. Later, when this scheme eventually came to nothing Hochhauser arranged to pass on Ashkenazy to Mrs Emmie Tillett, the doyenne of European agents, and the Managing Director of the famous firm of Ibbs and Tillett. As a condition for arranging the 'marriage' with Ibbs and Tillett, he received a share of the commission from Ashkenazy's bookings for several years until Ashkenazy finally heard about the arrangement and insisted that it should be stopped.

By this time, the whole affair had been picked up by the international press, although Ashkenazy had done everything possible to avoid publicity until the last concert on the tour had been completed. They went to stay with friends, the kind and hospitable Mr and Mrs Bibby in Cheshire, hoping that they could avoid any unnecessary interviews there. However, the press had got hold of the story from some sort of Home Office release and *The Times* even went so far as to announce that Ashkenazy had applied for political asylum – this was quite untrue and Ashkenazy remembers being bitterly disappointed with such flimsy sensationalism, especially from a newspaper of the reputation of *The Times*. Fortunately, when the press could not find the Ashkenazys for a few days, and the story looked as though it might die, he hoped to be able to avoid most of the pressure of questions and interviews. Only *Life* magazine kept up the pursuit and pestered Dody's parents relentlessly. After a few days of this, Ashkenazy felt that it would be best to face the press in a controlled situation and so a press conference was arranged in the Adelphi Hotel in Liverpool. There the Ashkenazys explained that their decision was a purely personal one and that there was no political dimension. Ashkenazy wanted to cause as little distress as possible to his parents and to minimize the risk of any adverse repercussions for them and for his sister. It all turned out very well and Ashkenazy feels sure that the Soviets were reasonably satisfied with his controlled behaviour on this occasion. He also believes that if he had made anything political out of their decision at that stage, nothing would have persuaded the Soviet authorities to allow him to return with the newly issued multiple visa. At that stage, Ashkenazy began to think that there might indeed be some hope of living like a free man, with the right to come and go from the Soviet Union just as he pleased. After all, the whole affair was so unprecedented, and he was still very inexperienced.

Some days later Ashkenazy went to the Soviet Embassy with his and Dody's passports to get the new visas, and met the Ambassador. 'He was terribly friendly and charming. He said, "Well, here you are – a young couple, and your lives are just beginning. It's only natural there should be some friction between you. It will probably all settle down and you won't in the end want to leave the Soviet Union – such a wonderful country." The clichés followed, of course – they always mix up clichés and propaganda with all sorts of human considerations.'

It was by then early May and the visas had actually been issued; on 14 May they flew back to Moscow, leaving Vovka with Dody's parents.

'To leave our son behind was Dody's idea and a very sound one. When Stepanov at the Ministry asked her, "What is this, you have left your baby behind – don't you trust us?" Dody immediately replied, "You're absolutely right, I don't trust you.

You don't trust us, so why should we trust you?" They never expected that sort of reaction. They don't expect people to speak their minds because from childhood in the Soviet Union you learn not to.'

Ashkenazy himself admits that at this stage he really did not know what to think about their new status; he began to think that it really might be a new departure and that it might be possible to live abroad for a while and yet have the ability to travel freely back and forth between Moscow and the West.

'I was mostly concerned about my parents who took the whole thing very badly. Indeed their whole future became uncertain and I began to feel that the responsibility for all of this might be too great for my shoulders.'

In such circumstances the pressures are enormous. There are always people to remind you what is at stake, how much your family and friends can suffer. Ashkenazy was deeply conscious that for his mother in particular the whole affair must have been profoundly shocking. After having achieved for a few short years some sort of real standing within the Soviet state by virtue of her son's success she could now see this structure crumbling around her. Inevitably, she blamed much of it on the influence of Dody and these new difficulties only confirmed her original view that marriage to a foreigner could bring nothing but trouble and disappointment. One of the most impressive things is that everyone understands the consequences of political disfavour; it is almost as though the breaking of unwritten rules of the game affects everyone and so the transgressor is made to feel that he is blighting the lives and opportunities of everyone he knows.

It soon became clear that even though the Ashkenazys' original plan had been to stay in Moscow only for about ten days to two weeks, they were not going to be able to leave as soon as they had hoped. The Soviet authorities wanted to make as much capital out of their return as possible and asked Ashkenazy to play some concerts to prove to those in Russia and abroad who knew of this whole affair that he had decided to return home of his own free will and that everything was back to normal. They must also have taken into account the mounting pressure on him from his parents and from others in the musical world to persuade him to change his mind, so the longer he stayed the harder it would be to leave again.

'I agreed in the end to play some concerts, and at one point we decided just to go to the airline office to buy our tickets and leave, since in theory once one has one's exit visa and passports, the ticket office could supply the airplane tickets without further formality. But I soon realized that if the Ministry of Culture and the KGB didn't want us to go they could always stop us at the airport anyway, and this was what I was most afraid of. I decided that it was wiser to pretend to be undecided rather than to risk a point of no return, which would certainly have happened if we had been stopped at the airport. So we pretended that we were absolutely fine, that there would be no problem about our going when and if we wanted to, but that for the meantime we didn't want to leave immediately. Once, when I did ask Stepanov about our request to return to London, he replied, "Are you not still a Soviet citizen?" When I replied "Yes" he said, "Well, in that case, just wait" – just like that, without an explanation.

'At this or another meeting I had with Stepanov, he suddenly referred to the fact that he knew we had put our names down to buy a car. Of course, even today this can be an incredibly long drawn out business in Russia since far too few vehicles are made to satisfy the demand from private citizens who would like to own one – not that it is easy to afford a car on Soviet salary levels. Stepanov then said that he assumed we were waiting our turn in the queue and that this might well mean a delay of two or three years. This was certainly quite normal in the 1960s, although the situation appears to be better now. When I replied that we knew we would have to wait a long time, Stepanov picked up the telephone and had a call put through to the Deputy Minister of Trade. After a brief conversation, he turned back to me and said, "Well, that is fixed. You can go tomorrow to choose your car. You will be able to pick it up immediately." And we did. It is possible that Stepanov simply wanted to show off his power and influence, or perhaps he wanted to do something to make amends for the difficulties I had suffered in the past. The intention may also have been that I should see what sort of special privileges could be available if I behaved myself and returned to the fold.

'Later, when I had finished all the concerts they had arranged for me, I said to Stepanov, "Look, I have done all that was required of me, so why can't we go now?" He then replied,

"Listen, there is a plenum of the Central Committee going on at the moment so everyone is very busy up there on top. Our Minister Furtseva has had no chance even to meet with her colleagues." This was said with special emphasis and with a particular look in the eye, as though he was telling me something very significant. What he in fact meant was that Furtseva had had no chance to meet Khrushchev in order to put the problem to him. It was the old problem of who would take responsibility and it was obvious that despite visas and passports, no one at the Ministry of Culture, not even the Minister herself, was prepared to take such a decision without involving the highest authority.

'We continued to pretend that we really wanted to go back to London only to prove that we were free to do so, just as we had proved to the outside world that we had returned to Moscow at our own wish. After all, our visas proved that we were now free to go but I needed time to discuss everything with my parents. Then, on the assumption that we would eventually decide to stay in Russia, as we were beginning to say we would probably do, we had to show that this would be of our own free will and not as a result of official pressure. The Moscow representatives of the British press kept telephoning, to find out about our plans. A few days before our departure, the *Daily Express* asked when we were going back to London. We replied that we didn't know for sure, though it was likely to be soon, but that in any case we had decided to stay in the Soviet Union and so we would simply return to London in order to pick up Vovka and to spend a little time with Dody's parents before returning to Moscow. This was my idea – I felt that we had to lie like that in order to get out; it was certainly the greatest lie of my life. I did not feel that I could even tell my parents of our real intentions; we left the matter of our return open but I am sure they sensed that we would probably not come back.'

Meanwhile British newspaper reports in mid- and late June 1963 reconfirmed the impression that they would not stay long in London, and the American pianist Malcolm Frager who was in Moscow at that time on a concert tour, including some performances of works for two pianos with Ashkenazy, helped to reinforce the picture. On 21 June Mr Frager left Moscow for New York, but stopped over at Heathrow airport in London. There, he told *The Times* that Ashkenazy was to have left with him on the same Aeroflot flight but had decided to postpone his departure at the last minute because they had been recording together 'up to two or three in the morning' that very day. He felt he needed a few more days to organize his short return visit to London. Frager went on to say that he felt sure that Ashkenazy had decided to stay in Moscow after he had collected Vovka from his parents-in-law: 'He has a new apartment, a car, and a piano, so I think that it is definite that he is going to make his home base there.'

Ashkenazy continues, 'As it happened, the authorities very cleverly induced me to surrender my foreign passport in exchange for the internal identity pass. I needed some money from the Philharmonia of which I was officially a member but in order to draw this I had to have my identity pass. This I could not hold simultaneously with a foreign passport. You see how subtle the system is – even when certain privileges or facilities are granted, their usage is very strictly circumscribed! Still, I think the fact that I did give up my foreign passport also helped to persuade them that we trusted them and that we had accepted the fact that we would only go when it was officially permitted. I suppose they had also been impressed by the fact that we had returned to Moscow at all, particularly Dody, so perhaps all these things together convinced them that we really would come back to Moscow again after the next London trip.

'The day finally came when Furtseva was able to see Khrushchev and she then called us into her office. This time, instead of reopening the whole discussion with us in order to try to persuade us to change our mind about going abroad again as she had done on a previous occasion, she said right out of the blue, "Very nice to see you; when are you leaving for London?" I immediately realized that she must have got clearance for us to go, so instead of saying something like, "Are you finally letting us go then?" I said, "We haven't really decided; maybe next week, say on Monday or Tuesday." (This was on a Friday.) "Very well," she replied. "You should certainly see your parents-in-law again and we know that you want to come back soon, so you had better collect your passports now." Interestingly enough, she was also going to London for an official visit a few days later, so this too may have played its role. She said, "I am going to London, too, so

I'll see you there. There'll be a reception at the Embassy and I hope I'll meet you at it."

'I went straight from her office to the relevant department of the Ministry and asked for my passport. I still had to wait for about half an hour, even though they obviously only had to open a safe to give it to me. Funnily enough, this time I wasn't nervous at all about the delay – I was quite sure that I would get my passport and would be able to go. After all, when a Minister herself tells you that you can go, that is pretty conclusive. Even so, we went to the lengths of buying tickets for the return journey from London to Moscow by train to confirm the impression that we would indeed be coming back soon.'

In his memoirs,* Khrushchev writes as follows about the whole incident:

> When I was head of the government, the young pianist Ashkenazy married an Englishwoman who had studied in one of our Conservatoires. They had a baby and went to visit the wife's parents. Shortly afterwards Gromyko reported to me that our Ambassador in London had cabled the following story; Ashkenazy came to our Embassy in London and said that his wife refused to go back to the Soviet Union. He loved her very much and asked our Embassy what to do. Now I should mention that I had heard Ashkenazy play and had personally congratulated him when he won first prize at the Tchaikovsky Competition. He's an excellent pianist and I often hear him on the radio. I consulted with my colleagues and proposed 'Let's give Ashkenazy permission to live in England however long he wants. That way he will always be able to return to the Soviet Union. We really have no alternative. If we insist that he leave his wife and return home, he'll refuse. He's not an anti-Soviet, but we could turn him into one if we put him in the position of having to choose between staying with his wife and obeying the government. He would immediately fall into the clutches of emigrés and other types who would start working on him, beating all sorts of anti-Soviet ideas into his head. We don't want that to happen. What's wrong with him living in London while keeping his Soviet citizenship? He can come back to Moscow anytime to give concerts. After all, he's a musician and that's a fine profession.' Everyone agreed, and my suggestion was accepted.

* *Khrushchev Remembers*, trs. and ed. S. Talbott, Andre Deutsch, 1971.

Khrushchev went on:

> It always gives me special pleasure when I turn on the radio and
> hear it announced that Ashkenazy has come to Moscow to give
> a concert. I'm glad we protected his good name as a great Soviet
> pianist and saved his family life in the process. Perhaps the time
> will come when Ashkenazy and his wife will want to come back
> and settle in Moscow for good. Or perhaps they will settle in
> London. I'm not excluding that possibility. So what. Let them
> live where they want. I think the time has come to give every
> citizen that choice. If he wants to leave our country and live
> somewhere else for a while, all right; we should give him that
> opportunity. It's incredible to me that after fifty years of Soviet
> power, paradise should be kept under lock and key.

This passage is revealing for a number of reasons. Khrushchev may, of course, have been under the impression that Ashkenazy did indeed return to Russia on subsequent occasions as a
consequence of his, Khrushchev's, wise and humane decision.
Alternatively, he may have been given this impression by officials
who were anxious not to have the waters muddied further after
the failure of this experiment. Whatever Khrushchev may have
known about subsequent events, his masterly exposition of the
obvious, all mixed up in his characteristically human way with
half-truths, factual errors and lies, sums up nicely one of the
essential paradoxes of Soviet life. Ostensibly the Soviet citizen
has all sorts of freedoms and rights enshrined in the law. But the
Soviet mind is not concerned with the inviolability of these rights
but only whether it is expedient for the citizen to be allowed them
when he needs them. In other words, the rules are there for all to
see, but everyone knows perfectly well that it is for the authorities
alone to determine when and how these rules may be applied or
suspended.

The Ashkenazys finally left for London on 2 July 1963. They
packed only such luggage as would be necessary for a short trip
and left their apartment as though ready for imminent re-
occupation. But after the stresses and anxieties of the last few
weeks and the obvious fact that multiple visas and passports
meant nothing to the Soviet authorities, they knew that
they could never take the risk again of setting foot on Soviet
soil.

In a footnote, the editor of Khrushchev's memoirs pointed

out that in 1969, Soviet diplomats in London referred to Ashkenazy as a Soviet artist who could travel freely in and out of the Soviet Union. Presumably, they must have believed that this convenient fiction had become one of the unwritten rules of the game being played by the Soviet authorities with Ashkenazy. In other words, that he would keep a low profile and would make no anti-Soviet statements in return for his conveniently anomalous position as a Russian living in the West with a Soviet passport. They must have counted on the fact that the threat of sanctions against Ashkenazy's family in Moscow was enough to maintain good behaviour and that they could use him as a convenient example of the freedoms enjoyed by Soviet artists. However, when the Soviet Press Attaché made a statement in the *Guardian* to this effect, with the assertion that the writer Kuznetsov who had recently defected could have applied for the same 'privileges' afforded to Ashkenazy, the latter was stung into action. He gave a long interview to the *Guardian* branding the statement as a manifest falsehood. He said, 'When an official Soviet spokesman says that I move freely between Russia and the West, as I only wish I could, it is a gross and unfair distortion of the truth.'

In a strange way, Ashkenazy seems to have found this cynical piece of misinformation on the part of the Soviet authorities a sort of turning point; up to that time, he kept his disgust and contempt for the Soviet system to himself, almost as though politics were not a matter to concern himself with. Thereafter, he obviously felt that the rules of the game, if indeed there ever had been any, had been broken on the Soviet side and that the gloves were off.

9

By THE TIME that the international press had finally lost interest in the story of the defection that was in the end never proved to be such, the Ashkenazys were at last left in peace to get on with the business of establishing their lives anew in London. At the beginning they had to live very modestly, staying for some months with Dody's parents in their semi-detached house in Sunny Gardens Road in Hendon. Gradually the financial picture improved as the demand for Ashkenazy mounted worldwide and as his fees began to flow in; soon they were able to buy a house for themselves in a quiet close in Hendon not far from the Tryggvasons and some sort of ordered routine could at last be established.

As a pianist Ashkenazy had success everywhere and especially in England, the Low Countries, Italy and Scandinavia. His popularity with British audiences was particularly striking, but for many years Ashkenazy had difficulty in accepting this as his due, rather than as the result of the publicity generated by his original decision to leave the Soviet Union. Nonetheless, he has reciprocated the loyalty of his public in Britain by making London the centre of his activities from that time onwards despite two later changes in abode.

From a business point of view, this centring on London was obviously convenient. All his concert activities were already coordinated by his new agents Ibbs and Tillett, at that time certainly the most influential and best known management in Europe. Then, after some skirmishings with EMI, he eventually signed an exclusive recording contract with Decca, partly because that company was prepared to confirm their positive interest in more decisive and concrete terms. Decca offered a down-payment of £1,000 in recognition of their exclusive rights and thus enabled the Ashkenazys to buy a car. For them this was more than just a luxury; they both disliked travelling by train to get to the concerts soon scheduled for him all over Britain.

One of the most bewildering things about Western musical life for Soviet émigrés has always been the whole concept of management. In Russia there are no independent managers and all opportunities for concerts at home and abroad or for recordings are controlled by agencies under the direct control of the Party and the government. These offices have very little interest in the artists themselves or in the music that will be performed. They are primarily concerned with the fact that music, and indeed all the arts, need a bureaucratic infrastructure if the necessary budgets, allocations, and permissions are to be secured. In the Soviet Union, people in all walks of life are accustomed to the fact that every aspect of their lives will be controlled by these bureaucracies, and they develop an extraordinary resilience in spite of the endless obstacles and frustrations they must daily endure at the hands of the officials in charge. The wheels can be oiled to turn a little faster but this requires contacts, special influence or *blat* of one kind or another. As a result, many of the most ambitious performers in the Soviet Union become very skilful at achieving what they need for their careers by manipulating anyone who can be of help in their climb up the ladder.

The idea, therefore, that an artist should engage a professional to take care of his business so that he can concentrate on his work and his performing is unnervingly alien to most Russians, even though it also has, at least in theory, its attractions. It is beguiling for an artist to think of being relieved of all responsibility beyond that of actual performance and many émigré Russians have suffered painfully from the delusion that only the lack of an all-powerful, all-knowing manager stands between them and the fame and riches which they feel are their due. Unfortunately, the quest for this mythical champion is confused by an often paranoic mistrust of everyone in the field, a symptom no doubt of the scepticism and cynicism about the motivation of all those officials who had to be bribed, cajoled or pressured back in the Soviet Union. Every piece of advice has to be checked out with ten other people, and since this may result in ten different opinions, the resulting state of indecision and insecurity becomes all the more distracting.

Fortunately for Ashkenazy, his contact with the Western approach to management was more gradual and less unsettling.

His first experience of it had been when he was very young, when most decisions were made for him anyway. Apart from questions of repertoire, or relatively ordinary matters of arrangements connected with his itinerary, he had very little influence on the management of his foreign tours while he still lived in the USSR. His American manager, Sol Hurok, was of course a famous figure among Soviet artists and much kudos was attached to a tour under his aegis.

'As for my relationship with Sol Hurok, I didn't exactly feel affection for him but certainly respect. He had a certain sort of intuition about artists, whom to push, whom to put on his posters under the banner "Hurok Presents", and he very seldom made a mistake about who was going to be a success. He tended to make these judgements himself rather than relying on others, as so many agents and impresarios do. Most of them never risk a decision until someone else has made it first.

'Even with this respect, however, the relationship remained essentially commercial right until the end. I never felt that we communicated on a personal level – indeed I don't believe that he felt there was any need to do so. For him, it was always a question of an impresario and an artist, even though one could be led to believe that there was something more when he would invite us to an exclusive restaurant or to his apartment after a concert. In fact, I always felt that this was simply part of the business relationship, just the frills on top and nothing more.

'In Russia he was looked upon with great awe, as someone who could apparently open all doors; the great, fantastic impresario. And maybe this lasting impression had some bearing on my subsequent feeling of being let down by him when we moved to London. He came to London quite shortly after we decided to stay, and I thought that following two successful tours, I would quickly be invited by him for a third tour – naturally, at that stage this was something I wanted and needed to have. When we met in the Savoy he started to say that I should go back to Russia, that all my family and friends were there and that it's very difficult in the West, difficult to live here, with so much competition and so on. I just couldn't understand why he was saying these things and painting such a black picture of the West. I still don't know why he did it. It wasn't as though he was the sort of person who would take instructions from the Russians – he was really much too powerful and they needed him too much. Besides, he knew them too well to think that he would ever get me again if I did go back. He just didn't look honest about what he was saying; he looked false, downright false. After all, he could easily have organized a tour for me in 1963/4, or certainly 1964/5, but he didn't lift a finger for two years so my first tour was not until 1965/6. Even so, I thought that I should not leave him because his office had such a good name and it would be better to be patient. But this really turned me against him, for I could never find an explanation for his actions. Whereas with Hochhauser, I feel sure he hoped that if a multiple re-entry visa could be arranged for me by the Soviet Authorities he could continue to represent me without creating problems for the rest of his business with the Russians, I don't think that Hurok had this sort of solution in mind. Also, he was touring Nureyev at exactly that time, although apparently he got Khrushchev's personal agreement that it would be acceptable for him to do so while still dealing with all the rest of the Soviet business. Nureyev defected in 1961 and, since Hurok was already touring him by the time I stayed out, maybe he thought that he should not add another controversial figure to his plans quite so quickly. All of this influenced my attitude to him for the rest of his life. What it really came down to was that although I knew him to be completely anti-Soviet, here he was painting a rosy picture of the Soviet Union for me. What was it all for?

'Now with Mrs Tillett it was certainly different. When it was arranged that she would represent me, I had no clear idea as to what I could or should expect from her or from the agency. This was not only because I was completely new in the music business of the West but also, being still very young, I had no real concept as to how my life should be. I had no basis for making relative judgements of people. My reaction was quite irrelevant – I liked her as an individual and felt comfortable in her presence. She seemed a solid person, with nothing contrived about her, and she genuinely tried to do the best in her relationships with the artists in order to support them. But she didn't have any very clear idea what to do with me or my career. She just followed up all the leads from where I had played before, or from people who were interested in having me. There was no question of a plan for, say, the next three years; in fact, I don't think that I could possibly have thought three years ahead anyway – maybe just a few months, so that I could begin to make a comfortable living, while deciding which engagements I could really handle. I wasn't thinking dispassionately of what I had to do in order to make my career. I started to plan what I should learn, what repertoire I should play for my forthcoming concerts, how I could grow artistically. I certainly didn't leave things to fall into place on a day-to-day basis, because I'm not that sort of person.

'Inevitably, some of these early experiences made me feel extra suspicious of people in business – Dody says that I am alternately suspicious and naïve anyway, by nature – so I certainly devoted some energy to trying to figure out how this or that person treated me and what his particular motivation or priorities might be. If you begin to think about it carefully and see all the details of the way people behave in their relations with you, you can quickly establish for yourself whether you want to work with someone or not. I have in fact parted company with a few people in my professional life precisely because I was disgusted by the way they behaved on certain occasions. One of the things I couldn't stand was the way that so many people would never admit to mistakes they had made but always tried to evade the issue and find a way out of the responsibility. I really hated this.'

In those early days in the West, Ashkenazy presented a complex picture to those who observed him. Shy and retiring by disposition, his small stature and his somewhat gaunt and preoccupied expression did not command immediate attention, even though in performance the sense of electricity and charisma were all the more compelling. His head of thick black hair was often only cursorily combed and then, as now, he showed not the slightest interest in how he dressed. At that time most clothes seemed to fit him badly, not least because he is in fact extraordinarily strong and broad-shouldered for his size. Later, perhaps in an attempt to accommodate Dody's patient efforts to make him more presentable, he took to wearing an endless succession of plain grey suits for almost every occasion. For his concerts he complied with the still prevailing custom of white tie and tails, even though this outmoded and unpractical outfit suited his build badly and made him extremely uncomfortable. Later, first for his solo recitals and then for orchestral concerts as well, he abandoned tails and wore a light-weight dark blue or black suit over a cotton polo-neck shirt. He finds the relative looseness and lack of restriction of this outfit infinitely more comfortable; it also suits him better.

In his professional dealings with his agents and with others to whom he looked for services for which he was, of course, paying, he could be unnervingly particular and precise. Mrs Tillett, indeed, who could look back on several decades of service to some of the legendary musical figures of our time, never seemed quite at ease with him. Once he had found his feet, he seemed to know his own mind too precisely and to remember too accurately exactly what he had requested in previous conversations. As a result, after a couple of years she began to delegate more and more of her dealings with him to a young member of her staff who was keen, and green, enough to attend to every detail as though his life depended upon it. The first few months of this new collaboration were, in fact, quite sticky. Ashkenazy obviously felt somewhat sceptical about having this inexperienced, if willing, novice wished upon him. Relations were at first formal, if friendly, and Ashkenazy was careful to check and double-check that everything was done according to his precise instructions. A closer and warmer relationship only blossomed when the young man managed to make a dreadful mistake, to which in fear and trepidation he immediately confessed. This apparently disarmed Ashkenazy completely, perhaps because he had been so accustomed in the Soviet Union to the way that everyone always tried to cover up or disown their mistakes; he had even discovered, to his dismay, that this seemed to be almost as prevalent in the Western music business. From that day, a very unusual rapport began to develop, one which the co-author has been privileged to enjoy up to the present, first for four years at Ibbs and Tillett and then after 1969 under the aegis of his own agency Harrison/ Parrott Ltd, of which Ashkenazy was the first and crucially important client.

If at first impression Ashkenazy's reserve, intensity, attention to detail and occasional sharpness are most striking, those who get to know him better soon discover with pleasure how much more there is to be found in him. His shyness can give way to the most winning warmth and charm; the intensity of his concentration can be redirected from its normal fixation on music to a generous and unstinting interest in his friends, not to mention his family. His kindness, loyalty and generosity, not only to close friends, but even to passing acquaintances are remarkable. He takes a keen and intelligent interest in the widest range of intellectual, political and philosophical topics but is also genuinely diffident about his grasp of some of the more complex issues. If he does not know something or does not fully understand it, he is the first to admit it. There is no shadow of intellectual vanity or pretension, no display of spurious knowledge.

He is extremely well-read in world literature – one thinks of his earlier story about acquiring and reading the Balzac volumes – and yet he laments large gaps in his reading. His knowledge of music is enormous, covering not only the most peripheral piano literature, some of which he likes but does not have time to perform, but also an astonishing range of orchestral works. Here too he accepts that there are many lacunae, maybe even some conscious omissions. Apart from a life-long devotion to the works of Beethoven, Mozart, Chopin, Brahms, Schubert and Schumann, he is also a tireless advocate of Russian music of all kinds, even some which displays certain weaknesses of which he is fully aware. He is drawn to music which is full of passion, colour and commitment. Amongst his many favourites are Richard Strauss, Ravel, Debussy and Sibelius. He is less drawn to Haydn, Mendelssohn or to the later works of Stravinsky; Liszt he plays very little, and Bruckner and some of Mahler's more emotionally extravagant symphonies he prefers to leave alone. But he tries to avoid prejudices. He is prepared to study any and all music in depth if he can find the time and if he thinks that the quality justifies the effort. He sees music as a universe of many ages and many worlds, all of them worthy of exploration or examination, if not conquest. One man's life, alas, is all too insufficient, and so a process of selection, a schedule of priorities must be the inevitable fate of the performing artist.

The London musical scene onto which the Ashkenazys arrived in the early 1960s was an extraordinary one. After its relatively provincial status between the wars, when if anything the only really international orchestra had been the BBC Symphony under Sir Adrian Boult, the situation after the Second World War had been promising from the start. This was partly due to the enterprise and foresight of Walter Legge, who had taken advantage of his war-time contacts to make what many still believe to have been the finest orchestra of its time, the

Philharmonia. He harnessed to it many of the most outstanding conductors and instrumentalists of the day, both for his London concert series and for the gramophone recordings he arranged as virtual artistic dictator of HMV's classical division. His championship of conductors such as Herbert von Karajan – in itself remarkably far-sighted given the taint of Nazism which stuck persistently for many years and which long made him unacceptable in America – Klemperer and Kempe among others did much to make the post-war development of musical life in London immediately and strikingly international. This may well have forestalled a tendency which has too often beset the British scene, a prejudice that foreign artists are valued only because they are exotic and that protective barriers must be maintained to nurture home-grown but neglected performers and composers.

The fact that so many Jewish musicians had made their homes in London as refugees from Nazi Germany and Austria had also borne fruit; they were followed in the fifties and sixties by exiles from various Eastern European countries taken over by the Communists. In due course, a further wave of talented young artists fled from Hungary in the wake of the abortive rebellion in 1956. By the mid 1960s, a talented colony of young performers from all over the world had made its home either temporarily or permanently in London, drawn there either as a political refuge or, increasingly as the years passed, by the rich and varied range of opportunities.

London already offered five competing symphony orchestras, none of them organized on a subscription basis and each of them in need of a large number of soloists and conductors for their long and varied concert season. Given the dislocations suffered in Germany immediately after the war, the London-based recording companies had something of a head start in the international market, not least because the American scene was still relatively inward-looking. Soon, following a decision by the American musicians' union to establish recording rates for its musicians far in excess of what their European counterparts were willing to work for, the centre of the international recording business shifted to the London orchestral market and effectively remained there for the next fifteen years.

Although extremely under-subsidized by comparison with the equivalent institutions of most European countries, Britain's musical life showed a remarkable initiative and flexibility. An impressive list of regional orchestras including such relatively famous ensembles as the Hallé and Scottish National Orchestras offered further employment to soloists at low fees but very acceptable artistic levels. Scattered throughout the country, several thousand music clubs and choral societies offered bread and butter income and invaluable professional experience to countless aspiring artists. Alas, by the early 1980s many of these organizations have either disappeared or fallen on hard times, badly hit by inflation, the difficulty of securing the right sort of artists for their increasingly sophisticated audiences, and sadly out-dated attitudes towards promotion. This is a sore loss since the extraordinary flowering in the 1960s and 1970s of British performers, particularly singers, must in part be due to this unique infrastructure.

In the mid-1960s, then, at precisely the most auspicious time, some very remarkable artists burst onto the London scene; Daniel Barenboim, still only in his early twenties but already able to look back on a long career as a child prodigy, was now waiting impatiently to occupy the role to which everybody knew he was entitled; Jacqueline du Pré, surely one of the most naturally gifted artists of the post-war years; Zubin Mehta, soon to be snapped up by the Los Angeles Philharmonic Orchestra; Alfred Brendel, at that time somewhat older than many of his friends and relatively ignored by the musical establishment until the early 1970s; Fou Ts'ong, at the time married to Zamira Menuhin; Itzhak Perlman and Pinchas Zukerman, the first and most extraordinary of a whole new generation of Israeli Juilliard-trained violinists, were amongst the most outstanding. The atmosphere amongst these and many other lesser figures was exceptionally cordial; they socialized interminably, played chamber music together incessantly. They all seemed willing to help one another and, for a time, a heady atmosphere of artistic fraternity prevailed.

The English Chamber Orchestra, itself made up of young and ambitious players reluctant to settle for the anonymity of symphony orchestra life, became the focal point for much of this activity, not least because of Daniel Barenboim's increasing involvement with it. Christopher Nupen, at that time a young television director on the staff of the BBC, encapsulated the mood

Evstolia, Vladimir's mother, 1966.

David Ashkenazy, Vladimir's father, 1979.

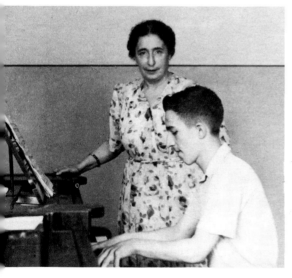

Music lesson with Anaida Sumbatian, 1948.

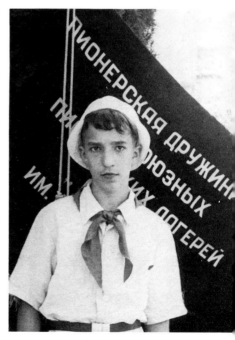

In Pioneer uniform at Artek summer camp, 1952.

With Emil Gilels in Brussels for the Competition in 1956.

With his Ministry of Culture 'companion' in New York during his first American tour, 1958.

Boris Zemlyansky, Ashkenazy's teacher 1955–63.

Recording in London with Kyril Kondrashin, 1963.

At the prize winners' concert after the 1962 Tchaikovsky Competition

Reception at the Kremlin after the Competition. On Ashkenazy's left are Krushchev, John Odgon, the violinists Gutnikov and Oistrakh. On his right stands the cellist Shakhovskaya, also a first-prize winner, and behind them Suslov, the Soviet ideologue.

After the 1962 Tchaikovsky Competition in the Large Hall of the
Moscow Conservatoire.

Leaving London with Dody and Vovka for concerts in Holland. At this stage they had not confirmed that they would stay in the West.

Многократна**Визы. Visas.**
ВИЗА № 203312
19 и _апреля_ 1963 г.
ВЪЕЗДНАЯ-ВЫЕЗДНАЯ ТРАНЗИТНАЯ

Эхспедиции СССР
Фамилия _Ашкенази_
Имя _Владимир Давидович_
с _один_
следует _в Москву_

ДЕЙСТВИТЕЛЬНА
однократно
для въезда в СССР в течение _____
суток со дня выдачи, пребывания и
многократного _до 19 октября_
выезда из СССР в течение
1963 с момента переезда границы
пограничные пункты
любой

О № 017158

— 22 —

Ashkenazy's exit visa: 'This visa entitles the holder to cross the border of the USSR at any point an unlimited number of times for a period of six months.'

In Iceland with Dody, Vovka and Nadia, 1964.

Conducting the Philharmonia in London, 1982.

With Jasper Parrott, 1983.

The Ashkenazy family, 1983. From left to right: Vladimir Jnr (Vovka); Nadia; Vladimir; Thorunn (Dody); Alexandra (Sasha); Sonia; Dimitri (Dimka).

of the times with a documentary called 'Double Concerto'. This featured the preparation and performance of the Mozart concerto for two pianos played by Daniel Barenboim, Vladimir Ashkenazy and the English Chamber Orchestra. The amazing intensity and artistic maturity of these young but indisputably brilliant artists, combined with their almost adolescent *joie de vivre*, seemed to be exactly the recipe that the new, much younger, public of the late 1960s and 1970s was seeking. The concert-goer in London at that time was unusually fortunate; he had the opportunity of hearing the widest range of concerts featuring not only many famous senior artists, but alongside them and often working harmoniously with them these new, charismatic young Titans.

Ashkenazy was swept up into this magic circle; a very considerable draw for the public in his own right, and by general acknowledgement the most outstanding all-round pianist of his generation, he was much cultivated and seems for a while to have found the excitement and stimulus of this way of life irresistible. However, as the years passed, and as the leading lights in this community followed the different routes of their brilliant international careers, the earlier sense of homogeneity began to fade. This was probably inevitable and even necessary; truly creative artists are and must be individualists and, as time passes, the style and artistic personality of other equally self-possessed performers become inevitably less and less compatible.

For Ashkenazy, the major problem was that this sort of life was too distracting. It interfered with the regime of steady, disciplined work which he had by now found to be essential. By 1968 he had decided that family life – the Ashkenazys had two children at that time, to be followed by three more born between 1969 and 1979 – had its own essential priorities which consumed virtually all the time that was left over from the demands of the piano. It was bad enough that London was the centre of Ashkenazy's recording activities and the hub of the administration of all his affairs. When he came home to London from concert tours abroad, the telephone would ring non-stop. If it was not his agents seeking his approval for future arrangements, there were other musicians with social or musical plans of one kind or another or, to his dismay, people from the press wanting interviews, although as a general rule Ashkenazy declined to give these at that stage of his life.

After five years in the West his career was formidably established. There was no hint of that syndrome which often bedevils brilliantly successful prize-winners, whereby too much exposure too soon leaves them drained of available repertoire after a few short seasons at the top. There can be a moment of truth for many promising young artists when they discover that the hurly-burly of those first few seasons, when promoters seemed to vie for the chance to engage them, has left them no time or energy to expand their repertoire nor to review those works which they have used as war-horses since emerging from the chrysalis of studenthood. The Western concert circuit can be cruel in this respect; young artists can be put on the highest pedestal of celebrity, inundated with offers and lauded to the skies. Then, if they falter, they can be as easily displaced by a newer, apparently brighter star in the firmament. And yet the process of maturation is seldom an even trajectory. When artists of great talent are very young, they are often afraid of nothing and find every new challenge exhilarating. After a few years on the international scene, as they begin to face reappraisal the second or third time round in cities where they have previously had success, the sense of responsibility, even of unpreparedness, weighs ever heavier.

In the Soviet Union, artists have perhaps found it easier to pace their careers. With relatively infrequent foreign tours it is possible for an artist to husband his best repertoire for the most important occasions and in the intervals to prepare new works in relatively unexposed circumstances in the Russian provinces. Even so, it is interesting to observe that comparatively few Soviet artists who have either played extensively in the West, or left the Soviet Union for good, actually put this opportunity to good account. Perhaps because of the tendency already noted above for Soviet artists to be expected to play a limited number of very brilliant or effective works on their foreign tours, many become lazy about enlarging their repertoire along more catholic lines. Richter, of course, was in this as in so many things the exception; the range of works he has offered during his career has been always eclectic, and even at times eccentric. Amongst the younger generation, apart from Ashkenazy, only the violinist Gidon Kremer has seemed able to cope with the demands of a top-flight career whilst still finding the time to renew and expand his repertoire.

Between 1963 and 1968, the number of concerts played each year by Ashkenazy tells quite a story. In 1963, a much interrupted and improvised season, he played fifty-four concerts. In 1964 and 1965, the total each year came to just over ninety concerts. In 1966 he played 107, in 1967 114 and in 1968 129 engagements, a level of activity which he went on to maintain for many years to come. The range of concerto repertoire was impressive; the works he performed during these five years included all the Beethoven concertos, Tchaikovsky 1, Brahms 2, Chopin 2, Prokofiev 2 and 3, all four Rachmaninov concertos, Mozart K.271, K.246, K.466, K.595 and the Double Concerto, the Bach D minor and Schumann.

Much of this repertoire has remained as arrows in his quiver ever since; although he has dropped the Tchaikovsky and Bach concertos he has added a significant number of new works as the years have passed. This long list of concertos, matched by an equally wide range of recital programmes, enabled him to build up an ever broader international career without having to repeat works in the most important centres until many years had elapsed. He could keep on returning to crucial cities such as London, New York, Paris and later Tokyo without stretching his artistic resources too thin. Hence the intensity of activity; each work would be performed through a long circuit of different cities. Interspersed amongst the great capitals would be many smaller places where he could begin to offer works planned in due course for the most exposed platforms perhaps two years later.

Thus, in those years in London the subsequent pattern of his career was broadly established. His third American tour in 1965 was a triumphant re-affirmation that the brilliant young talent of 1958 and 1962 had matured into an artist of ever-growing stature. Thereafter, he toured the United States at least twice a season, constantly sought after by the most important orchestras and conductors. In Europe it was the same; his managers were in the happy position of being able to select his schedule of engagements largely according to his wishes from the great number of prestigious invitations constantly on offer.

On the other side of the world, he made his first tour of Japan in 1965. This country with its enormous record market and large and devoted concert public has played an important role in the careers of many of the great artists of our day, and Ashkenazy's success was instantaneous. He made a second tour in 1968, and since then has returned every two or three years for up to twenty concerts at a time.

Meanwhile, as a background to all of this arduous if artistically and financially rewarding touring, the Ashkenazys felt that the apparent advantages of living in London constituted something of a trap, depriving them of any real privacy, peace or family life. Dody had in any case always seen herself as Icelandic through and through, despite her British upbringing, and she wanted the children to learn to absorb some of the attributes of that independent island breed. Most of all, they simply wanted to escape. Somewhat impulsively, therefore, the decision was made to sell their house in London and move to Reykjavik; they moved into their new home there in the autumn of 1968.

Ashkenazy has always felt an intense affinity with northern people and in particular with the Norwegians, Icelanders and Finns. Each season, he devotes what many consider to be a disproportionate slice of his availability to Scandinavia, taking particular pleasure in performing in small towns in scenically beautiful areas. In this way, he has given concerts all over Sweden and Finland, including even the Åland Islands in the Gulf of Bothnia. He has also played in the Shetlands and Faroes, in Malta and Fiji, and on one occasion while on tour in New Zealand there were serious discussions about a visit to Antarctica – alas only to be frustrated by the difficulty of getting a piano there on time.

Another as yet unfulfilled ambition is to play in Greenland; when the chairman of the Royal Danish Orchestra came round to see Ashkenazy recently after a concert with the Philharmonia in the hope that he might persuade him to conduct his orchestra at some time in the future, Ashkenazy, who has a high regard for the orchestra and was happy to try to find a mutually convenient date, suddenly asked, 'Do you ever get sent by the Danish Government to play in Greenland? I should love to go with you!'

This love for Scandinavia is partly emotional and obviously has much to do with his marriage to Dody. But Ashkenazy also values very highly the prevailing attitudes and atmosphere of Scandinavian society with its concern for the individual and respect for man's right to live in an unadulterated environment. He values the traditional and lasting sense of reliability and integrity in human dealings which is still very much the rule in these countries, although he is perhaps less drawn to Sweden, with its exaggerated emphasis on forced equalization, than to some of the others. In the field of music and the arts this seems to lead to a gradual dissipation of creative energies, replaced instead by an arid sense of routine. His favourite country has become Finland and each summer the Ashkenazys spend some weeks in a simple wooden cabin in the lakeland of the interior of the country. They find the peace, the wholesome air of forests and lakes, and the simple way of life an enormous tonic after so many months of hurly-burly in the airports, hotels and concert halls of the world. Perhaps this Finnish cabin is an unconscious substitute for the ubiquitous country *dacha* of Russian literature much beloved of artists both before and since the Revolution.

Improbable though Reykjavik might seem as a base for someone whose life is at the constant mercy of airline schedules, the years spent in Iceland were happy and fulfilling. The main objective, that of enhancing the quality of their family life, was triumphantly achieved. Whenever they spent time together at home in Reykjavik there were few distractions or interruptions and their privacy was very much respected by the Icelanders despite the celebrity of these intriguing new residents. They lived in the outskirts of Reykjavik moving, when their enlarged family led to their outgrowing the available accommodation, into a house specially designed for them with a large studio and plenty of room for the children.

They did not feel, however, that it would be right for them to enjoy the privileges and tranquillity of their new found haven without making an appropriate contribution to Iceland's musical life. Ashkenazy agreed to become artistic adviser to the Reykjavik Festival, which up to that time had been a largely local, or Nordic affair. With his assistance the biennial festivals which started in 1970 were able to offer to the enthusiastic Icelandic audiences the most extraordinary line-up of musical talents from all over the world. Among those who appeared were Yehudi Menuhin, Mstislav Rostropovich, André Previn, Daniel Barenboim, Jacqueline du Pré, Birgit Nilsson, Itzhak Perlman, Pinchas Zukerman, André Watts, Victoria de Los Angeles, Martti Talvela, John Shirley-Quirk, Elizabeth Söderström, Renata Tebaldi, Henryk Szeryng and John Williams, and in 1974 the London Symphony Orchestra gave two concerts under André Previn. A visit by the Philharmonia is planned for 1984. Since leaving the country in 1978 Ashkenazy has continued to provide as much help as he can as Honorary President of the Festival Committee in their continued efforts to maintain this very high artistic level.

During those years, too, Ashkenazy was slowly coming to the decision that he should do some conducting and, in the initial stages, this was partly justified by the fact that he could be of use to the Iceland Symphony Orchestra. This was semi-professional but fielded some excellent players and maintained a very competent standard, considering that it was drawn largely from Reykjavik with its small population of around 100,000 inhabitants. The orchestral management appreciated that regular work with Ashkenazy as conductor, even at a relatively early stage in acquiring his technical expertise, could offer the orchestra and public more in musical terms than the succession of second or third class conductors they often had to make do with from the open market.

As an added benefit, Ashkenazy refused to be paid for these concerts, so more money was available in the budget for interesting soloists; they in turn were more likely to come to Iceland to play with Ashkenazy than might have been the case otherwise. Many of the distinguished visitors to the Reykjavik Music Festival performed there for fees well below their normal terms, or even for expenses only on the understanding that a similar favour would be done by Ashkenazy to a musical cause near to their own hearts. John Dankworth and Cleo Laine, for instance, appeared at the Festival in return for Ashkenazy giving more than one recital at their musical centre in Wavendon. More recently, Gidon Kremer agreed to play in the 1982 Festival, by which time of course Ashkenazy and his family had long transferred their home to Switzerland, on the understanding that Ashkenazy would return the favour at Kremer's Lockenhaus Festival in Austria in 1983. Similar arrangements were made with Martti Talvela, Daniel Barenboim and Yehudi Menuhin.

The concerts with the Iceland Symphony Orchestra were most valuable for Ashkenazy. If too much time had to be devoted to the relatively mechanical business of getting the notes right in performances of works as complex and demanding as Shostakovich's Eighth Symphony or the Rachmaninov Second, he became convinced that whatever his professional shortcomings as a conductor might be at that stage, one essential ingredient was already present. When it came to getting behind the notes, to making the music flow as he wanted it to, he had the ability to get his wishes across to the orchestra, sometimes to the degree that they could find the resources to play far beyond their limitations as instrumentalists. Those few concerts undertaken in the protected and isolated circumstances of this remote island convinced Ashkenazy that he had something to offer as a conductor as well as a pianist. This decision, once made, had momentous repercussions on the later development of his professional life.

The time slowly came for other changes to be made. The years in Iceland had been happy and fulfilling, and precious space had been won not only for family life, but for the achievement of precisely the undistracting circumstances in which Ashkenazy felt he could lay down his best work. But there were major drawbacks as well. Airline links with the rest of Europe are limited, with very few direct connections. Most flights leave early in the morning in order to allow the outgoing aircraft time to manage a return to base within the same day. Iceland's international airport, Keflavik, is rather far from town, which means that almost every trip involves an unpleasantly early start. As a result, it often proved impracticable for the Ashkenazys to return home for two or three days between engagements, as they would certainly have done if based in a more accessible place. The journeys themselves tended to be unnecessarily exhausting and were disruptive too to Ashkenazy's rhythm of work. He found increasingly that the benefits of a peaceful stay in Reykjavik could be easily dissipated by the journeys to and from the island.

By 1978, therefore, the Ashkenazys had reluctantly decided that they would have to give up their Icelandic home as their principal residence. They thought for a while of returning to London, but knew that their original reasons for leaving would still remain. Instead, like so many other émigrés – and musicians – before them, they turned their attention to Switzerland. After some explorations through other cantons, they finally settled on Luzern, partly because they had friends there, perhaps influenced too by the fact that Rachmaninov had made his summer home there. But other, more practical considerations carried most weight. Luzern is a little under an hour away from Zürich airport, which provides one of Europe's best networks of direct flight connections. There is even a regular rail link from Luzern to the departure terminals at Zürich airport. By road, the Ashkenazys can reach many of the cities on their concert itinerary within three or four hours drive; often they have even been able to return home after a concert. Such gains in convenience, not to mention many whole days now spent at home instead of in hotels or at airports, are precious indeed. Luzern, too, is a beautiful old city with a magnificent lakeside position. It is small enough to be peaceful and unpolluted and yet offers all the facilities of a larger metropolis. Schools, in particular, are excellent and conveniently close. The Ashkenazys live practically in the centre, only a few minutes from the lakeside, but it feels like a quiet suburb.

Luzern is also famous, of course, for its annual music festival, one of the most distinguished in Europe with a programme featuring the greatest of the artists and orchestras of the day. This fact was not itself of any significance to the Ashkenazys in their decision to settle in Luzern, but some two years later Vladimir was asked by the Festival Committee to join another distinguished Luzern resident, Rafael Kubelik, as artistic adviser.

Family life has certainly been a great bulwark against the loneliness and insecurity from which many successful artists suffer all their lives. His marriage, built on complete trust and loyalty, has blossomed in a manner increasingly rare in the volatile world of music. The Ashkenazys have five children ranging from Vovka (Vladimir) born in Moscow in 1961, Nadia (1963), Dimitri or Dimka (1969), Sonia (1974) to Sasha the youngest who was born in 1979. While the children were young, they travelled the world over with their parents, Dody always ensuring with the help of a succession of Icelandic nannies, some of them relatives, that her husband could enjoy the company of the children to the full without being distracted from his work. Now, with the two eldest already grown up and with Dimka and Sonia at school in Luzern, only Sasha can still travel regularly on her father's international tours – and not for much longer. The pattern, therefore, begins to change a little, as they try to keep the tours reasonably short with as much doubling back home as can possibly be contrived. Vovka, after studying at the Royal Northern College of Music in Manchester for six years, is already launched on his own career as a pianist.

The children have, on occasions, had some direct influence on the planning of Ashkenazy's tours; two trips to South Africa were made as much as anything because he wanted the children to see the game parks there. Australia has a very special importance in Dimka's life for two quite separate reasons.

In 1969 Ashkenazy was preparing for his second tour of Australia at a time when Dody was expecting their third child. About one month before the tour commenced, Dody had a miscarriage, so she undertook the long journey from Europe in an inevitably sombre mood. Ten days or so after her arrival, she was still feeling poorly, and consulted a doctor. He promptly informed her that she was pregnant, and that she had previously lost one of two twins. The survivor was Dimka.

Dimka's second point of connection with Australia started with a near tragedy. While on a family holiday in Greece in 1979, he fell out of a motorboat and although an excellent swimmer, was caught in the propeller of the outboard engine, suffering appalling injuries to his left leg. The accident, itself horrifying, turned into a protracted nightmare as his parents rushed him by taxi first to the nearest doctor some ten miles away and then to a hospital in Corinth. From there, after interminable delays, he was transferred first to one and then another hospital in Athens, with the result that some eight hours passed before the surgery necessary to save his leg, and probably his life, was finally performed.

The worst was at least averted but after one week in the hospital it was clear to Dimka's parents that Greek standards of hospital care and hygiene, let alone surgical expertise, were simply inadequate unless they were prepared to accept that Dimka would remain crippled for the rest of his life.

By a strange piece of good fortune, the Ashkenazys had become friendly during their last tour of Australia with the eminent and pioneering microsurgeon Dr Earl Owen, who is a great music lover and had himself studied the piano to an advanced level. The day after Dimka's accident, the Ashkenazys telephoned Dr Owen in Sydney, and he advised them to remove the child from Athens at the earliest possible opportunity and to put him into the hands of a top-class microsurgeon. He assured them that new and highly successful techniques could be employed to repair and where necessary re-graft nerve, arterial and vascular tissues in Dimka's leg so that as many of its functions as possible might be restored. The Ashkenazys immediately asked

137

Dr Owen to take Dimka into his own personal care, and so, after five weeks of first-class nursing in a Swiss hospital so that he could recover from various infections contracted in the Greek hospital, Dimka was flown out to Sydney with his mother for a series of complex operations.

This was a bleak time for Ashkenazy; he had agreed to go to Shanghai to make a television film for the BBC*; just before his departure he received the news that his mother had died. Then, although he knew that Dimka had arrived in Sydney safely, the actual operations had to be delayed because of continuing problems with his liver and spleen.

In the end, however, the Ashkenazys' faith in their friend was more than justified. The surgery proved to be overwhelmingly successful despite the apparently irreversible damage the leg had suffered and, some four years later, after a continuous and arduous regime of exercise and physiotherapy, Dimka had regained nearly all of the functions of his leg; indeed, he is proving to be an athletic and enthusiastic tennis player.

In gratitude for Dr Owen's support in these traumatic times, Ashkenazy determined to do something in return for his pioneering work in micro- and laser surgery, fields to which the Australian medical establishment seems to be strangely indifferent. He agreed, therefore, to take up an invitation for a third Australian tour in 1982, on the express condition that a major fund-raising concert for Dr Owen's Microsurgery Foundation should be scheduled at the Sydney Opera House. Dimka, who now has only happy memories of Australia, joined his parents on the tour and the Microsurgery concert was a huge success, raising in excess of A$ 50,000 for the Foundation as well as a great deal of invaluable publicity.

* 'Music After Mao'.

138

IO

SINCE ASHKENAZY is by now one of the most recorded classical artists of the day, and since the development of his record catalogue has had a major impact on the evolution of his artistic plans, a little space should be devoted to the unusually close and fruitful relationship he has enjoyed over the years with the Decca record company.

In the 1960s Decca was at the height of its international reputation at a time when the making of gramophone records was enormously profitable; the market seemed unlimited and it appeared that any artist of established reputation could record almost any work, however obscure, and it would be snapped up by a host of voracious collectors. Over the previous ten or fifteen years it had acquired a formidable list of artists, admittedly mostly conductors and singers, but including amongst its pianists Julius Katchen and Clifford Curzon. This in itself was significant and made the signing of Ashkenazy a particularly good decision, since neither Katchen nor Curzon was likely to inhibit him from recording the sort of repertoire he was able to offer at this early stage in his career. Katchen was very much involved in a series of Brahms recordings and Curzon, though greatly valued and at the height of his powers, recorded so unwillingly and so infrequently that there was little risk of conflict of repertoire.

Soon it became clear that recording was an activity which suited Ashkenazy particularly well. Prior to his departure from Russia, he had recorded very little, although one can still buy recordings made at the time of his participation in the Chopin Competition in Warsaw as well as an extraordinary performance of the twenty-four Chopin studies made in Moscow in 1959–60.

'Since I recorded so little in Russia, I certainly found it difficult at the beginning, but gradually I discovered a way of dealing with the problem of not having an audience in front of me. It is basically a question of your state of mind; you should play as though you are playing for an audience and I think that it is perfectly possible to do this even when playing at home. After all, I very often practise as though I were playing a concert, and this helps me to build up my playing to the level of an actual performance. My work benefits from this and it means that my recorded performances can reach the same level of spontaneity and immediacy of communication as a public concert. I'm not saying that they always do – just that often they can do.'

As the years passed, an extraordinary relationship of mutual trust, unusual in the volatile music business, developed between Ashkenazy and Decca. With rare sensitivity to his personality and method of work, the managers in charge of the planning of artists' repertoires left him a largely free hand to decide what and when he would record.

It should be said that an exclusive contract of any kind is not normally the sort of arrangement which appeals to the recently liberated Soviet mind. Many other famous émigrés or defectors have preferred to record with as many different companies as possible, often playing one firm off against another. After years without any choice whatsoever within the Soviet Union as well as comparatively meagre financial rewards for their recording activities, Soviet émigré artists tend to think of the gramophone record business in the West as an El Dorado where as many different claims as possible should be struck at the same time.

In the end, this often results in confusion, distrust and, in the depressed markets of recent years, lack of responsible development. In trying to exploit their sometimes transitory appeal to the record buying public, many artists have ended up by being exploited themselves. It is the old story; with an imperfect grasp of all the factors at issue at any one time in the record business, many ex-Soviet artists seek advice from all sides but heed only those who feed their expectations the most.

Ashkenazy remembers that he too was prone to many of the suspicions and misconceptions to which the Soviet mind can easily fall victim, but his solid relationships with Ibbs and Tillett and Decca in his early life as an émigré helped him to concentrate on the quality of his work.

The life of any successful artist is often more lonely than might be apparent; despite the exhilaration of performance and public adulation, many sensitive artists often feel isolated in a long and relentless struggle to realize some of their creative aspirations. For Ashkenazy, who is not by nature gregarious, there seems to have been some sense of compensation in transforming these outwardly professional contacts into something much more personal, based on a real reciprocity of interests. He seems uneasy about a purely formal, commercial arrangement where services are merely rendered and paid for. It is important to him to have a home team committed to his support, but by the same token he is often disposed towards a particular course of action because it will bring tangible benefits to others as well as to himself.

The commercial objectives of a company such as Decca can act as a useful catalyst and Ashkenazy has often justified certain projects because Decca wanted them for their catalogue or for a particular sales offensive. If this suggests a willingness to subordinate his real inclinations to marketing considerations, the true explanation is much more complex. Like many artists, he admits to finding the burden of responsibility in his performances hard to shoulder day after day without some respite. Pressure from those with a different sort of interest in his playing can provide relief by leading to a slight, even if illusionary, sense of sharing in this responsibility. A mood of liberation can result, rather in the same way that a difficult acoustic or a badly prepared piano can sometimes heighten the focus of a performance. When expectations are diminished for reasons beyond a performer's control, he can sometimes feel a strange sense of release, almost as though some degree of unavoidable compromise can legitimize the taking of correspondingly greater artistic risks.

Seen in this light, Ashkenazy's consummate professionalism is a curious inversion of the more typical Soviet response to matters of personal and artistic responsibility. After growing up in and living with a system where these concepts hardly exist, or where they are travestied by subjection to a dogma which no thinking person can respect, many Soviet artists seem to feel few obligations to anyone apart from themselves. In other instances amongst some of the most gifted and self-possessed Soviet or ex-Soviet performers, artistic integrity is replaced by an egotistical complacency that apparently suppresses all self-criticism or humility.

Consciously and unconsciously Ashkenazy has striven to leave this sort of Soviet conditioning behind him. He faces his artistic responsibilities with unflinching resolution and his unremitting application keeps him in peak mental and physical condition for the challenges of his concerts and recordings. As we have seen, his method is to work up his repertoire through long arcs of performances, starting off each new or revived work in small towns in Europe and extending through perhaps two whole seasons or as many as twenty concerts before he is prepared to play them in such key cities as New York or London.

If a consequence of this approach is that Ashkenazy tends to play a larger number of concerts each season than most of his peers, it brings the happy benefit that he is one of a very few top international names who do not disdain to give concerts outside the main metropolitan centres or festivals. In recent years, as demand for the great names continues to outstrip supply, it has become fashionable for many of them to reserve themselves for those engagements which will bring them the greatest prestige, a sad state of affairs for those music lovers who live far from a major concert-hall or opera house. Ashkenazy clearly enjoys his excursions into the provinces and accepts any less than ideal circumstances with good humour and tolerance. On a human level, the response from people who do not often have the chance to hear great music played at the highest level seems especially rewarding.

In the early 1970s Decca laid out for him some very ambitious plans as far as solo piano repertoire was concerned, and by 1983 he had already recorded all the Beethoven piano sonatas as well as the sonatas for violin and piano with his long-standing duo partner Itzhak Perlman. Plans to cover most of Rachmaninov's solo piano literature as well as the ten sonatas of Scriabin are well advanced, and his monumental project to record all of the piano works of Chopin is nearing completion. In the field of chamber music, the Beethoven trios with Itzhak Perlman and Lynn Harrell will be finished in 1984 but will be released by EMI, for whom Perlman records, since the earlier recordings had gone to Decca.

If recording plans have often been the catalyst for projects in the concert hall, the process can work equally well in reverse. In 1983 for instance, the Brahms 150th Anniversary year, Ashkenazy and Perlman performed the three Brahms sonatas for piano and violin in Manchester, Geneva, Paris, Munich, Berlin, Vienna and London and then recorded them for EMI. Recordings have also played an important role in the development of Ashkenazy's conducting activities, but this will be described in a later chapter.

These combined recording and concert projects have done much to avoid any hint of routine in Ashkenazy's career, a pitfall which can beset any successful artist with some twenty-five years touring behind him. In Ashkenazy's case, he has been playing concerts intensively and at an important level since the age of seventeen; if he takes after many of his venerable colleagues, he may still be going strong forty years from now, and so new challenges are always stimulating. In order to ensure some special focus to his concert activities Ashkenazy has endeavoured to incorporate a major artistic project into his plans every few years: the Rachmaninov concertos performed as cycles in London and New York, the Beethoven concertos first in London with Bernard Haitink and the London Philharmonic (also televised by the BBC), and then a few seasons later in Amsterdam, New York and Washington also with Haitink but with the Concertgebouw orchestra; all three Bartók concertos. Perhaps the most ambitious was reserved for the Adelaide Festival in Australia in 1984 when Ashkenazy conducted the nine Beethoven Symphonies as well as playing all five concertos in a six-concert series with the Philharmonia as part of a world tour.

If gramophone recordings have been an area of activity to which Ashkenazy has taken with apparent ease, the same cannot be said for television or indeed the press. In the early years of his career in the West, he showed extreme reluctance about appearing on television except when his public concerts were relayed direct from the concert hall. He was equally unwilling to give interviews to the press, stating that he preferred to be judged as an artist through his performances alone. Part of the reason for his reticence was the continuing ambiguity about his actual status in the West; for many years he remained a Soviet citizen and travelled on a Soviet passport with all that such unwelcome documentation involved in the form of an endless succession of visas and re-entry permits for whichever country his concert itineraries included. His contact with the press in the spring of 1963 had not been a happy one and he was resentful of the fact that even reputedly responsible journalists had shown so little sensitivity to the extreme delicacy of his position at that time. It seemed wiser not to give interviews at all rather than to shy off from questions which such situations inevitably provoked.

'It was very difficult for me to meet journalists and talk to them about my reasons for staying. I didn't know how to treat the press or how to express myself exactly, and I was often misquoted or misunderstood. It still happens now, but to a much lesser degree. It is difficult but experience helps. I felt very insecure for many years in the West psychologically and in many other ways. Obviously you don't want to expose yourself to the press for interviews, if you feel insecure. Now things are different: I make arrangements in advance to meet members of the press when they want to talk to me, or if Decca requests it for publicity reasons. Now I give interviews of all kinds for television, radio and the press.'

Other considerations had some bearing on his earlier attitude, particularly when it came to television. Directors are understandably anxious to persuade the television public that artists are first and foremost communicators with whom even the most uninformed viewer can have some contact. This means that artists are often prevailed upon to talk about what they do as though this often alien medium is comfortable to them. Very few artists have an easy gift of verbal communication, although many will unfortunately not admit this even to themselves, and it is surprising how often television producers put performers into moulds which manifestly do not suit them. For the serious artist, television can be a treacherous and trivializing vehicle.

Even today Ashkenazy tends to be shy about speaking in public, partly because of a continuing if unnecessary diffidence about his command of English. In the 1960s he had infinitely less self-confidence but even then he could on occasions be persuaded to take the plunge, as Christopher Nupen demonstrated not only with the influential 'Double Concerto' programme already mentioned but also a couple of years later with a most engaging television portrait entitled 'The Vital Juices are Russian'. In this and many subsequent programmes, Ashkenazy was able to show that, provided that he felt at ease with the people working on the programme, he could communicate on television with remarkable intensity and persuasiveness. It seemed that he could forget all about the cameras and studio if the musical or conceptual challenges were absorbing enough. The crucial thing was that there had to be something for him to get his teeth into, some problem which would really engross him.

On another much less successful occasion he was interviewed by André Previn, a close friend whom he rightly believes to have a special gift for television communication. Ashkenazy was so much in awe of Previn's effortless mastery of the medium that he simply left all the talking to him, thus keeping the interview decidedly earthbound. By contrast, his many films with Christopher Nupen as well as a few programmes for the BBC including 'Music after Mao' in Shanghai, a programme on Scriabin, and an interesting workshop in which the role of the pianist-conductor was explored not only in a Mozart concerto but also in the Beethoven Fourth and Brahms First Piano Concertos, have enjoyed well-deserved success. If the material is substantial enough, he will communicate it with conviction and intensity, yet his manner remains modest and unpretentious. As in the concert halls of the world, it seems to be a formula the public finds hard to resist.

Ashkenazy himself has the following to add: 'I suppose that we artists have to play on television because this is a development of the times and if an important percentage of our public wants to hear and watch music on television, we simply have to comply with their wishes. After all, millions of people who like classical music live far from any city where there are regular concerts of international calibre and, to these people, records and television are the only real way of hearing a lot of music, apart from the radio. Television offers the advantage of radio in that live concerts can be heard, but with the added bonus that the viewer can get some sort of idea about the personality and charisma of the performer. I suppose that is always very fascinating to a lot of people. I don't think they will stop going to concerts, but they can at least stay at home to watch something interesting, maybe from another country, if they feel like doing so. With the development of satellite television and cable arrangements, many interesting concerts may be available to people who could never afford the money or time to hear the performances live.

'If we turn our backs on television, some of us may slip a little in the consciousness of the public; for our careers not to progress as they should, only because we are not seen on television and are therefore not sufficiently in the public eye, would be silly and counter-productive, however disagreeable it may be for some of us to be on television. These factors even apply in the Soviet Union to a certain degree. Music is seen on television there too, and featured in the rest of the media, and one might almost say that since the media as a whole are insufferably tedious, anything worth watching may have a correspondingly greater impact. Interestingly enough, in Hungary every few years they have a conducting competition organized by state television. Every stage is covered by TV, and the public as a whole has the opportunity of voting for a special prize for the conductor they like the best. This competition arouses the most incredible interest throughout the country and the winner, if he happens to have the sort of personal magnetism which the public likes, can enjoy subsequently the sort of following normally reserved for pop stars.

'So although it is true that television is very much concerned with superficial and immediately discernible qualities of magnetism and charisma which may not necessarily go very deep, and which may have a cheapening effect when abused, this is not essentially very different from what can happen in public performance where the public can just as easily be deluded – for a while, if not for ever. And those erudite and self-important critics are just as easily deceived. It all comes back to what sort of people are involved, both performers and public. Those who want to search for what is important in life will look for it on television just as they would in the concert hall. Television is a fact of our lives and we should all aim to make the most of its incredible power to instruct and inspire.

'I confess that I am also interested in the technological side of things. I am fascinated by things like the new compact discs or the prototype video-disc – they are really beautiful in their own right, and electronic gadgetry which makes life easier or more fulfilling seems to me to be altogether desirable. The more we can make our tools serve us in the spiritual and artistic objectives we set ourselves, the more we are the gainers. It depends upon human nature as to whether we put these things to good or harmful uses; in the end each individual has to decide this for himself. In the West at least there is some possibility of choice, whereas in the

Soviet Union it is all decided way above the heads of ordinary people including, of course, creative artists.

'I may be particularly susceptible to the appeal of electronic gadgetry, particularly when it touches my own field of music, because of the poor quality and general lack of availability of such things when I was growing up in Russia. To those of us who accepted the squalid and deprived conditions of daily life in Russia as being the norm, any labour-saving or technologically ingenious device seems an incredibly positive advance, even if we do not admire the uses to which these devices are sometimes put. This can affect one's attitudes in other areas. Russians find little charm, for instance, in old-fashioned hotels or houses. People in the West who have had some choice as to where or how they live can allow themselves to be affected by atmosphere or nostalgia; to us functionalism, efficiency and service are symbols of the ability to escape from uniformity and total disregard for the most elementary consideration for a person's well-being – things which surround one every day of one's life in the Soviet Union.'

11

MOST SOVIET EMIGRES find it immeasurably more difficult to adjust to the different mores and pace of life in the West than they could possibly imagine before they leave the Soviet Union. This is still true in the 1980s after more than twenty years of extensive cultural exchange between Russia and the West. One of the biggest problems is to know whom to believe, since the very diversity of opportunity and motivation in the West tends to produce almost as many conflicting opinions about any one subject as there are apparently qualified experts. For many Russians this has been their undoing; as they bounce uncertainly from one adviser to another, they have changed their plans and loyalties with damaging inconsistency, often alienating in the process the very people who were initially most willing to help. Sadly, but perhaps inevitably, many émigrés have tended to believe those who have painted the rosiest picture of their prospects, whereas those who have pointed out the pitfalls of too precipitous a rush toward the legendary spoils of success in the West have gone unheeded – at least until it was too late and irreparable damage has been done.

Too often, also, Russian émigré musicians of undoubted talent have suffered from their own cunning and gullibility – a fatal mixture. The cunning, Ashkenazy is convinced, is learned from years of finding one's way within the Soviet system; the gullibility may result from the fact that Soviet artists of talent have always been privileged with the USSR and have come to expect certain material advantages as being their natural due. Ashkenazy remembers well that since he was always something of a celebrity in Moscow amongst his friends and contemporaries and since he generally had more money than he needed for his limited and simple requirements, he and his friends would treat it almost as a matter of course that he would always pay the bill. Money, therefore, tends to occupy a special position in the minds of émigré Russians. On the one hand they deeply resent not having it and on the other they often squander it as though there were no tomorrow as soon as they get hold of it. Unfortunately, it does not always seem to matter whether the money is actually theirs to spend and so one is often faced with an ostentatious open-handedness with funds supplied by someone else.

This seems to be in part a product of the Russian view of the artist as someone Byronic, romantically contemptuous of responsibility and order. It is also consistent with the emphasis on expressiveness when it is at its best, or display when, as is too often the case, it remains anchored in the superficial. Russians so often make a positive virtue of disorder and unreliability, as though these were necessary aspects of genius, the trappings which point to true talent. Not that this is a purely Soviet phenomenon; on the contrary it is deeply rooted in the Russians' historical view of their national and cultural characteristics. One can see many examples of this state of mind in the novels of Dostoevsky or Tolstoy or the plays of Chekhov and it seems to add up to an almost obsessive national preoccupation with the theatrical. It is no accident that Diaghilev and the Ballets Russes enjoyed such enormous success in the West in the 1910s and 1920s; the sheer energy and creativity, the juxtaposition of the Asiatic and European elements in Russian history and culture were simply breathtaking to a European society which was still to a large extent rigidly ordered.

Russian émigrés of all generations have learned how to exploit this seductive blend of the exotic and the familiar; in each generation there have been those who have made brilliant successes in the fertile soil of the West, hungry for sensation; there have been many others, perhaps with less robust talents or more fragile personalities, who have set out on the same routes with the highest hopes, only to reap a bitter harvest of disappointment, disillusion and poverty.

The ebb and flow of history has naturally played its usual unpredictable role. The most fruitful times for Russian artists in the West have tended to be periods of prosperity following years of austerity or hardship. It is surely no coincidence that the 1920s and 1960s seem to have been the times when Russian artists enjoyed their greatest vogue; each period followed prolonged spells of national isolation as the countries of the Western world repaired the lacerations of two world wars. In the 1960s, as we know from so many other areas of life, Western societies began to break away from and to reject that rather staid and stifling sense of order, patriotism and materialism which the war years had inculcated. In music too, there was an appetite for large emotions, for theatricality, for star performers with charismatic personalities. The central-European conception of music as being something serious, something that you would put on your best suit for, became gradually discredited amongst the younger generation of audiences. And it was more and more these younger people who had the spending power and the motivation to go to concerts or to buy records. Even among German musicians the most astute, and in this category Herbert von Karajan must surely carry away all the prizes, adapted to meet this new challenge. For many Russian artists this Western appetite for the dramatic, and the theatrical, so evident in the phenomenal growth of audiences for opera, was a God-send.

To a great degree, Ashkenazy's own success in the West owes much to this trend but, as we have seen, much of what is involved he rejects totally. It may be exhilarating on occasions to face up to some of the most demanding challenges of the piano repertoire but unless this is with some greater end in view, he does not feel that the effort and the achievement has any real worth. As a result there are areas which he leaves well alone despite the enormous range of works in his repertoire; he plays very little Liszt, as we have seen, and despite Decca's wish that he should record the two piano concertos, he has never agreed because he finds little substance in them. Another odd instance is the Tchaikovsky B flat minor Concerto, which was, one would say, the very vehicle which finally established him as a major international pianist. In 1963 he recorded it for Decca with Lorin Maazel but he has always said that he never felt particularly drawn to the work and found it particularly difficult to play to his satisfaction because of his relatively small hands. Now that the original record is old, although a best-seller of its time, Decca would dearly love to have a new digital recording from him, but he has steadfastly resisted all their pleas. The problem, he says, is that in order for him to prepare it to the required standard – and who needs another version of this over-recorded piece unless it should be of really surpassing brilliance? – he would have to work at it non-stop to the exclusion of far more worthwhile and artistically challenging works. So he has decided to drop the concerto from his repertoire permanently.

However, there are times when the ability to display a little virtuosity can come in useful; in the summer of 1978 he was engaged to conduct the Philadelphia orchestra for the first time, in a programme including a Mozart piano concerto and, appropriately for an orchestra so closely connected with the composer, Rachmaninov's Second Symphony. During the break in the one and only rehearsal for the programme, Ashkenazy astonished those around him by launching furiously into the Bartók Second Piano Concerto as the members of the orchestra filed off for their interval refreshments. On being asked why he had decided to warm up with this concerto which he was not to play for many months, he replied with a laugh, 'Well, I had to show them that I can still play the piano despite my conducting!' So natural facility, raw talent, human experience, unceasing work, the memorizing of scores – all of these things are simply the basic tools with which the music itself must be confronted, absorbed and penetrated. One of his rare but scathing criticisms of other pianists comes when he believes that they have stopped short of the music itself and are simply playing the instrument, however attractively.

Yet it would be quite wrong to deduce from all of this that he has fanciful ideas about himself as a sort of high-priest of an arcane mystery out of the reach of those with less self-discipline and dedication. The regime he has adopted is one that happens to suit him personally; it will be remembered that even while at the Conservatoire he felt aware of how fortunate it was for him that he was not co-opted into the class of the great Heinrich Neuhaus, because although the imaginative side of his make-up would undoubtedly have been stimulated, he might never have acquired the habit of work essential to him; if his whole life is to be dedicated to the idea of excellence in music, he sees no alternative to a constant and unremitting review of his ideas and the means of expressing them.

All this may suggest that his self-confidence is less secure than his characteristically positive and direct behaviour might indicate. Certainly at times in the 1960s his closest friends were familiar with bouts of comfortless depression when he would bewail the fact that nothing he did was good enough, and that he did not have sufficient resolution or capacity to achieve the minimum of his aims. On such occasions he could be seen to be possessed by a kind of doggedness, slightly blinkered in his obsessive dedication to his work, as though he were oblivious to the thought that his art and his whole spiritual outlook might be enlarged or refreshed by a wider range of stimuli or by broader horizons. He could not accept that repose and reflection could on occasions achieve as much as another few hours of practise at the keyboard. More recently he has admitted on one or two occasions that he sometimes practises because he cannot think what else to do. Significantly, this is said in self-criticism.

This single-mindedness sometimes meant that he could be unforgiving of the frailties of other less committed or capable beings. To this day, unlike most Russian artists who seem to flourish in a Latin environment, Ashkenazy has little time for the countries of the south; although he is normally willing to go almost anywhere once, out of curiosity – and for some reason he feels that he should play wherever he travels, almost regardless of circumstances – in most Latin countries once is normally enough. Most Russians seem to thrive on the special type of adulation which is bestowed on artists in these countries, but Ashkenazy is easily infuriated by the general atmosphere of inefficiency and unreliability so inescapably connected with the southern way of life and the Latin temperament.

Recently he was persuaded to play for the second time in his career in Mexico and was engaged for recitals in Mexico City and in Guanajuato by the Cervantino Festival, a plaything of the Mexican First Lady of the day. She had musical and artistic aspirations and indulged them lavishly and ostentatiously at the expense of the national exchequer. The fees were handsome by any standards but when Ashkenazy was asked by a friend how the Mexican interlude had gone, and in particular whether the arrangements had been satisfactorily made, he replied, 'Well, all sorts of small things went wrong all the time and the organizers had to be reminded about everything, but they tried hard to be efficient and were very attentive. The most bizarre thing of all was the fact that in the concert programme for my piano recital I was described as "the violinist and occasional Principal Guest Conductor of the Philharmonia". What the bemused public must have thought about my versatility when I came out to play a *piano* recital really intrigues me. In the end, sadly, the best thing about the whole experience was when the plane took off for Los Angeles and I suddenly thought that I'd never have to play in that part of the world again, however much they might pay me. Still, I suppose I may end up touring in Latin America at some time in the future as conductor with an orchestra. Somehow it always feels different when one is on tour with a large troupe of friends. Who knows, maybe the fact that I thrive on tours is some sort of throwback to my father's enjoyment of his life as an Estrada artist.'

The Festival management also got into a fine tangle over its finances, despite being able to call on the full panoply of executive privilege to overcome the bureaucratic difficulties which are so much a part of Mexican life. When Ashkenazy's fee was paid, a negotiable dollar cheque was issued by the Festival's bank on a corresponding bank in Germany. The cheque was promptly dishonoured when it was presented for collection but unfortunately neither bank took the trouble to inform the Festival management in advance. While efforts were being made to disentangle the mess, a substitute cheque was issued, this time payable on a more cooperative American Bank. When this second cheque had been duly presented and cleared, the German bank suddenly decided to honour the first cheque after all and paid the funds into Ashkenazy's bank in Switzerland. Frantic telexes were exchanged across the Atlantic between the Festival management and Ashkenazy's London agents in an attempt to unravel this puzzle and it must have been one of the very rare occasions in Latin America when an artist ended up being paid twice rather than facing the much more common problem of default.

Ashkenazy's attitude to Latin America may indeed be somewhat coloured by the fact that his first and only visit to Argentina in 1973 resulted in his losing half of the fees due to him as a result of the bankruptcy of the local promoter; ironically, the half actually received had been paid in advance in accordance with the contract, and it was precisely the punctuality with which this first payment had been made that persuaded Ashkenazy to trust the impresario over the balance. His first visit to Mexico a few years earlier had been spoiled when he caught a virus; he had to cancel one of his two concerts, although he managed to drag himself to the piano to play the other. Since he felt like death and hates cancelling anything, the memory was not a happy one.

In Italy, in the days when he used to play there regularly, he often travelled with those of his children who were small at that time. This required formidable organization, particularly as far as Dody was concerned, and also made them especially vulnerable to the vagaries and disruptions of international travel. It is the Italians' particular talent for a combination of disorder and disinterest in this area which alienated the Ashkenazys more than almost anything. It reflects badly on the reputation Italy enjoys for the cult of the family and of children that so little courtesy or assistance is forthcoming at its railway stations and airports for the weary, troubled or elderly traveller or for those accompanied by small children.

These things may seem small when set against the incomparable grandeurs of Italian culture, but to Ashkenazy they are symptomatic of a fundamental lack of respect for the weightier values in life, as are the eternal gossiping and unwrapping of sweets which used to be the principal preoccupations of Italian audiences at concerts. In the 1960s Italian musical events tended to be excuses for social gatherings for the richer and idler members of society; audiences were notoriously inattentive and ignorant.

In fairness, Ashkenazy is the first to admit that some recent experiences, in this last respect at least, have been a lot happier. In the 1970s a new generation of music lovers seems to have emerged and their genuine passion for music and rapt attention to its finer exponents have been widely appreciated; Ashkenazy remembers with particular pleasure a recital in Rome in 1981 when he played a difficult programme including the "Hammerklavier" Sonata, never exactly an easy work for those whose powers of concentration are weak. He said that he had never performed this sonata in such an atmosphere of total stillness and attentiveness. He has similarly positive memories of concerts in Milan in May 1983.

As in so many other places, the old guard who tended to hold sway in musical circles the world over and who often treated concerts as an extension of their and their audiences' social lives have begun to give way to a new generation of promoters, organizers and festival directors whose boundless enthusiasm and considerable knowledge are combined with a desire to serve the artistic community in a way which has earned the loyalty and gratitude of many performers. This is particularly true in France, where alongside an official music establishment remarkable for its backwardness despite the millions pumped into it by way of public subsidy, a number of enterprising individuals both in Paris and in many provincial centres have achieved miracles in building a new musical life. As a result, many of the world's most interesting artists who had been systematically ignored by the officially supported organizations began to return to France and to play there regularly. If he feels that they are motivated by a genuine love for the arts and for artists, Ashkenazy is willing to be enormously supportive to this new breed of promoters, even when this may require him to accept greatly reduced fees or even no fee at all. Indeed, he finds it so difficult to say no to a request made personally to him by someone who appears to have a genuine case to plead, that he can get taken advantage of; some well-meaning amateurs show more enterprise in making these approaches than competence and professionalism in carrying their projects out. Ashkenazy's belief that any letter written to him directly warrants not just a personal reply – an attractive if unrealistic belief – but also in many cases agreement to whatever is asked of him, has been the despair of his advisers; it hardly helps in the constant battle to reduce his commitments.

Questions of human dealings are of the greatest importance to Ashkenazy. He believes passionately that man's relation to man, in the sense of each person's essential individuality, is the key to all our finest hopes and aspirations. Not that he feels sanguine about mankind's collective progress in this respect – indeed, he often finds an explanation for some particularly contemptible or disreputable action by saying, 'Well, as I always say, this only goes to show how rotten mankind is.' But even if he believes this in moments of disgust, he remains one of the most irrepressively positive people in the world and is all the more convinced that each man has a duty to overcome in himself this fatal tendency to deteriorate morally.

In the Soviet Union he knows that there is little hope in this respect. All the forces of government, of the internal infrastructure, even of the metaphysical ideology upon which social and intellectual life is based, conspire together to accentuate the irreversible decay of man's finest and most exemplary attributes. If everything depends upon what sort of person you are, what kind of a person can you hope to become in the suffocating climate of repression and lies which has been institutionalized within the Soviet Union and in other communist states?

An interesting feature of Ashkenazy's consideration for the public he serves is his quite unique record as far as cancellation of his engagements is concerned. Over the last twenty years of intensive concert-giving from one end of the world to another, totalling in all something like two thousand performances, he has cancelled only three or four times and then only when confined to bed. He takes very good care of his health by ensuring that he eats well and that his rest at night is, as far as is possible, undisturbed; even so he is as much prey to colds, 'flu or worse as those of his many colleagues who seldom get through two or three months' work without cancelling one or two performances on the way. It is partly a question of taking reasonable precautions: he does not smoke, drinks very sparingly and then only wine, and conserves his strength carefully in order to be able to redirect it all the more unstintingly to areas where it is needed. On tours, his energy is apparently inexhaustible; day after day, in addition to full rehearsals and concerts, he will practise for several hours, even using up the breaks in orchestral rehearsals to work at the piano as though not a second can be lost. But the thinking behind all of this is simple and logical; orchestral breaks are dead periods of little use to anyone except the orchestral player who needs a little relaxation from the tedium of a life-time routine. If he uses this time profitably, he can rest at other times and conserve his energies when it is most rational and practical to do so.

If he feels in less than top condition because of a cold or 'flu, he reasons that the combination of determination and physical work which his daily life requires is likely to accelerate the process of getting back to top form. Since the human metabolism varies according to cycles as well as to external conditions such as climate, environment, diet and change of time zone he sees the battle against these often very debilitating factors as an unavoidable part of his performing life. They may even produce unexpectedly creative results, if overcome. So much that is best in art comes out of struggle, and Ashkenazy feels convinced that the will to persevere, to go on aiming for the best results, is a habit that must be learned and cultivated like any other human activity of any worth. The acceptance of defeat by failing to honour a commitment for any but the most irresistible reasons is a failure not just in duty to the public – and this Ashkenazy takes exceptionally seriously – but in the artist's duty to himself.

It is not surprising that many artists who have left the Soviet Union and live in the West have a rather different view about their responsibilities in these things; many are notoriously willing to cancel engagements on the flimsiest pretexts, often merely because a decision made in advance no longer suits them when the date of the performance actually approaches. These bad habits are learned early in life in the Soviet Union, where few engagements outside the most important in Moscow and Leningrad have any real career significance. In any case, the concerts are so likely to be cancelled, rearranged or mismanaged by the officials that a similar unreliability on the part of the artist is hardly a matter for special comment. These factors coupled with the traditional Russian view of the artist as a person whose genius lifts him above the need to concern himself with such trivialities as punctuality, or responsibility to others, has made it difficult to many émigré artists to change their attitudes in the face of more censorious public opinion in the West.

Ironically, reactions to such behaviour have also changed greatly in the last ten or fifteen years in most Western countries. As the power of artists of the top calibre to act as they please has grown, promoters and public alike have become resigned to an ever-increasing scourge of last-minute cancellations in their concert and opera seasons. There have been one or two court actions against artists by the more intrepid victims of such behaviour but in the end everyone recognizes that there are very few artists who really draw the public, and an indulgent attitude to a cancellation in one season may result in the artist making things good the next. The only country where these things are taken very seriously indeed is Japan; this is partly because almost all tours by foreign artists are planned long in advance and involve enormous investment in pre-tour publicity and promotional overheads, not to mention the rental for halls and the running costs of the management concerned. Perhaps predictably, Ashkenazy feels himself to be very much at home in Japan; the combination of immaculate organization with the fundamental seriousness of the public provides exactly the sort of conditions in which he feels at his best. There is the added incentive of excellent financial terms. In Japan, ticket prices are very high and the public has very decided ideas about which artists are deserving of their custom. The Japanese are a great reading nation and books and magazines about music abound. Concert goers, a high proportion of whom are girls in their late teens and early twenties, prepare themselves very well for the concerts they attend and a last minute substitution by another artist is simply not acceptable.*

Many artists have only the vaguest idea of what their commitments are, even though they have agreed to them; it is often left to their agents or wives to keep them primed with their schedule when engagements come too close to be ignored. Ashkenazy carefully plans with his manager every detail of his schedule of engagements even though this may stretch three or four years ahead; he cannot understand how people can function at their best in any other way. For those who do not plan, there is often no hope of avoiding over-commitment or lack of preparation, and a cancelled concert may well be the life-line which will save a more important engagement a week or so later.

In the end, it all comes back to man's expectation of himself; mistakes or misjudgements are inevitable from time to time, especially in a *métier* where the pressure builds up inexorably as the distances separating each section of the international music community shrink with the acceleration of transport and media communication. Too much is undoubtedly expected of artists, especially of many who are too young to have formed a clear picture of their own proper rhythms of life. Fierce competition among performers for those opportunities which may enhance or

---

* No less experienced a person than Walter Legge discovered this to his cost in 1966 when his wife Elizabeth Schwarzkopf had to cancel a major Japanese tour for valid medical reasons. The promoters suffered a great financial loss and pressed Legge to find time for a replacement tour at the earliest possible opportunity. Legge proved to be somewhat cavalier in his negotiations with them, insisting that although Schwarzkopf would certainly consider a tour in the future, this would have to wait until a convenient period in her very full diary could be found. The Japanese became more and more pressing, probably the type of approach least likely to persuade Legge to do anything and in the end, to everyone's immense surprise, they instituted proceedings in the Japanese courts. These led to a settlement out of court, which proved to be very expensive for the Legges.

establish their careers encourages them to seize upon attractive engagements without proper consideration, in case a valuable stepping-stone might otherwise be missed. It takes a courageous, unusually mature, or exceptionally fortunate young artist to decline today what he knows he may never be offered again tomorrow.

If many Russians find the uninhibited, intuitive type of response to music and the arts cultivated so often by Latins very congenial to their own ill-disciplined attitudes, Ashkenazy once admitted that he wished that there were a greater percentage of intuition in his own make-up. On being reminded of this recently, he qualified his original statement: 'Perhaps what I should have said was that I sometimes wish that I could bring out this intuition more in myself. On further reflection, I think that I do have the intuition, in fact we all do, but it is a question of drawing it out and developing it. I am similarly convinced that in some unspecified future we shall be able to use faculties such as ESP, telepathy and other powers which we know we have but which we still have no real idea how to use. It may be a question of physical faculties or attributes which we have never used or never had cause to develop, but which could release talents we did not know we possessed.

'When it comes to intuition, I have decided that I shall try to bring it out in myself in whatever way I can. I see this as a delicate, continuous process, which I believe can only come out of a sense of freedom; this for me means in practical terms that I have to prepare myself as perfectly as I can, both in my playing and conducting, so that these aspects of performance become as much as possible second nature. It is not just a matter of my professional life though; it also concerns everyday life and deal-ings with people. I believe in developing a good balance of the two essential parts in our make-up; the animal background and the more recent attributes of *homo sapiens*. It has been argued that our emotions are related to our pre-human origins and that it is our more recently acquired faculties of reason which have to organize these instinctive, animal characteristics. To me this is too crude an explanation for the dichotomy within us.

'There is, clearly, an irrational element within us and this may indeed relate back to the various stages of our evolution as a species, but it has very little to do with emotions. After all, even though we may have been fishes and reptiles and are still mammals, we have also been *homo sapiens* for a very long time by now, which means that the emotional elements in our composition have developed over several millennia of intercourse between the irrational and rational elements of our biological inheritance. One could say that the irrational part is no longer what it was. Reflected as intuition or instinct, it is already a trained, intelligent faculty based on an immense experience of rational thought and action.

'I seek to achieve a proper balance in everything I do by trying to develop my intuitive responses in tandem with my rational processes.

'In music, that balance may have to be adjusted in favour of one side or the other. The proportions will be different for, say, Bach or Tchaikovsky, but both elements must still be there. I find it helpful to remind myself of a stanza by the poet Samuel Marshak who translated Shakespeare's sonnets into Russian — rather well, incidentally. It comes from one of his verses for children, for which he was famous:

> I wish for you throughout your life that your heart
> be intelligent and your brain be kind.'

12

IN THE SEVEN YEARS between 1969 and 1976, Ashkenazy was much preoccupied with his growing interest in conducting, and with constantly recurring doubts as to whether he was really prepared to move on from his occasional concerts with the Iceland Symphony Orchestra to more exposed but obviously more challenging arenas elsewhere.

The decision to persevere was taken with painful deliberation and a great deal of soul-searching, much of it in the course of endless discussions with those closest to him about the advantages and disadvantages, the rewards and pitfalls of such a step. On many occasions he wavered and thought seriously of giving up; after all, it was obvious that as a greatly celebrated pianist he would be vulnerable to the most ferocious criticism from those who would wish to make unfavourable comparisons between his long-established reputation as pianist and his still fledgling skills as conductor. At times a truly Russian quixotry seemed to manifest itself; he could be so persuasive about his total lack of technical qualifications for the task in hand as to persuade even those most convinced of his real talent for conducting that he should after all eschew this particular challenge. Such signs of wavering support would then make him all the more determined to continue. In the end, his passionate involvement with the music he wished to perform, the intensity of his power of communication, and a disarming lack of pretension about his technical skills won over those who would be the most important arbiters, the orchestral musicians themselves.

He hopes that his conducting, and the expanded range of musical experience encompassed by it, have done much to sharpen and refine his artistic attitudes and thoughts. In principle he believes that it has had a very positive effect on all of his music-making.

One of the insoluble problems facing an apprentice conductor who is already a performer of great public standing is that almost every work conducted will be, for him, a first performance, whereas the public and the critics will judge each occasion, quite rightly, without any special indulgence and with the heightened interest and expectations due to an artist of great celebrity.

In the early days, Ashkenazy tried to diminish the risks inherent in this dilemma by getting some experience with orchestras of good quality based away from the most exposed musical centres. In England, his first engagements were with the Northern Sinfonia in Newcastle and at Lancaster University and then, in 1976, with the Royal Liverpool Philharmonic in a programme including the Shostakovich Eighth Symphony in Liverpool. He also conducted several programmes with the excellent Swedish Radio Orchestra both in Stockholm and elsewhere in Sweden and there were even some discussions about a more permanent association. But this was in 1978 and the moment for such an arrangement had already passed, largely because of a successful series of concerts with the Philharmonia, then still called the New Philharmonia and only just beginning to restore its fortunes after years of decline at the end of the Klemperer era.

These introductory concerts with the Philharmonia established an immediate rapport and persuaded the initially sceptical Decca management that a recording relationship could also be entered into with advantage. As a result, Ashkenazy felt that any position that might eventually be offered by the Swedes would inevitably become subsidiary to the new relationship with the more prestigious London orchestra, not least because of Decca's strong preference for an orchestra with an established recording reputation, such as the Philharmonia had retained from its era of glory in the 1950s and early 1960s. Ashkenazy decided not to encourage expectations in Stockholm which he might not later be able to satisfy, but a less formal collaboration with the Swedes continued, first in concerts and later in a series of television programmes directed by Christopher Nupen featuring the music of composers as diverse as Respighi, Mussorgsky and Sibelius.

For the Respighi programme, which subsequently won an American Emmy nomination, Ashkenazy learned a whole list of scores ranging from the familiar 'Pini de Roma' to the obscure Toccata for Piano and Orchestra which he directed from the keyboard. The entire programme was successfully recorded in two three-hour sessions despite the fact that much of the music was unknown to the orchestra. London orchestras rightly pride themselves on the speed and accuracy of their work in the studio but one wonders whether the Swedish Radio Orchestra's performance would have been bettered in equivalent circumstances in London.

The Mussorgsky programme also led to some interesting developments. The original intention had been to film the famous Ravel orchestration of "Pictures at an Exhibition", contrasted with a performance of the original piano version which Ashkenazy subsequently recorded for Nupen a year later in London. This plan eventually had to be modified because the publishers of the Ravel orchestration made financial demands for the television license which were out of all proportion to the budgetary possibilities of the programme. After considering all the alternatives, and in view of long-standing reservations he held about some aspects of the Ravel version, Ashkenazy finally decided to record instead the orchestration by the Finnish composer Funtek. If much less known and certainly less brilliant than Ravel's inspired score, Ashkenazy found the approach to be in some important respects truer to Mussorgsky's original conception.

In the event, the necessary modification of the original plan for the Nupen film accelerated another project under discussion at about that time. It first came up over dinner in Amsterdam on the occasion of Ashkenazy's happy and successful debut as conductor with the Concertgebouw Orchestra. He was explaining to a group of close friends why he finds the Ravel orchestration disturbingly untrue to Mussorgsky, including the fact that Ravel had carried over many errors from a very inaccurate piano edition of the work. As a pianist brought up since childhood with the correct score, these errors of transcription were both unnecessary and annoying, so he thought that some day he might try not only to perform a small act of homage to Mussorgsky by cleaning up those errors but also to offer some new thoughts about an orchestration more faithful to the essentially dark colourings and moods of the original masterpiece.

These musings came to the ears of Decca who pressed him to proceed with these plans, as a coupling for a new digital recording of the piano version, since they wanted him in any case to

163

replace the excellent but sonically dated recording he had made in the late 1960s.

Ashkenazy worked on the orchestration during the winter and spring of 1982 and put the finishing touches to it during a long and gruelling tour of Japan in May and June of the same year. The new orchestration was performed by him with the Philharmonia at the Royal Festival Hall at the opening concert of the orchestra's 1982/83 season, and was heard at the same time at the Windsor Festival and in Chatham.

'I admire Ravel's orchestration tremendously and think that it is a fantastic piece of work. But I think that it has very little of Mussorgsky in it. One only needs to listen to *Boris Godunov* in Mussorgsky's original orchestration to see what I mean.

'Mussorgsky's conception is very dark, revealing perhaps a limited knowledge of the orchestra, but even if he had been more expert he would probably have wanted the same effects. He really needed a special orchestra for his music, and wasn't interested either in brilliance for its own sake, or in a lot of light colours; he wanted deep, heavy, muddy colours and that is what I think Ravel did not want to understand. Ravel was probably too great a genius himself and I suppose somewhere deep down inside, he looked a little condescendingly upon Mussorgsky who was not an educated musician but an amateur. He had hardly studied music but was a natural, a sort of rough diamond. He had never studied orchestration and had very little background in harmony or counterpoint – so, to this refined genius, Ravel, he must have seemed rather primitive.

'Ravel altered many points of notation, including dynamics, and incorporated all the misprints from the first piano edition. This means that he never even tried to find the manuscript or a facsimile to see what was right or wrong, which is a pity. In any case, Ravel's affinity with the orchestra was very peculiarly his own; I find it organic only in his own music and not in Mussorgsky's "Pictures". His version sounds fantastically brilliant, of course, and very inventive, but to my ears the invention is all for the sake of achieving fabulous sonorities rather than to bring out faithfully all the idiomatic nuances of what Mussorgsky wanted to express.

'I am not alone in this assessment of his orchestration. I find that nine out of ten of my colleagues say the same thing, but very seldom publicly, because of the danger of seeming to be too arrogant about a great master. I hope that people will understand that I am not arrogant but am simply speaking my mind, and that of my colleagues. In any case, I'm not trying to compete with Ravel – I know that I could not possibly do so. But if I have revealed a little more of Mussorgsky, I shall be happy. That is all I was aiming at.'

For its first performance, Ashkenazy wrote the following in the accompanying programme note:

> I always think in terms of orchestral colour when I play the piano and since this masterpiece evokes the strongest orchestral associations for me, I have developed my own personal vision of how the piece should sound when transposed from the piano to the larger canvas of the symphony orchestra. The result of this slow and irresistible process is what I offer tonight. My approach to this challenge has been based on complete loyalty to Mussorgsky's idiom and to what I believe was in the composer's mind when he conceived this cycle. I have not been concerned with effect for its own sake, however inventive or brilliant a certain passage might sound, but instead I have been guided by the deeper undercurrents of this predominantly dark coloured piece. In other words, I have tried to work from within the music rather than from without and I hope the result has a certain validity.
>
> It is important to note that in Ravel's masterly orchestration there are a number of textual errors which probably resulted from his use of a poor edition of the piano score while working on his version. Unfortunately, all currently available recordings reproduce practically all these mistakes, although they could be so easily corrected by referring to an edition of the piano version based on the manuscript. I must confess that it feels good that at least in my version these mistakes can be put right.

The new orchestration was enthusiastically received by public and critics alike and aroused considerable interest among other conductors. The almost Asiatic, old-Russian flavour of the work in Ashkenazy's conception contrasts dramatically with the brilliantly urbane, but perhaps over-cultivated images created by Ravel.

Returning to his developing activities as a conductor, Ashkenazy soon came to the conclusion that the lack of exposure involved in performance with orchestras of secondary rank might be comforting but that there was also diminishing value in the experience acquired. He simply could not afford to set aside enough time for conducting to allow for performances with a large number of different orchestras without risking serious encroachment on the routine and discipline indispensable to his piano playing. He also realized that only the best orchestras would be capable of the type of performances which would make his own technical shortcomings matter less. He admits that in the early stages of his conducting relationship with the Philharmonia, he sometimes needed to rely on the instinct and experience of some of the orchestra's most outstanding musicians to ensure that his musical intentions were carried out satisfactorily. Consequently his own process of learning accelerated more rapidly through regular work with the Philharmonia than it could do through intermittent exposure to orchestras of lesser quality. He did not want to squander too much time and energy correcting technical problems of ensemble or intonation, or even instrumental playing, since these would obscure the main objective, that of making music. Between 1978 and 1982, therefore, Ashkenazy accepted very few engagements with orchestras other than the Philharmonia. Instead he conducted as many out-of-town concerts as possible with the Philharmonia to ensure that the ensuing London programmes and recordings were as well prepared as possible.

These concerts served many useful purposes simultaneously. They provided extra employment for the Philharmonia in places where low budgets often require them to work with conductors below the first rank. If skilfully scheduled they could also ameliorate the uncomfortable and wasteful system by which programmes are often rehearsed for only one London performance; on the continent or in America, by contrast, orchestras generally give several performances of the same programme in their home town because of different subscription series, a system long held to be unworkable in London because of the enormous range of conflicting events available for the public to choose from.

Ashkenazy often made the whole package more attractive to the public by including in the programme a Mozart concerto directed from the keyboard. He was the first to appreciate that at the early stages of his conducting career, the public would be more inclined to hear him in his new role as a conductor if they could listen to him perform as pianist as well. In any case, these additional Mozart concerto performances were essential preparations for recording sessions, since in the late 1970s and early 1980s he was working his way through the complete set of Mozart piano concertos for Decca.

In his regional concerts, he normally managed to vary the programme a little from concert to concert in order to add an extra symphony here or there to his repertoire and, by the end of 1983, the list of works he had performed was beginning to look very impressive, considering how late he had started and how few months each season he had been able to devote to conducting.

He has by now conducted works by Brahms, Bartók, Rachmaninov, Mozart, Mahler, Richard Strauss, Stravinsky, Scriabin, Sibelius, Berg, Schoenberg, Shostakovich, Prokofiev, Wagner, Walton and Elgar. His appetite for new repertoire is enormous, with a range of interests which even his gigantic pianistic repertoire cannot match. With the piano, of course, different factors come into play. Since there are only a limited number of works each season which he feels that he can perform to the very highest level of quality, he has to relate the range of his repertoire to what is practicable and realistic. With conducting, he is prepared to take on almost anything, provided he finds it musically appealing and there is space enough left in his brain to absorb it. Very little contemporary music appeals to him, although he certainly does not have a closed mind; he simply feels that with time pressing so rapidly he only wants to take on works which to his mind and heart have something substantial to say. He does not feel the need to be a pioneer; he would prefer to leave the more ephemeral works to others fascinated with innovation for its own sake. If something new were to impress him, he would certainly wish to perform it.

'I don't really know what to think about the long-term future of music. It may be that it is at a dead end, but on the other hand there are always extraordinary people, one or two geniuses who appear in a lifetime. If there was a Beethoven or a Wagner, maybe there will be another composer of similar stature who will find the appropriate musical terms with which to convince us that true musical expression on the most exalted and communicative level is not dead.

'What I hear at the moment does not inspire me, regardless of whether it is extremely advanced or based on traditional tonal music. I very rarely find that anything new is expressed; so much sounds to me merely experimental without having anything very much to say. For me the crucial value of music is as a means of self-expression, not just about oneself but revealing one's understanding of the world around us.

'It is not so important what we actually experience in our lives, but much more how we respond to these experiences and how we communicate our understanding of them in whatever is our chosen means of expression. Of course, there are very few individuals who can do this on the most transcendental level, but at least we know that a Raphael, a Michelangelo, a Beethoven and a Shakespeare have really existed and have proved that it is possible to understand something of the inner meaning of life and to express this so that others can catch a glimpse too. By contrast, most new music that I have heard so far sounds to me shallow and insignificant.'

Ashkenazy's relationship with the Philharmonia between 1977 and 1983 was seminal to the growth of his conducting activities and he enjoyed the work he did with them so much that he tended to invest the collaboration with an almost romantic glow. He felt that he had an exceptionally good understanding with many of the members of the orchestra on a personal and musical level, and this high regard seems to have been largely reciprocated on the orchestra's side. There was certainly no doubt about the wide range of commercial benefits he was able to bring with him in the form of a steady flow of recordings, many television sessions and major international tours. Since London orchestras are subsidized at a very low level in comparison with equivalent bodies abroad, and suffer the additional disadvantage of having no permanent home base to which they can devote a substantial part of their annual activity, any additional engagements play a very significant role in the orchestral musicians' welfare and income.

Ashkenazy's many performances and recordings of Mozart piano concertos with the orchestra did much to enhance a special, almost chamber-music, approach to rehearsals, with the result that each musician was able to feel some individual share in shaping the final performance. It could be argued, however, that this approach worked less well at the beginning of the collaboration. There is in every orchestral player's mind a dichotomy; on the one hand, he resents any conductor who denies him his individuality by imposing too rigid a conception of how the music should be played; on the other, the conductors who are most admired are often precisely those who through force of will achieve the submersion of each musician's separate entity within the musical framework the conductors choose to dictate.

In his early years with the Philharmonia, Ashkenazy was inclined to blame himself immediately and publicly if anything went wrong in rehearsal or if the artistic results of a performance were less than satisfactory. Despite the advice of some of his friends within the orchestra who were perhaps more attuned to the orchestral musician's mentality, he tended to be excessively apologetic and self-effacing, giving too readily the impression, which he undoubtedly felt, that he was not yet fully worthy of the privilege of conducting so fine an orchestra. As time passed his confidence in his technique grew, and with it a better appreciation of the inescapable fact that artistic responsibility rests in the end with the conductor alone and that a democratic approach to music making may have to be modified when the results are unsatisfactory. One or two inferior concerts, including a strangely demoralized performance in Munich in 1979 in the middle of an otherwise excellent tour, taught him that the conductor must always be able to maintain a clear perspective of what is happening in a performance. He must both stand back from the music and immerse himself totally in it. If the impetus or sense of purpose within the orchestra begins to flag, and this can happen all too easily in the middle of a long and exhausting tour, the conductor alone can and must impose his will in order to restore the integrity of the performance.

This may call for an element of asperity, something very alien to Ashkenazy's whole way of dealing with people and something which he feels should be used only to overcome a real psychological block. Authority should come out of a truly mature understanding of the musical material and must be based on superior creative gifts. Ashkenazy has no wish to emulate those conductors who resort to tricks of the trade or personal eccentricities in order to bluff their way past a lack of preparation or conviction.

All in all, Ashkenazy is not interested in a career as a conductor in the conventional sense. The ladder of fame and power which fascinates so many of his able and ambitious colleagues holds no allure for him. He will have nothing to do with the jockeying for position, the manipulation of commercial assets such as recording or television contracts, or the lobbying with boards and managements which many conductors see as inescapable if they are to get on.

Ashkenazy declines almost all invitations to appear as a guest conductor, preferring to build a few solid and lasting relationships which will enable him to perform a wide range of orchestral music in the best possible artistic conditions. He has, for instance, remained loyal to the English Chamber Orchestra with whom he regularly performs both in England and abroad. He has also developed a thriving rapport with the Concertgebouw Orchestra, following his first appearance with them in Amsterdam in 1979. It might have been easy to predict that this collaboration would work well after so many weeks together in 1978 when he played three complete Beethoven piano concerto cycles with them in Amsterdam, New York and Washington under the baton of Bernard Haitink, a conductor for whom he has the warmest admiration and affection. Nonetheless, it is often foolhardy to assume that a respected and admired instrumentalist will necessarily be readily accepted by an orchestra in the new role of conductor. Decca was delighted that all went so well with an orchestra with which they wished to work more extensively and, as a result, Ashkenazy has now recorded the three Rachmaninov symphonies in Amsterdam, to be followed in the near future by 'The Bells', a work which was commissioned by the Concertgebouw Orchestra from Rachmaninov to texts by Edgar Allan Poe in 1913.

Decca was also extremely anxious that Ashkenazy should conduct and record in America, a market of the greatest importance to the company under its 'London Records' label. Record buyers in the United States tend to be chauvinistic about their own orchestras, with the obvious exceptions of the Berlin and Vienna Philharmonics, and Decca has long maintained recording relationships with the Chicago Symphony under Solti, the Los Angeles Philharmonic while Zubin Mehta was Music Director there, and with the Cleveland Orchestra, which many consider to be the most refined and musical of all the North American ensembles.

Initially, a plan was devised for Ashkenazy to record with the Boston Symphony, following two successful programmes he gave with the orchestra at Tanglewood* in July 1978.

Originally, a two-week guest period had been agreed for spring 1980, but later discussions about more precise arrangements became bogged down, largely because the Boston Symphony management insisted upon an onerous quid pro quo in the form of a one-for-one package of recordings for their Music Director Seiji Ozawa, if Ashkenazy was to be allowed to record with the orchestra. Terms with Decca could not be agreed and, in the event, Ashkenazy had only one week with the orchestra and no recording. Moreover, the good rapport of July 1978 was unaccountably missing in April 1980. The resulting concerts were less than satisfactory.

Happily, other experiences in North America have been more positive. Ashkenazy conducted the Philadelphia Orchestra for the first time in summer 1978 and then again in the winter season 1982/3, at which time he also made his debut as conductor with the Cleveland Orchestra. Here the chemistry was right from the start; Ashkenazy marvelled at the professional pride and artistic excellence of this highly committed body of musicians, and was delighted with the performances of a Mozart piano concerto followed by a long orchestral suite made up from Prokofiev's *Cinderella* ballet; after the concerts, the complete score was then recorded by Decca. Ashkenazy was immediately offered engagements by the orchestra for concerts in each of the three following seasons, and he felt that he had found the right base from which to develop his conducting activities in the United States while at the same time accommodating Decca's own recording strategy for him.

Sadly, at the very time when this new relationship with the

* Tanglewood is a large estate situated in the beautiful countryside of the Berkshire hills in the heart of New England. This was donated to the Boston Symphony between the wars and has been the orchestra's summer home ever since. In addition to a regular series of concerts throughout the summer months, attracting large audiences from all over New England as well as from New York and Boston, there is also an ambitious teaching programme for young orchestral musicians, singers and conductors. Apart from providing continuous employment for its orchestral musicians when concert life could not be maintained in Boston itself, Tanglewood generates substantial income for the Boston Symphony because of the very large seating capacity of the main auditorium, somewhat overmodestly named 'the shed'.

Cleveland orchestra was being established, a cloud was passing over his rapport with the Philharmonia, or rather with its management. By the autumn of 1981 Ashkenazy had begun to play an increasingly important role in the orchestra's activities in view of his many London concerts, tours at home and abroad and his substantial recording programme. It seemed entirely appropriate, therefore, that the orchestra should invite him to accept the title of Principal Guest Conductor.

In this new capacity, Ashkenazy's work with the Philharmonia intensified during the ensuing eighteen months, and many interesting projects were devised for future seasons. Unfortunately, this harmonious rapport proved to be all too short-lived. In the early spring of 1983 it emerged that the orchestra's management had, in Ashkenazy's opinion, failed to live up to some important understandings reached during the preceding year, when arrangements for his new appointment were being worked out. As a result, he no longer felt that it would be appropriate for him to continue with the formal position of Principal Guest Conductor, preferring instead to return to the looser and non-exclusive connection which had existed previously.

By the beginning of 1984 it was becoming clear that approximately one third of his activity was being devoted to conducting. He does not believe that this will alter very radically during the foreseeable future, because any further extension of his conducting might make it too difficult for him to maintain his piano playing at an appropriate level. Unlike some of his colleagues who have become conductors after first being known as soloists, Ashkenazy does not wish to become a sometime pianist; indeed, he knows that he could not function satisfactorily as such. He may do fewer concerts as a pianist now than he did in the past, but his work at the instrument never ceases. Even so, Ashkenazy does admit – with something of a twinkle in his eye – that his conducting may bring one more long-term benefit. If when old age approaches, he should ever feel that he can no longer live up to his own expectations of himself as a pianist, he knows that a continuing creative life as an artist will probably remain open to him as a conductor, a *métier* which seems often particularly suited to the over-eighties!

13

LIKE MANY RUSSIANS, Ashkenazy has always had a complex and ambivalent attitude towards Germany and the Germans. He made a successful tour of West Germany as early as 1957, and a further tour was planned for two years later including a concert with Herbert von Karajan and the Berlin Philharmonic. This was cancelled after the first American tour and the black-listing following his 'trial' at the Ministry of Culture.* Later, when his international career was fully established, he received many invitations to perform in Germany at the most important level and for very high fees, but he declined all such offers for more than a decade.

His unease about Germany is in many respects hard to understand, because there is much in the typical German approach to music which fits in admirably with his own. In the first place, there is a general seriousness of commitment, a basically sound level of education and understanding of music, even amongst critics, although Philistinism and pretentiousness can be found everywhere. Secondly, arrangements tend to be immaculately efficient and this he very much values in the midst of the complex and pressured itineraries to which all busy concert artists are subject.

Yet, despite these favourable auguries, for many years Ashkenazy felt alienated as soon as he set foot in Germany. Not that this is so unusual a reaction among artists, in particular Anglo-Americans and those from Slav countries. For the Slavs, the reasons must be largely historical and may stretch back to the times when those proto-fascists, the Teutonic knights, first prom-

---

* Ashkenazy has always had the highest admiration for von Karajan as conductor and musician. After his original engagement to play with him in 1959 was cancelled, twenty-four years had to elapse before the two artists eventually performed together in concerts in the Philharmonie in Berlin on 29 and 30 January 1983. Ashkenazy played Beethoven's Fourth Piano Concerto.

oted the concept of *Lebensraum* for the Germans with concomitant attitudes of hostility or at best indifference towards their Slav neighbours.

Historically and politically, these confrontations have reaped a tragic and bitter harvest, and the scars of the life and death struggle of the Second World War in Russia – significantly always known there as the Great Patriotic War – have been slower to heal than with any of the other protagonists. Even when the Germans have welcomed with enthusiasm the most brilliant artists from Slav countries it is hard to avoid the impression that there is an element of condescension enveloped within the approbation, almost as though special allowances must be made when a basically Asiatic culture and mentality aspires to grapple with the mysteries of the greatest in Western music.

This is most obviously manifested in a tendency to belittle or reject much Russian music, with the possible exception of Tchaikovsky whose music has been too well integrated into the programmes of the large numbers of orchestras with which Germany has long been so liberally endowed. When it comes to Rachmaninov, Prokofiev, even Shostakovich, they are seen at best as appropriate vehicles for the many brilliant but somehow superficial artists from the East, and at worst – and the most damning judgements tend to be reserved for Rachmaninov* – as little more than *Unterhaltungsmusik* (light music).

Many Russian artists have found this painfully undermining, especially since they can often agree that there is an element of truth in the most discerning of the evaluations. Ashkenazy, for one, would never claim for a moment that the genius of Rachmaninov could be equated in any meaningful way with that of Beethoven, Mozart or Brahms, and there is never the slightest doubt in his mind that it is with the masterpieces of these giants that he will live, ponder and work for the rest of his creative life. Indeed, although he does play a great deal of Russian music with exemplary brilliance and authority, it is the music of Beethoven, Mozart, Brahms and Schumann which remain, with that of Chopin, the central pillars of his repertoire.

There remains the conviction that the Russian masters are

---

* Ashkenazy remembers reading in a Berlin paper a review of a recent performance of the Rachmaninov Third Symphony given by Lorin Maazel, and the Berlin Philharmonic. The symphony was described as 'music for Dr Zhivago'.

undervalued in Germany for the wrong reasons. The over-tidy German mind rejects as superficial or over-emotional elements which may provide clues to different but equally important parts of the artistic persona, and which may revitalize the energy needed to face the challenges posed by the most sublime and inspiring musical masterpieces. It may be that the ability to respond naturally and without affectation to the plangent soulfulness of Rachmaninov will help an artist to open himself more easily to the full range of emotions needed to reflect not only his highest aspirations, but also those insecurities, doubts and introspections which are such significant aspects of the darker side of the human experience.

It is interesting to note, in this context, that although the Germans and Austrians still consider themselves to be the proper torch-bearers for their rich musical heritage, with the notable exception of such giants as von Karajan or Fischer-Dieskau, few performers of real stature have emerged from those countries during the last fifty years or so. Those who have achieved widespread fame and acceptance have often done so late in life and bolstered by the formidable power of the Austro-German music establishment; the efficient marketing and promotion provided by Deutsche Grammophon has been particularly significant. If, with advancing age, figures such as Karl Böhm or Wilhelm Kempff became accepted as Popes of German musical art, the opinion has also been expressed in some musical circles that they are short in creative imagination for all their weighty seriousness. Among the last two generations of German and Austrian performers too – essentially those who matured since the end of the Second World War, including those whose careers were delayed because of it – early promise has seldom flowered into a really creative individuality. Instead, we have the curious paradox of musical life in Germany and Austria being increasingly dominated by artists who are basically extraneous. And yet there remains the feeling that many Israelis, Slavs and Italians who have found these countries their happy hunting ground are really glorified artistic *Gastarbeiter*, whose places will be unceremoniously re-occupied when truly national exponents of German culture eventually emerge.

Many Slav artists therefore feel that they are accepted in Germany or Austria on sufferance, provided that they devote themselves primarily to non-German music. As soon as they set themselves up as interpreters of Beethoven, Mozart or Schubert, they face condescension or downright rejection. This seems unavoidable in Vienna, too, with its peculiar blend of sophistication and provincialism and is an attitude all too frequently encountered in Munich, now restored, as before the war, as one of the musical crossroads of Europe. There the critic Joachim Kaiser has ruled as King for a long time, and his tendentious* but impressively presented utterances tend to be treated as gospel by large sections of the German music world.

Of course the psychological inheritance of the last war cannot be underestimated. Unprepared for the German repudiation of the Nazi-Soviet Non-Aggression Pact and the subsequent invasion, the Russians suffered the horrors of war to a degree no other European nation has ever endured. The brutalities committed on both sides beggar belief. For the Germans, the Russians were largely beyond the pale and Ashkenazy remembers as a child how the Germans were thought of as a nation of ghoulish killers. The austerities endured in Moscow during the war, although far less severe than those suffered in Leningrad, were attributed to the perfidious barbarism of the whole German race, thus setting a scene calculated to leave a lasting impression on any young mind.

Today, of course, Ashkenazy sees things very differently. He understands that however bestial many of the individual protagonists undoubtedly were, a national obsession with the iniquities of the entire German race was an invaluable forge in which Stalin could temper the steel of national resistance. He also knows that Soviet inhumanity to its own citizens during the 1920s, 1930s and 1940s matched any atrocity perpetrated by the Germans, with estimates that Stalin accounted for close to sixty million deaths during his various purges and terrors, including the war.

'I think I became a victim of Soviet propaganda during the war and the years immediately afterwards. This formed my general attitude to the German nation, but added to this was the fact that we were very much brought up on Russian music, with a

---

* In a concert review of a Sibelius symphony, Kaiser wrote: 'The themes from which Sibelius builds his symphonic cosmos remain, however artfully elaborated, often wishy-washy, in the style of film music.' [author's free translation]

corresponding neglect of German music. These two different aspects of my upbringing formed my irrational and unconscious response to this great central-European nation. On the other hand, when I listened to the music of Richard Strauss or read Goethe, I could not reconcile what I heard about Germany as a nation or the general attitude towards German music with the unbelievable depths I found in the greatest German poets and writers and later, as I became more familiar with the repertoire, in their composers. At first I just could not make any sense of these contradictions, so I thought, well, all those wonderful things are from the past and now all is different – that is, in so far as I thought it out at all! I feel it as a black mark against me, because having now played quite a lot in Germany and having met many Germans, my attitude had begun to acquire a proper perspective and has become quite different.

'The irrationality of my earlier conditioning has left its mark, and when I feel low, or not at my best, these basic responses come back and are difficult to fight. At times I find it hard to believe that Germans can behave in such an insensitive and arrogant way, when they have such a wonderfully cultured and civilized background. With these advantages they have every reason to be refined, sensitive and thoughtful. In any case, there is no doubt that the Germans and other German-speaking peoples are among the most advanced on our planet.

'As for the condescension shown by so many Germans towards non-German music, it is really nothing but narrow-mindedness, I think. I no longer feel insecure as a result of it, whereas before I sometimes felt that my system of values could be undermined in view of my personal commitment to so much music which the Germans have tended to despise. This is partly because nowadays I meet more and more Germans who say that they not only like Russian and other non-German music tremendously but that it touches something deep within them. Many of these people admit that their fellow Germans have been horribly narrow-minded in the past, and that there is much wonderful music that has been neglected which they feel it is essential to be able to appreciate. This development strikes me as very significant and brings me to a slowly evolving assessment of what sort of people the Germans really are – how they understand or perhaps misunderstand the world around them.

'It seems to me that the Germans contain in their characters a peculiar combination of tremendous elemental forces, full of contained cataclysms – in them there is to be found earthquake and air and volcano. But somehow this nature or these natures were put together with an incredible aptitude for the methodical and logical aspects of life. How it happened, I don't know, but the result is what we see both in history and today. It appears to be almost a freak of nature, as though so many cataclysmic elements have to be tightly organized and harnessed if they are not to erupt. And it is as though the Germans instinctively know that this cannot be contained all the time and so, as with volcanoes, there are fissures which allow some of their elemental energies to escape. On some occasions, if the pressure builds up enough and the fissures are unable to dissipate it, then the volcano erupts.

'I suppose that Bismarck may have come to some of the same conclusions when he saw that the unification of Germany was essential in order to fuse the chaotic energies of so many diverse peoples and states. After all, considering what Frederick the Great could achieve with the resources of Prussia alone, how much more could be done once all those petty kingdoms and principalities had transferred the energies previously squandered in wars and rivalry to a common purpose. The result was the incredible new machine which was first seen to practical effect in 1870 with the whirlwind defeat of France. That was a case of eruption engineered and planned by design. Successive German governments, and especially the military dictatorships culminating in Hitler, seem to have been all too aware of these characteristics and to have manipulated them with ever more terrible results.

'In my view, some of this can be transferred to the consideration of music which does not fit well with the traditional German view of the world and of nature. If they approach the music of Debussy, Rachmaninov or Sibelius too dogmatically they soon see all sorts of shortcomings which they cannot easily accept on their purist, logical level. If, on the other hand, they manage to get away from this preconditioned state of mind for a moment and allow themselves to listen to their most fundamental and elemental natures, they begin to accept and appreciate much that is wonderfully uplifting and inspiring in music they have previously rejected.

'There are different considerations when it comes to performance, since it is one thing to compose great music and quite another to perform it creatively. In my experience, many German performers seem to have difficulties in opening themselves up sufficiently at the act of recreation; maybe as a result of so much preconditioning the brain tells them that the music speaks for itself and has its own innate powers of expression – almost as though their respect for the greatness of the music makes it futile or impudent to try to add anything very personal to it in its performance. If, of course, this approach is adopted with non-German music the result is worse than death – straight to the mortuary. But even with German music, I have often found this tendency to offer duty, respect, even intellectual understanding instead of body and soul and the essence of life itself. Of course, there are important exceptions, especially now that Germany is part of the international stream; among the post-war generations, too, a much more open nature seems to be developing, combined with a great deal of soul-searching in an attempt to understand their past and their real nature. Many people have realized the full horrors of Nazism and the war, what they did to other peoples, the whole image they presented to other nations. As a result, they have started to ask themselves, "Why are we like this?" There are exceptions, of course, but I think that it is all very positive. I think that the German nation has changed a lot.

'When, for example, I play some of the most important works of Beethoven, Schubert or Schumann in Germany, I no longer have such a sense of insecurity about being pre-judged because I am a Russian. Earlier I was easily upset by these seemingly relevant but actually unimportant factors. Not that I am totally secure now, but I trust and believe in my own judgement and that of Dody and some very close friends who have values which coincide with mine, values which in their implications go beyond how one should play German music.

'In my recent experience with many Germans I find that one can be confused by a veneer of characteristics which suggests that they are typically German in accordance with popular perceptions of what that means, only to realize later that there is something very deep within them which is trying to get out. When you discover this you appreciate it all the more since you discern a real need for release in order that they may, in the end, be true to their inner selves.

'They really are a great nation but what they did in the war may be the logical culmination in their minds of their own conception of their greatness. Once this attitude became institutionalized, became national policy in the broadest sense, the logical conclusion was that they had to eliminate some other nations irreconcilable with this concept. Of course, these are incredible lengths to which to develop an argument, but with that type of cohesive national outlook and mentality it could and did happen in the special historical circumstances which prevailed. It was also potentially convenient for the leaders – and so led to such an unbelievable tragedy for the Germans, for their victims and for the world as a whole.

'Such a disaster could never have happened had there been any sense of humility before nature and one's fellow men. Maybe humility was effectively filtered out of the national consciousness by a gradual elimination of weakness in the German way of life, its social organization and educational structure in order to achieve the greatest military and industrial efficiency. In such a programme there is no room for humility since it obviously slows you down and makes you re-evaluate and reconsider all your preconceptions and aspirations.'

Slav artists are not alone in their ambivalent attitude to Germany despite life-long commitment to the German classics. In a recent book entitled *Conversations with Arrau*,* the octogenarian master pianist ruefully admits how difficult it was for him to achieve acceptance in Germany as an interpreter of Beethoven, even though he spent the formative years of his youth in Berlin, studying with the eminent teacher Krause. As a Chilean he was somehow expected to devote himself to more colourful, less intellectually demanding repertoire. He, too, suffered from the idiotic misconception, still often held by many who should know better, that nationality is a clue to interpretation, as if only Frenchmen can truly express the peculiar 'Frenchness' of Ravel or Debussy, or an understanding of Elgar is the exclusive preserve of the English. If this were true, a Chilean pianist would indeed have scant scope for self-expression. National attitudes are significant – it would be absurd to pretend otherwise – but interpreters on the highest level are not only able to discover much of what is

* By Joseph Horowitz, Collins, 1983.

essential in the cultural background of the works they perform, but are also capable of transcending these often superficial characteristics in order to achieve something on a higher level.

It took many years before Askhenazy finally decided to accept engagements in Germany; in the end, the promptings of Decca were probably as cogent as any, as they constantly complained how difficult it was for them to distribute his recordings adequately in one of the world's most important markets when he never appeared there personally. It was probably true to say that the Germans were more familiar with the veteran Polish pianist Stefan Askenase, with whom Vladimir was sometimes confused. In the end, he took the plunge, and from the mid 1970s began to accept a few engagements in some of the more important centres. It was gratifying to find that his success on most occasions was instantaneous, particularly in Berlin where he played the Prokofiev Second Piano concerto with Lorin Maazel in 1974 to an ovation of astonishing warmth. Latterly, he has begun to play regularly in Berlin, Hamburg – a particular favourite of his – Munich, Stuttgart, Frankfurt, Cologne and Bonn, as well as in many smaller cities where excellent pianos, fine halls and long-standing subscription audiences provide unusually satisfying conditions. In Vienna, too, he now feels at home and has three times appeared in the Vienna Philharmonic Orchestra's own series of concerts, a privilege enjoyed by very few soloists. In 1981 he finally played at the Salzburg Festival, having declined persistent invitations for many years. He returned for a second engagement there in 1983, this time to play the Brahms First Piano Concerto with Claudio Abbado and the London Symphony Orchestra; he had in the meantime recorded the Second Concerto with the Vienna Philharmonic, and the first with the Concertgebouw, both with Bernard Haitink conducting.

Even so, despite perhaps ten or fifteen concerts each season in Germany, Decca complain that compared with the standing which he enjoys in Britain, the United States, Japan, and most of the rest of Europe, Ashkenazy is still too remote a figure in the German-speaking territories. In a curious way, Ashkenazy seems to find this appropriate and reassuring, as though it would be unnatural for him to enjoy too easy acceptance in what is essentially an alien environment. Perhaps it is one more peak to be climbed, one more area of struggle, one more way of honing his creative edge which too easy a success might begin to blunt.

If Germany has been a relatively new field of activity for Ashkenazy, the United States have always been central to his career. In the 1960s and 1970s, Ashkenazy had responded rather positively to those aspects of American life which have always tended to impress visitors from abroad – the raw energy, the spirit of making good, the range of opportunity. Recently his evaluation has become more discerning.

'Probably in the early visits I was just much more forgiving, and recently different priorities have asserted themselves. I'm sure that even at the beginning I saw things as I do today but now it disturbs me much more. If I try to put my finger on the problem, I would say that many things in the musical world in America are dominated by hyperbole, sensationalism and the desire for effect; there is the feeling that it is essential to attract attention by any means possible. Maybe it originates from the fact that America started as a huge, open country and the people who settled it went there to make good. So, in a way, you had to be a success to succeed; to get on, you had to make it very publicly and as a result the most important element in American society became fame, in other words, being attractive and well-known to the general public. And let's not forget – it is a very big country! As long as the impact of something was sufficiently impressive, it had to be good. As a result materialism became so overwhelmingly important that most other values were excluded.

'On the other hand, in a nation of so many brilliant intellects there is inevitably a reaction against materialism, but the reaction itself tends to be counter-productive because of all sorts of distortions in thinking and in the appreciation of values. A good analogy is to be found in religious attitudes; American materialism is the very antithesis of a spiritual life and yet all sorts of incredible sects and religions mushroom all over the States. I don't think that the nation has found a real scale of values and yet there is a constant but totally chaotic search for some solid under-pinning for people's lives. Even marvellously talented writers and thinkers seem inclined to treat knowledge possessively as though truth can somehow be owned, given a sufficient investment in research or equipment, whether human or mechanical. Novelists often give the impression that they cannot be satisfied with the books they have written if they are not exploited in some other form; one has the impression that they will leave the door open for that screen adaptation or television series. Marketing often seems to be more important than what is being sold, not necessarily because of any specifically manipulative approach to people – although that is also very much in evidence – but because people begin to believe that nothing can be important unless it has stood the test of intensive marketing and packaging.

'In music this often means that pre-conditioning is all-pervasive, with the public, the critics, even musicians themselves being almost programmed in their responses and expectations. Artists, performances, emotions tend to be assessed according to easily identifiable categories. All of this, in my view, leads to a dangerously sterile type of uniformity, even though it may on first sight appear to be quite the reverse. It would be foolish to pretend that some of these tendencies are not found in Europe as well, but my impression and conviction is that there remains in the Old World a far more secure basis for individual value judgements than is the case in America.'

In comparing the Old World and the New, Ashkenazy sees himself as inescapably European. From a political viewpoint, however, he looks to the United States as the last safe retreat in the face of the inexorable process of Soviet subversion whereby those freedoms and creative aspirations of the individual which he values so highly are all at risk. In Europe, all too often, he sees signs of a fatal willingness to appease the Soviet Union in the interests of short-term economic advantage, regardless of the danger that these foot-holds will subsequently be exploited by the Soviet machine. He favours a policy of confrontation for the West, since he is convinced that it is only through strength, both military and moral, that the West can preserve its liberties. He has little patience with those who, despite admirable motivations, allow themselves through their enthusiasm for socialist princi-ples to ignore the travesty and abuse of those same principles in the communist bloc. He deplores the widespread abuse of power and contempt for human rights all too often found in countries supported economically, politically, or militarily by America and other Western democracies, but is frustrated and angered by the readiness of so many socialists and left-wingers to condemn the United States for policies of imperialism or subversion, whilst at the same time turning a blind eye to Soviet machinations in pursuit of world domination.

From his own personal experience he knows for certain what so many Western left-wingers choose decade after decade to ignore, despite all the available evidence. Communism as a creed is seldom espoused for long for reasons of idealism; few who have once been attracted by its basic precepts in search of a juster society have been able to square its realities with their own personal integrity. Clever people who are interested in ideas are often self-deceiving when faced with evidence which conflicts with the neat structure of theory they have chosen to adopt; under totalitarianism many of those same people become the upholders of party dogma and the most fanatical suppressors of independent thought. But many communist recruits in Western countries are people without any real commitment to principle; they are people who find the normal paths of advancement too laborious because of lack of talent or perseverance. Resenting setbacks or obstacles to their personal ambition, they want to overturn the society in which they live in order to find themselves on the top of the pile, enjoying the spoils of success without having had to earn them. Many of the apparently endless line of major and minor spies and traitors who have come to light since the end of the war have been this type of person; it is certain that many more are still at work burrowing away behind the walls of legitimate society, often carrying out at the same time perfectly legal functions within unions, civil services or established political parties. Perhaps the greatest tragedy of Senator McCarthy and the Committee of Un-American Activities was that it rendered disreputable investigations of any kind about covert political activity by people in the public eye. And yet, if there were effective screening of scientists, politicians, diplomats and civil servants in the West, perhaps some of the insecurities which beset us on the international scale might be reduced.

Western observers who begin to comprehend some of this are often appalled by their previous gullibility, but Russians such as Ashkenazy only point to the evidence of their own experiences and those of others in countries such as Czechoslovakia and Poland. They know that the whole system works only because of the interplay of spoils and repression. If from childhood on it is clearly understood that advancement, a reasonably civilized life and material well-being can come solely out of connivance and collaboration with the whole hierarchy of power, only the most intrepid, perhaps fanatical, will not go along with it. In Russia it is easy for all to see that it is the most unprincipled and self-seeking amongst the community who succeed the best, and everyone with any intelligence knows that their lives are enveloped in a largely impenetrable fog of lies, half-truths and propaganda.

14

In October 1979 Ashkenazy visited mainland China, his first visit to a communist country since he left Russia in 1963. The visit came about because the BBC had secured permission from the Chinese to make a programme about the Shanghai Conservatoire and about the revival of interest in, and official tolerance for, Western arts in Shanghai and Peking following the traumas of the Cultural Revolution and the interregnum of the so-called Gang of Four. The BBC needed a major name to act as a pivot for the programme, preferably someone who could give concerts and master classes at the Shanghai Conservatoire, and who could also conduct the local symphony orchestra. The arrangements had to be made at short notice but when Ashkenazy was approached he had, somewhat miraculously, a few days free. He was intrigued by the prospect of visiting the one communist country where he could feel sure that he would be safe because of its long-standing quarrel with the Soviet Union. He threw himself into the project, therefore, with his customary energy and commitment.

During the hectic week he spent in Shanghai, Ashkenazy devoted several afternoons to rehearsing the pitifully isolated Shanghai Symphony orchestra, whose enthusiasm was matched only by the woeful inadequacy of their instruments and of their library of scores and orchestral parts. Their contact with the outside world had been minimal for the last fifteen years, and the orchestra's permanent conductor and some of the players volunteered many heart-rending stories about the times during the Cultural Revolution when the performance of all Western music, and indeed of all but a handful of the crudest Party-inspired Chinese works, was prohibited. Ashkenazy also gave a full-length piano recital at the Conservatoire, as well as a series of master classes, and entered willingly into any interview or discussion that could be arranged by the television director or his Chinese hosts. Some filming was also done in the streets and this attracted huge crowds of curious onlookers. In the evenings his hosts from the Shanghai radio and television offered lavish and convivial banquets.

On a personal level Ashkenazy found the whole experience touching and fascinating. Such devotion under seemingly impossible circumstances to an aesthetic and spiritual world far removed from China's own incomparably rich history and culture was undoubtedly heart-warming. At the same time, whilst most of the members of the BBC party were caught up with enthusiasm for what seemed to be a dramatic process of renewal and liberalization in post-Gang of Four China, Ashkenazy remained undeceived. Without denying the many positive aspects of Deng Xiao Ping's modernization programme, he was very aware of the high degree of manipulation employed by the Chinese even if in the most subtle and sophisticated manner. The BBC party, like many other Western visitors at that time, were astonished by the freedom with which the excesses of the Cultural Revolution and of the Gang of Four were discussed whenever an opportunity presented itself. Ashkenazy observed how seldom Western commentators perceived that these much vaunted errors of a discredited past provided an excellent scenario for the new policies of Deng Xiao Ping, allowing him to clean the slate more abruptly than might otherwise have been ideologically plausible.

Though very much taken by the simplicity and friendliness of most of the Chinese musicians and students he met, he was depressingly aware of the baleful lack of personal freedom so reminiscent of his memories of the Soviet Union. He could see once again how suggestible most Westerners are when confronted with the workings of a type of regime of which they have no personal experience or understanding. With so many stories, enthrallingly recounted, about the excesses of the Cultural Revolution, it might appear that in the new China of Deng Xiao Ping such abuses of human rights were definitely a thing of the past. Ashkenazy could see beyond all the clever rhetoric and stage management and was not duped. Whatever the China lobby in the West would have us believe, the Chinese state remains the most totally controlled and marshalled society in the history of the world. Nowhere else are all personal liberties so totally circumscribed, including where one lives, when one marries, how many children one may have, in which city or commune one may work, which clothes one may wear. The power of the state is all-pervasive in a way that even the Soviet Union cannot emulate. People may well be incomparably better off than before from a material point of view – and Ashkenazy would not dispute the supremacy of the need to eat and to have shelter over all other human requirements – but to talk of freedom is to distort the very meaning of the word.

Not long after Ashkenazy returned from China, there was ample proof of how effectively the Western conception of what was happening in China had been manipulated, with the reappearance of show trials, and the unceremonious suppression of the much vaunted 'Freedom Wall'. Much of what the Western media saw as being liberalization was gradually perceived to be astutely primed propaganda, part of the armoury adopted by one faction within the ruling hierarchy to discredit the leaders so recently ousted. Deng Xiao Ping – and presumably Nixon – had seen the opening of China to the West and the rapprochement with the United States as geo-political stages in the struggle for power with the Soviet Union. Exchanges of symphony orchestras, cultural programmes, highly controlled tourism, well-publicized political visits were and are all part of the process of cosmetic disinformation needed to screen the grand design. The visit to China led to further reflections about the impact of totalitarian systems such as those in the Soviet Union and China upon individual creativity.

'The essential difference between these countries and the West is the respect and concern for the development of the individual. In my mind what is important is what a person can make of himself as an individual, rather than excellence in any particular field of activity. If the latter is achieved in the process, it is of course wonderful, but if everything is subordinated into making you a first-class sportsman or astronaut or musician provided this is of use to the state, as happens in Russia, then in a way it is like trading your soul to the devil. Your personality and individuality are never important; on the contrary, you are discouraged or even prevented from developing them freely. As a substitute the system gives you every opportunity to develop your physical capabilities, so it is just like Faust selling his soul in return for remaining young for ever. You may become a giant, you may be able to play all the Liszt Transcendental Studies, but what do you have inside you? The system cannot give you anything as a person, as an individual. In fact it ruins you while at the same time pretending to give you every opportunity.

'The greatest danger is that when you are young, you don't know any better; you think it is all exciting and marvellous. Later, when you grow older, you begin to see that you run the danger of having nothing inside you, of becoming a hollow shell. You can play very efficiently, very fast, very attractively and so with much success. You also probably realize that the majority of people don't know any better. They just see that you have terrific abilities and then your success is assured.

'Of course, one should avoid ascribing to the Soviet system those negative properties in human nature which you find in mankind throughout history regardless of political regime – things like greed, pride, ambition, hypocrisy. The only difference is that in the Soviet Union they have become institutionalized. You cannot find any way of being yourself except secretly. If you want to be honest, survival in the system makes this impossible, unless you are prepared to pay the incredible price of shutting yourself out of society altogether as some of the dissidents have done. In the West, you can at least try to be honest to yourself; you can rebel against society – in fact you can be almost anything you like.

'This means, paradoxically, that certain basic instincts, which can no longer be channelled naturally into the pursuit of self-betterment, evolve without any restraining licence. Personal ambitions can only be realized through the élitist, privilege-orientated system, and this is by definition amoral, or even immoral. In fact morality as it is understood in the West, morality as a concept that has evolved over many centuries of civilization, does not have any room in the Soviet system; it has been replaced by the so-called "Soviet morality". What "Soviet morality" is is not hard to detect from the preceding paragraphs.'

Alexander Zinoviev has pointed out that the most immediate and striking result of Soviet suppression is the cult of mediocrity. He even propounds the view that in recent years the levelling effect has achieved a more effective tyranny even than that of the KGB, based as it is on the surveillance and control of each man's life by his colleagues, neighbours and contemporaries. In a society where advancement is contingent upon every factor but

189

individual worth, anyone who is truly outstanding or unarguably gifted threatens to disturb the accepted parameters. Mediocrity will not damage the fabric of this type of society; individual self-expression, a search for personal excellence, these threaten the lives of everyone. Seen on the broadest canvas, spread across the vast territory and population of the Soviet Union throughout its lengthening history, the prospect is not edifying.

Music, in this wider context, plays an almost irrelevant role and Ashkenazy feels sure that when and if world-wide communist ambitions are realized and classical music no longer has any value as a propaganda tool, it will be simply neglected or even suppressed entirely. He points to the very real and recent example of the Chinese Cultural Revolution to demonstrate that this is not as far-fetched a proposition as it might at first appear to be. The Chinese Red Guards – manipulated from above, of course, since a spontaneous movement as it was claimed to be is an impossibility in a country under such intense regulation as the Soviet Union or China – decided to be consistent and abolish all music except the most primitive type of political songs, the rest being considered a part of bourgeois 'decadence'. In a way, this was the inescapably logical development of revolutionary theory. In the Soviet Union, there were always too many conflicting interests to be accommodated for anything quite so radical to be adopted as policy, and the Party shrank from a rejection of the historical and cultural traditions so intertwined with the development of music. Music was also seen to be useful as a source of prestige which provided a human face in international relations, and it served as solace of a harmless kind for a public starved of entertainment and escapism in their difficult, austere and tedious lives.

In some respects there has been a considerable loosening up of official attitudes to music since the late 1950s. Before that, the Party saw the danger of revisionism or counter-revolution in everything and music was no exception. The apparatus for control remains in place and periodically someone in the leadership does some sabre-rattling about the danger of formalist tendencies in the arts, but classical music is by now very much a political backwater.

'Control was really very rigid during the war – even more so before it – and right up to the end of the Stalinist period. I remember the first time that Debussy was played, at the end of the

1950s. It was his Nocturnes, and the sense of excitement in musical circles was incredible. Stravinsky, too, was never performed until 1962 when he was invited to come to Russia as part of Khrushchev's policy of reclaiming some of the more brilliant and successful émigrés as though they were both prodigal sons from the Revolution and still somehow products of it. A very intelligent policy really, because at that time few people could resist the chance to visit Russia, especially given the incredible fuss that could be made of celebrities. To this day, newly elected Western political leaders never seem to be able to resist invitations from the Kremlin; as soon as they are asked, off they trot, cap in hand, in order to enjoy for a moment the illusion that they may be able to make some newsworthy contribution to East-West relations. All they achieve, of course, is to be led by the nose by those wily old Kremlin foxes who are pastmasters at issuing meaningless and ineffective communiqués which gratify the vanities of the Western leaders without altering anything one jot.

'Nowadays, artists in the Soviet Union seem to be allowed to play almost everything, although permission has still to be secured for anything considered to be controversial. This in itself can act as a form of censorship because of all the bureaucratic delays involved. Every such request has to be approved by the administration of the Philharmonia where, if a controversial request is made, the official concerned will feel nervous about taking on the responsibility himself, and so, just to make sure, will refer the request to a higher official, who in turn may feel that it should go up to someone in the Ministry of Culture. This man will then feel that if it has come all the way up to him it must really be very sensitive, and so perhaps someone in the Central Committee should have a look at it. The Central Committee spokesman may not quite understand what all the fuss is about and is certainly not musically literate or interested anyway, so he will pass the decision back to the Ministry of Culture saying that the Central Committee has no objection provided that the Ministry of Culture feels that work in question can be performed. So by the same process, the matter is referred back to the original official at the Philharmonia, who will call in the artist or conductor and say, "Well, of course we have no objection to your performing whatever you want, but you know these things take time, so why not put it off until another concert and then no one will feel you are rushing things?" Of course, this snakes-and-ladder game only goes on when a performer of some standing and influence is involved, someone who might perhaps be able to make trouble if unreasonably thwarted. For a young artist without this sort of leverage, the request may simply be turned down immediately, or just lost in the paperwork.

'As for decisions as to which foreign artists should be invited to the Soviet Union, I don't think that the orchestras have very much to say about who comes. Everything is still handled by Goskoncert working under the control of the Ministry of Culture, and foreign artists are often invited under the auspices of an international cultural agreement. The relationship between the orchestras, Goskoncert and the Ministry of Culture is certainly a complex one, and if the Ministry feels that it has to invite a particular artist or someone nominated by a particular country for political reasons of one kind or another, the orchestra will just have to put up with it, regardless of what they think about that artist.

'In general, foreign artists tend to be invited if they are thought to be ideologically sound or at least well-disposed. In the late 1950s and 1960s – and even more significantly in the 1930s – there were always artists or writers who felt themselves to be alienated from their own societies in the West, often for idealistic reasons, and these people could often be manipulated very successfully when they were invited on official visits. To our ears much of what was said and written by European socialists, including people like Bernard Shaw, when they visited the Soviet Union in the 1930s, with the political purges going on under their very noses, seems unbelievably blind and foolish, but this type of gullibility continues today, though perhaps in recent years it has been more often applied to Cuba, China or, for a time, to North Vietnam. The capacity for self-deception and wishful thinking seems endless; in the 1970s it seemed again to be particularly fashionable for certain eminent performers and composers, as well as many writers and poets, to make all sorts of pro-communist protestations, claiming to see in the Soviet bloc a model of how society should be organized. The irony of this is that their own personal lifestyles and liberties would have been the first things to have gone if their recommendations had actually come into effect. Most of them seem to be a little less enthusiastic now that we have seen what is happening in Afghanistan and Poland, but the Soviet Union has always been particularly expert at making capital out of this sort of nonsense.

'However, the Ministry of Culture is not solely politically motivated – or at least not expressly so, since everything ultimately has to have a political dimension – and so as well as many second-rate fellow-traveller artists, they do also invite the really great international names. Michelangeli has played there, and Rubinstein and von Karajan, although the latter case was certainly part of some sort of cultural offensive sponsored by either the German or Austrian governments. With these established artists, problems of currency have often intervened because the Russians, in common with most Eastern bloc countries, try to avoid paying large fees in convertible currency. Often they get away with this, and it is significant that East Germany, that most rigid of Soviet allies if certainly also the richest, imposes the strictest and most inflexible embargo on anything but the most derisory fees for foreign visitors.

'In the 1960s and 1970s the climate was such that many artists were prepared to accept whatever they were offered, just out of curiosity to visit the country and to play before such enthusiastic audiences. Sometimes, however, artists did get their full fees; I believe that Rubinstein did, for example, largely because though they kept on asking him to visit he always said that he wouldn't unless they paid him properly, and that he didn't care whether he went or not. This probably struck some sort of chord with the Ministry of Culture; they finally came to believe they had better pay his fee if they wanted him to come at all.

'There was and is, I think, a tendency to receive foreign artists uncritically. This was partly because Russia was so isolated in the late 1950s when things began to open up a little, and when for the first time since the 1930s foreigners were invited to come. Any show of individuality was especially appreciated. This was and is still very noticeable in the Tchaikovsky Competitions where some second-rate foreign artists receive ovations from the public, only really because they are Westerners. The audiences don't realize that playing differently doesn't imply validity in itself. Still, it is very touching in many ways because they are reacting to something different from the drab uniformity which overwhelms them in their lives, day in, day out.

'As far as Soviet artists are concerned, they are subject to two basic factors; one is the policy of the day as interpreted by Goskoncert and the Ministry of Culture and the other is how successful they are in the West. Even if there is a plethora of prize winners or a less positive international situation as a result of something like Afghanistan or Poland, it does not seem to me likely that either will have a significant impact on the way that the musical system works or will function in the immediate future. After all, for the individual artist, the challenge and fascination of going to the West to give concerts or to take part in a competition is still too great. I doubt whether any young artist is likely to pass up the opportunity of going to the West for any reason and, if the talent is big enough, it will assert itself regardless of how congested the field is. In any case, I suppose all young artists have to feel that they have a good chance of doing well when they enter a competition or play abroad. There is a lot to prove to yourself personally, whatever the outcome is in terms of prizes or engagements. Everyone also feels that they must seek out and take advantage of whatever opportunities present themselves before the policy about these things is changed and the changes are lost, perhaps for ever.

'As far as the Communist Party is concerned, in the end it may be decided that all types of cultural manifestation may have to be reduced or cut out because they provide too much scope for individuality to assert itself, which is basically anathema to communism. It is significant, for instance, that the number of good books published in the Soviet Union recently, including the classics, has begun to decline rapidly. People who have come out of Russia recently say how difficult it is to buy a volume of Tolstoy or of Pushkin, whereas in the past I used to be rather surprised that so many good books of all kinds were published there. In fact, it became illegal to take out of the Soviet Union any books printed before 1976; then, in 1982, the sending or taking of any book or music abroad became prohibited.* In the 1960s and even the 1970s, some of the magazines and periodicals contained some reasonably lively material, but that is now a thing of the past. In a way it may be symptomatic of two things;

* As a further example of unpredictability, late in 1983 it again became possible to send music abroad, though no explanation for this change of heart was made available.

firstly the realization that any good book, however apolitical, may stimulate and encourage independent thought and secondly, the safer those in power feel they are in terms of the world situation, the less they feel that they have to worry about the image they present to the West. In time they may accelerate this process if they feel that they can do so with impunity. This is all speculative, but I feel very strongly that I am right.'

A factor which may have had some bearing on the current attitude of the Soviet authorities towards musicians and other artists in the Soviet Union has been the adverse publicity which has surrounded a succession of prominent defections by leading performers. Rudolf Nureyev was one of the first to make the leap and since he did so at a time when curiosity about Russian performers was at its most intense in the West, partly because of the preceding decades of relative isolation of the Soviet artistic community, the defection of so charismatic a figure aroused the keenest international excitement. Ashkenazy's own decision to stay in the West not long after the Nureyev scandal also attracted very great publicity as we have seen, but the ambiguity of his subsequent status and his own decision to keep a low profile did much to blunt the edge of the story. Indeed, it was only the Soviet Embassy's clumsy and ill-advised attempt to make propaganda capital out of Ashkenazy at the time of the Kuznetsov defection (cf. p. 119) that persuaded him to make a public declaration about his true position and his real feelings about the Soviet regime.

Since then there has been a succession of defections of greater or lesser significance and it could be argued that the West's greater familiarity with such cases and diminished interest in them has meant that they have become gradually less and less damaging to Soviet credibility. The focus of attention shifted in any case to the dissident movement and to such figures as Solzhenitsyn, Sakharov and Bukovsky, with the result that even the highly orchestrated banishment of Rostropovich made less impact than would have seemed conceivable in the early 1960s. Nonetheless, two most unexpected defections in 1978 and 1981 respectively do indeed seem to have coincided with a new tendency to re-introduce cold war policies into the business of artistic exchange with the West and, as such, merit more detailed description.

The first case was the sudden and unexpected defection by the famous conductor Kiril Kondrashin in Amsterdam in December 1978. Already in his sixties, Kondrashin had been for many years a member of the Party and an apparently reliable member of the establishment élite within the Soviet artistic hierarchy. He regularly travelled abroad without problems and enjoyed considerable prestige and a privileged position within the Soviet Union. He was the type of artist who was frequently called upon to take part in official concerts, and often gave first performances of important new compositions, most significantly Shostakovich's controversial Thirteenth Symphony. Despite these official endorsements, Kondrashin somehow managed to maintain a reputation for personal integrity and Ashkenazy, who had not known him well before his departure from Russia despite a few concert appearances together, commented a few times to friends during the 1960s that he was sure that Kondrashin had a deep-rooted contempt for the whole Soviet system and way of life; certainly he alone among prominent Soviet conductors seemed unconcerned about performing with artists from politically unacceptable countries like South Korea and became, for instance, an enthusiastic supporter of the violinist Kyung-Wha Chung in the early 1970s. Most of his Soviet colleagues automatically cancelled their appearances or had to withdraw, on orders from Moscow, if they found themselves billed together with any artist who could be thought to be the least controversial.

Kondrashin did not, in fact, seem to need to look over his shoulder all the time for official approval and this was widely interpreted as confirming how strongly placed he was as a Party man. His defection, therefore, was a major blow to Soviet prestige even though, after careful thought, he decided to avoid any public explanation for his decision. Originally he had wanted to speak freely and extensively to the press about his rejection of the Soviet way of life but in the end he was obliged to hold his peace because of the risk of retaliation against his children in the Soviet Union and because he wished to avoid unnecessary disturbance to his new life in the West. Nonetheless, in less public forums, Kondrashin's irrefutable knowledge of the inherent sickness of the Soviet system had a telling effect. When Volkov's controversial version of Shostakovich's memoirs was attacked by the Soviet press as being a forgery, Kondrashin expressed the conviction that they were in fact genuine – a belief also held not only by Ashkenazy but by other prominent émigrés including Rudolf Barshai, who knew Shostakovich well.

Even more damaging to Soviet prestige was the defection in 1981 of Maxim Shostakovich with his teenage son Dimitri. Maxim had enjoyed a very privileged position in the Soviet musical hierarchy and, as chief conductor of the Moscow Radio Orchestra, had one of the best jobs available. At the time of the controversy over the Volkov book, he did not contradict the official position that the memoirs were forged, so his much publicized defection so soon afterwards seemed to give the lie all the more dramatically to the official statements. Characteristically, Soviet disinformation went to work as soon as the initial shock had passed.

Whereas before, Maxim Shostakovich had been treated as a meritorious member of the Soviet establishment, he was soon subject to various attempts by the Soviet media to discredit him. He was described as a mediocre conductor who owed his advance to his father's prestige, and rumours were circulated that he was trying to avoid a court case likely to go against him after a serious car accident. Steps were also taken by Soviet agencies to interfere with his concert-giving activities in the year following his defection when, of course, he was of particular interest to concert promoters and orchestra managers looking for an interesting ingredient for their concert schedules.

In Japan, pressure was brought to bear on the New Japan Philharmonic Orchestra, which had engaged Maxim for a series of concerts in January 1982. Some of the concerts had been contracted for by a promoting organization which wished to maintain good relations with the Soviets; so when these concerts were suddenly cancelled, the orchestra was left in the embarrassing position of having brought Maxim to Japan for one concert only instead of the advertised series.

There was a similar story in Oslo in February 1982 when the Soviet Embassy tried to bring about the cancellation of a concert Maxim was scheduled to conduct with the Oslo Philharmonic Orchestra. The chief conductor of the orchestra at the time was the Soviet Mariss Yansons and there had already been evidence that Goskoncert had taken advantage of this fact to impose what amounted to a boycott on any defector or émigré artist as far as engagements with the Oslo Philharmonic were concerned. In 1981 the orchestra insisted that a contract with Kondrashin had to be cancelled, and although many of the other distinguished Russian émigrés would have been obvious candidates for engagements with the orchestra, no single defector or émigré was booked with the orchestra during Yansons' first two seasons as chief conductor. In the end, the Soviet attempt to block Maxim Shostakovich's appearance backfired. The Norwegian press got hold of the story as part of a detailed investigation into the activities of the KGB in Scandinavia and the resulting outcry led to some awkward questions from the Norwegian Foreign Ministry to the Soviet Embassy.

If it seemed that this type of covert manipulation by Goskoncert, which had been building up over recent years in many countries including Austria and Britain, had suffered at least a small setback on this occasion, there are no general signs of any abatement in attempts to interfere wherever an occasion presents itself. In 1981, for instance, the Vienna Festival decided to sponsor a production of the Tom Stoppard/André Previn play for actors and orchestra, EGBDF. This work is certainly anti-Soviet and the announcement of its inclusion in the Festival programme produced furious protests from the Soviet and other Eastern bloc embassies, accompanied by the threat that artists would be withdrawn if the offending piece were not dropped. The Festival Director held his ground and several Eastern bloc artists indeed had to be replaced. Some six months later the East Germans unceremoniously cancelled a signed contract for André Previn to conduct and record the Brahms 'Requiem' in Dresden with the Staatskapelle.

The case of Shostakovich is particularly interesting because of the transcripts subsequently published in the press of the conversations which took place between him and the Ministry of Culture representative travelling with the orchestra. Since the latter's appeals to Maxim Shostakovich to reconsider his decision fell on deaf ears, other members of the orchestra were induced to bring pressure on him. The thrust of their argument was that the defections of the Shostakovichs would make life all the harder for everyone else and was therefore a deeply disloyal act to all their friends and colleagues.

It later transpired that these were not just empty recriminations. Not long after Shostakovich's defection his orchestra, the second Moscow Radio Orchestra, was disbanded by the authorities. Instead, a new orchestra was founded some time later under the leadership of Gennadi Rozhdestvensky with the not altogether promising name of the Orchestra of the Ministry of Culture. Auditions were held and it was claimed that the new orchestra would be open to the best available musicians from all over the Soviet Union. Some of those who auditioned successfully did indeed come from outside the Moscow area, a few of them even residents of the so-called autonomous republics. Unfortunately, it later turned out that none of these could take up their positions because they could not secure the necessary permits to reside in Moscow; appeals to the Ministry of Culture for assistance apparently fell on deaf ears.

This was not the first time that an orchestra had suffered for political reasons. In the 1970s the mass Jewish emigration from the Soviet Union caused considerable turmoil because of the high percentage of Jews involved in the musical world. Jews who applied for permission to leave were normally disqualified from whatever jobs they held while they awaited a decision on their emigration papers, and many who intended to stay also found themselves victimized. In 1974, the authorities decided to expel the majority of Jews still employed by the first Moscow Radio Orchestra, whose conductor had for many years been Gennadi Rozhdestvensky. Since thirty-five or more musicians found their jobs at stake, the repercussions on the quality of the ensemble were obviously extremely serious and Rozhdestvensky's resignation from the post of chief conductor was known to have been forced upon him because of his opposition to these disreputable events. The expulsions were at least held up until Rozhdestvensky was replaced by Feodoseyev, a conductor whose career seems more strongly based on his record of obedience to the establishment rather than on any significant talent. Soon after he had taken up the position, the Jewish musicians were indeed dismissed; in fact, a greater number were removed than had been originally threatened.

None of this came as any surprise to Ashkenazy, who has lived through so many personal experiences of Soviet interference for political motives in the lives and activities of the musical community. On one occasion in the early 1970s, the Concertgebouw orchestra in Amsterdam wanted to book him to play as soloist with Rozhdestvensky. At that stage, Ashkenazy was interested in the idea of a collaboration with someone he had known in Moscow before his emigration, even though he had some doubts as to whether it would ever come to fruition. He accepted the engagements but pointed out to the Concertgebouw management that there might be problems if Goskoncert ever heard about the plan. A few months later Rozhdestvensky was duly withdrawn from the concerts on some trumped-up pretext.

On another occasion, Ashkenazy was booked to play with the conductor, Arvid Yansons,* in Helsinki and there, in view of Finland's uniquely non-aligned status, he felt that political considerations might not necessarily interfere. This time, Yansons actually arrived for the rehearsals of the concert, but before he had completed more than one or two of the sessions, and prior to the general rehearsal when Ashkenazy was due to appear, he was suddenly called out from the rehearsal hall because a representative of the Soviet Embassy had to see him urgently. From that meeting, he went straight to his hotel and a message was left with the distraught management of the orchestra to the effect that he had been suddenly taken ill and could not go through with the engagement. Since then there has been no single occasion when a collaboration between Ashkenazy and a Soviet conductor has even been seriously considered.

Ashkenazy has subsequently established why this is. In recent years Goskoncert has insisted that when Soviet conductors accept engagements abroad, their programmes and soloists must be submitted for approval well in advance. This helps to account for the fact that on so many occasions the ensuing concerts become 'package deals' featuring a Soviet soloist and a predominantly Russian, even Soviet programme. Fortunately, as so often in Russia, the system sometimes breaks down because of inefficiency or ignorance. Many of the people who work in Goskoncert know very little about classical music, and there have been instances where some quite extraordinary programme proposals have been passed on by Goskoncert to foreign orchestras or agents, sometimes as a result of practical jokes perpetrated

* The father of Mariss Yansons.

by Soviet artists who have suffered too long from the agency's ineptitude. Consequently, even though there appears to be no specific instruction which forbids a Soviet conductor from making music together with a defector or émigré, the requirement that all programmes and soloists must be cleared through the official channels has the same effect. No Soviet conductor will wish to increase the already high risk that his much anticipated visit to the West will be cancelled because the Soviet authorities suddenly take exception to his soloist. It is the old story; a tolerable life in the Soviet Union can only be achieved by avoiding wherever possible snags in the workings of the Party and state bureaucracy.

These and other developments may, in the long term, lead to a review by the Soviet authorities of the value of music as part of the international cultural offensive. If music proves to be less anodyne than was previously thought in terms of political language, then the whole process of music education and training may come under much more careful scrutiny. In other words, if musicians who win prizes and achieve great fame abroad prove to be unreliable and a source of embarrassment, then musical activity will be seen to be just as much of a threat as literature or painting. The prospects for future generations of Soviet performers are uncertain. On the one hand the whole system is still geared to produce prize-winning performers, with a heavy emphasis on the targets of the foreign 'markets'; on the other, there is a growing politicization on both sides of the iron curtain of the perceptions of audiences and authorities alike.

In very recent years, and in particular since the invasion of Afghanistan, Western audiences seem to be generally less well disposed towards Soviet performers, perhaps in part because their appeal is diluted by the large number of Soviet émigré musicians who are competing for the public's attention, while some of the most brilliant of the younger generation of soloists are forbidden to travel abroad. A climate of distrust prevails and it appears that official policy has accepted a slowing-down in the process of cultural penetration until more reliable disciplines can be established. Given the fact that a shift in policy, once clearly discernible, is often very hard to reverse, a gradual ossification of such attitudes could prejudice in the longer term the relatively privileged status music has hitherto enjoyed in Soviet life.

The Soviet-born violinist Gidon Kremer, who now lives in the West, provides an interesting example of how the attitudes of both the authorities and of the more sophisticated of the artists have shifted in recent years. Kremer gave his first concert in the West in 1970 but started touring regularly in the 1974/5 season, establishing a brilliantly successful career, particularly in Germany and Austria after he had been taken up by Herbert von Karajan. Capitalizing on his very considerable prestige, he managed to play what seemed at times like a strange sort of poker game with the Soviet authorities, winning for himself in the process unusual freedoms not only to travel much more extensively than normal, but even to take over the partial organization of his concert schedules himself while he remained outside the Soviet Union. Later on, he was also allowed to keep a larger than normal percentage of his hard-currency earnings during a two year period when he was allowed to move relatively freely between the West and the USSR with his newly married wife. She, however, did not have the same freedom, and on one occasion when they were both in transit at Moscow Airport en route from Japan to Europe, she was prevented from taking the onward flight because she did not have the additional exit visa required after any landing on Soviet territory.

One can only speculate as to the reasons for this unwonted flexibility on part of the Soviet authorities; a secondary objective may have been the desire to counteract Rostropovich's increasingly strident attacks on the Soviet regime following the Central Committee's decision to strip him of his citizenship. The Soviet authorities may have hoped that Kremer's relative freedom within the system would undermine the credibility of Rostropovich's jeremiads, an odd throw-back to the thinking of 1969 when they had attempted to use Ashkenazy's alleged freedom of travel to try to discredit Kuznetsov after his defection. However Kremer did have strong foreign connections and the arrangement may simply have been an experiment. Kremer's position nonetheless seemed oddly anomalous and his public statements were masterfully ambiguous. Some people wondered whether he had made some sort of deal with the KGB, thus providing a new, modern twist to the Faust legend. In fact, Kremer's personal history was in itself highly unusual since he had a Swedish grandfather as well as other recent German forebears. As such, the Soviets could always claim that Kremer's apparently exceptional status was justified by these foreign connections and could not be treated as a precedent. Later, as his agreement with the Soviet authorities reached the end of its validity, Kremer was reported to be negotiating for still greater freedoms. He felt a strong responsibility to try to help some of his colleagues, including such artists as Natalya Gutman, Oleg Maisenberg, and Alexei Gavrilov, and he was effectively seeking for them the right to come and go as they pleased. Later, it became clear that his efforts on behalf of other artists were considered as an impertinent interference and it soon emerged that Goskoncert no longer felt that Kremer's special status suited their purposes. It became known that other artists were asking for similar facilities at a time when it was also clear that comparatively minor concessions of this kind were being discounted as insignificant by Western public opinion in a political climate increasingly hostile to Soviet initiatives in international relations. Kremer was in the end unable to renew the agreement which had served him so well previously, and is now effectively, if not explicitly, an émigré. He has become a Soviet citizen living abroad who has the possibility of visiting the USSR, but is denied any opportunity to perform there. Furthermore he has been told that he does not represent the Soviet State in any capacity.

'When it comes to why certain artists are no longer able to travel abroad whereas others seem to have comparatively little difficulty even at times like these when East-West relations are cool, one can only speculate from case to case. A young pianist like Gavrilov could have had a bad report, like I did, and indeed there are rumours that he was just a little too outspoken a few times on his trips to the West. Funnily enough, on at least one trip to England when he was accompanied by an "interpreter" from the Ministry of Culture, it turned out that he knew rather more English than his companion, and so, as I heard from a manager friend of mine, poor Gavrilov had to translate for the interpreter to tell him what people were talking about in his dressing room! On the other hand, some people say that those in the Ministry of Culture who evaluate these things may have felt that Gavrilov's impact in the West would be lessened if he were too easily available, and that if they withdrew him from circulation altogether for a few years until he had matured more as an artist and had added to his repertoire, then they could really get the maximum hard currency out of his tours as well as great political prestige and capital. Perhaps they thought that with so many young émigré artists flooding the West, it would be better to save up some of the brighter Soviet artists until they could be more confident that they would not get lost in the crowd. If this is the case (and I personally am sure this is *not* the case), you could almost say that the Ministry was carrying out a rather sophisticated managerial game-plan – but one in which the wishes or interests of the artists would never be even considered.

'In some other cases, an artist may be thought to be very reliable, and maybe his family background is such that the risks are very small that he will talk too much, let alone defect. If an artist of this kind wins some prize and receives quite a lot of engagements as a result, they may well let him out without too many problems. Dimitri Alexeyev, for example, seems seldom to have been refused permission. Other artists are sometimes suspected in émigré circles to have close connections with the KGB, although I for one see little advantage or even plausibility in such arrangements as far as the KGB is concerned. It is different when an artist has been recruited by the KGB in his youth, as could have been the case with the distinguished violinist Leonid Kogan or might even conceivably have happened to me if I had willingly cooperated; then he is practically an officer of the service, and as such may have all sorts of tasks to perform both at home and abroad. But when it is suggested that a certain artist acquires the right to travel abroad in return for some sort of semi-espionage for the KGB, it seems to me to be very fanciful. After all, what real value could they get out of it? What sort of significant information could such an artist acquire? He might report what his colleagues tell him about musical gossip or even about what is going on in the private life of an eminent conductor or orchestral manager, but this is pure triviality and can never add up to anything of significant use in the areas of defence or political information. And even if some important contact were made on a social level which could later be developed with a view to encouraging indiscretions of one sort or another, artists tend to be too exposed, too visible. Once any such suspicion were to fall on them – and any sort of approach of that kind would probably seem surprising, since musicians are seldom thought to be interested in such things – rumours would fly and people would cease to be open with them. The KGB must understand this; there are not many fools sitting there – they are mostly intelligent and devious people who use all their cunning to achieve the, alas, all too many successes they have had in such fields.

'This seems to me to be particularly obvious with someone as controversial as Gidon Kremer. After all, in view of the great amount of speculation as to how exactly Kremer had managed to arrange with the Soviet authorities the considerable freedoms that were allowed him, it is all the more improbable that he could have been of any use whatsoever to the KGB. So many people thought that some sort of deal had been struck that they were likely to be all the more cautious in talking openly to him, and as a successful and highly visible personality, he could be kept very easily under surveillance by Western agents if they suspected anything. And as a fifth column he would be quite useless; the KGB is too well served by a well-placed network of people implanted in influential positions so that they can carry out their work discreetly and effectively. Even if he was supposed to make reports from time to time about people he met, he could still have done this and not harmed anyone. After all, I wrote those few papers about some of the foreign students in Moscow when I was still a boy but I took care not to write anything of any significance – just nothing. I thought that I ought to write something so that they would not think that I was refusing to cooperate, but what I gave them was of no value at all. Why couldn't he do that too? And just imagine how much time would have to go into checking any information that did come through from such sources. I am sure that Kremer had made no Faustian deal but was simply clever and determined enough to make the most of his prestige and his unusual background to win, temporarily, a little space for himself.

'One has to come back to the fact that nothing is so determined as to be predictable. In my own case, when they eventually gave me the *vid na zhitelstvo*, a kind of passport required by Soviet citizens who live abroad permanently, it was done on the authority of an office which deals with such special cases as and when they come up. The Soviet authorities may have thought, "OK – he has decided to live in the West, so we had better give him the right document to avoid giving him the impression that we haven't agreed, or rather that we cannot allow these things in special cases when circumstances require it. By giving him the document, we regularize the situation." I suppose that those particular officials genuinely thought that I could and would take advantage of the rights it granted and that I would now begin to travel back and forth as I needed. And maybe if I had actually done so, someone in the Central Committee might have decided to treat this as an experiment. Of course, I didn't trust them and so I never went back but it is perfectly possible that if I had done, they might have tried it out for some years – even in a communist state they do try things out.

'Rostropovich, on the other hand, was never seriously trying to get out permanently. He used to travel like any other Soviet citizen with each trip approved one at a time, except that he travelled much more because he was unbelievably successful and had great influence and wonderful connections with the Ministry. So, in practice, wherever he wanted to go the trip would be approved. Kremer may have temporarily received greater travel privileges but he was never outspokenly anti-Soviet whereas Rostropovich while still living in the Soviet Union openly flouted the authorities with his public letter about Solzhenitsyn. As a direct result of this letter he was deprived of the right to travel abroad. His Moscow performances were also strictly limited, although he did conduct a performance of the Tchaikovsky Sixth Symphony with a student orchestra just before his departure, and played as soloist with the San Francisco Symphony Orchestra under Seiji Ozawa. His wife Galina Vishnevskaya, formerly one of the great stars of the Bolshoi Opera, was banned from singing there completely. Later, after the terrific outcry from the West, he was actually allowed one trip abroad to play in Paris at Yehudi Menuhin's United Nations Concert, but this was effectively a one-day trip and he came straight back, presumably because his family was still in Russia. He may have thought that his permission to go on that short trip was the first sign that he would soon be allowed to do what he liked again, but this is only my guess. Within the Central Committee, however, he was already labelled as anti-Soviet, and when he later got permission to live abroad for two years with his family and started criticizing the Soviet Union in all sorts of ways they must have finally decided that he was beyond the pale and that they had no choice but to take his passport and citizenship away. If he had been more discreet there could perhaps have been a different outcome.

'Even though Kremer also gave some interviews, especially at times when he wanted to bring a little psychological pressure to bear on the Soviet authorities as a prelude to the next round in his negotiations with them, he never went beyond vague criticisms of how badly his and his colleagues' concert schedules had been organized or how he had never been free to make his own plans because of the interference of Goskoncert. That is hardly being anti-Soviet. If criticism is not ideological and doesn't really hurt the Soviets, they can sometimes put up with quite a lot. After all, the Soviet papers often carry stories which criticize the functioning of certain institutions, normally blaming the un-socialist behaviour of certain key functionaries. But when a celebrity like Rostropovich, a great and famous international artist, runs down the whole system in every interview, then they feel that a line must be drawn. Kremer belonged to a different generation so even if he had been less discreet, fewer people would have taken notice.

'On the whole I personally don't believe that defections, even of the apparent importance of those of Kondrashin or Maxim Shostakovich, will have much negative impact on music within the system, because the position it occupies is so insignificant anyway. As long as it suits the Party to export musicians to the West, they will see the benefits as being greater than any temporary embarrassment they may suffer over the occasional, highly publicized defection. And as we have seen, the Soviets have also learned that once someone has gone to the West, they cease to be a source of potentially more significant irritation within the country itself. They have realized that people as outstanding as Solzhenitsyn or Bukovsky have become somewhat neutralized as soon as they have been expelled. They would probably like to get rid of Sakharov too, if he cannot be made to die a natural death tucked away in obscurity, but they are obviously afraid that with his great knowledge of the scientific establishment he could be of use to Western intelligence.

'As for the merits of international cultural exchange, or rather that between the communist bloc and the West, I find myself rather undecided. On the one hand, visits by Western artists can and do have some positive effects by establishing contacts with people on a personal level, with the result that a

207

tiny proportion of people in Soviet Russia learn a little more about the West and distinguish a little better between truth and the lies constantly served up to them. But the number of people affected is so small that I think the importance of the whole process is greatly exaggerated in Western countries. On the other hand, the Soviet cultural presence in the West has had great propaganda value because Soviet artists are not impeded by Western restrictions from doing what they like, or meeting whom they please, albeit always under the complete control of the local Soviet representatives and with the full knowledge that if they abuse these privileges from the Soviet point of view, they may suffer for it when they return to Russia, not least by not being allowed out any more. Western visitors to Russia, by contrast, are strictly supervised and controlled, can travel very little and can make few contacts except through official channels. In sort, what the Soviet Union wants to achieve in the West through its side of the exchange programme it can do very easily, whereas the West can do very little of value in return. This imbalance is once again particularly striking in the case of China where visits by foreign orchestras, ballet companies or soloists are very well publicized in the Western media but probably pass virtually unnoticed by the overwhelming mass of the Chinese population. Even those tiny communities involved directly in the arts often cannot get to hear or see the Western visitors because most tickets are distributed to the Party cadres, regardless of the fact that they have nothing whatsoever to do with the arts.

'Cultural exchange has always been unequal because Western governments cannot interfere too much with the normal areas of free enterprise, which may carry on quite independently of what governments want or plan. If a particular impresario or sponsor wants to engage a Soviet artist or ensemble and can make the appropriate financial deal with Goskoncert, this may fall quite outside the context of a cultural agreement. Indeed the whole idea of these exchanges was incomprehensible to the Americans in the early days because they did not see it as being the proper role of government to intervene in the arts where normal market forces were thought to be the correct way of producing cultural life in all its variety and range. To the Russians, anything so haphazard was out of the question and they obviously saw the benefits of an arrangement which gave them total control of the form the exchange would take as far as visits to the Soviet Union were concerned, while at the same time giving pretty free access to those Western countries they were keen to penetrate more effectively. Added to which, most Western countries were prepared to pay the main cost of these bilateral agreements anyway.

'My feeling is that in the present world situation there is really no way any longer of keeping politics and music separate. This is, I suppose, because the Soviet Union has successfully connected everything in life with politics; they have divided the world and decided that every aspect of life is part of the grand design of the march towards communism. Of course, this tendency is not just limited to the Soviet bloc; more and more, the arts have come to be supported financially and even in some case administratively at government or municipal level, and this tends to mean that politicians feel more and more that they have the right or even duty to interfere in cultural matters. Perhaps this is all tied up with the inevitable growth of state power as the world has polarized during this century and if so, most of the responsibility for this must be laid at the Soviet Union's door. The individual, even in the West, is puny when facing the power of the state and since the Soviet political system has made such relentless inroads throughout the world, Western states have to a certain extent felt the need to follow suit. It would certainly be wonderful if we could all be convinced that the arts and cultural matters are so essential to the health and spirit of mankind that we must support them generously by saying, "Here is the money and now you must do as you think most fit!" In the Soviet Union the arts, in so far as they are approved, are supported entirely by the state and when the state dictates what should be done, there is no chance that those instructions will not be obeyed.'

15

WE WILL NEVER KNOW whether official circles within the Soviet government and Party seriously concerned themselves about Ashkenazy's status after he had left Russia or if there was ever any real interest in trying to persuade him or even to force him to return. The statement issued by the Soviet Embassy in London at the time of Kuznetsov's defection suggests that they found it convenient to pretend that Ashkenazy was living in the West with official approval and, at least until the fall of Khrushchev, this could have been the case. Ashkenazy continued to travel on a Soviet passport until 1972, and his documents were extended or reissued by the Soviet Consulates in London and Reykjavik without too much difficulty. But if the fiction was maintained at least tacitly for the first few years that Ashkenazy might return to the Soviet Union one day to visit his family and to give concerts, he himself was never deceived.

'As far as going back to play in Russia, I don't think I am or ever have been under any illusion that I could go back safely, although I did put out feelers from time to time because of my parents and especially my mother. I needed to show her that I was willing to try; even though I was quite sure that it would all come to nothing, she needed to have some hope to cling to, however slender. After all, given her devotion to me as a child and young adult and her own unquestioning acceptance of the Soviet way of life, my departure was an incredible trauma. Indeed, it became virtually impossible for us to communicate for quite a few years, except through my father. At one stage, in 1976, the Soviet Ambassador in Reykjavik seems to have had the idea that the mood was changing in Moscow; perhaps he wanted the personal credit for arranging my return, but I knew that nothing would come out of it and nothing did. The more you know about the Soviet system the less you believe such a thing could ever really happen. I went through all the motions, though. Naturally, it would be interesting to go back, just out of curiosity to see what it is like now, but I don't have a particularly strong desire to play there.

'It was, on the other hand, my constant aim to try to get my parents out of Russia to visit us as often as possible. This led to a sort of cat-and-mouse game on the part of the Soviet authorities, which is typical of the way they treat people.

'My father first visited me in 1967. I had sent him a written invitation, which is how the necessary procedures must be initiated, and then he applied formally for permission to visit me. The first time he applied, he waited three months for an answer only to be refused. I then decided to be a little deceitful and went personally to see the Soviet Consul in London. I told him that I was very surprised that my father had been refused permission to visit me. The Consul asked me why I so much wanted him to come – imagine such a question to a son trying to arrange to see his father! – but I replied, "Look, I haven't been back to Russia for some years now and I want to hear from my father what the situation is like in case I feel that it might be time for me to go back." I supposed that this encouraged hopes that I might indeed be contemplating a return, and within a few weeks my father received the permission to travel and was able to spend some weeks with us.

'After that it took many years before I succeeded again in getting my parents out. This was basically due to the *Guardian* piece and the interview I gave after Kuznetsov defected. When my denunciation of the Soviet Embassy's statement that I was free to travel to and from the Soviet Union appeared, it shattered the fragile relations I had maintained with the Soviet authorities up to that time. So when I next sent an invitation to my father, it was immediately refused and continued to be so for the next eight years. When we moved to Iceland we even had the support of the Icelandic government and the Icelandic newspapers, but all to no avail. Finally, after the Helsinki Agreement and after renewed intervention by the Icelandic Prime Minister at a very high level – and, of course, by that time I was an Icelandic citizen and fully entitled to that country's support and assistance – permission was granted in 1976 for both my father and mother to come to visit us. After that, for some reason, there was no problem with the next visit which took place at the beginning of 1979. Not long after my parents returned from that last visit my mother died and we soon decided that we should try to get my father and sister out of the Soviet Union permanently. We applied formally in 1980 and tried all sorts of ploys to make things go smoothly but without success. At first their applications were held up by one trumped-up reason after another, mostly of an unbelievably bureaucratic nature. Either the applications had been filed in the wrong way, or should have been made together or separately – I don't even know the correct sequence of events. This whole area of emigration procedures is positively Kafkaesque; there are certain papers and certain rules, but you never know why things are being held up, or whether the delay is a general one or applies just to you. In the meantime, if you ask too often what is happening the officials can be unbelievably rude and hostile, as though you have no business disturbing them when you want to leave the country anyway. So the state of insecurity is terrible; you feel that you may never get out but at the same time you have burned your bridges and life will be impossible if you fail.

'With typical Soviet inconsistency, however, it isn't always like that and in fact neither my father nor my sister have had any real problems since they applied. And now, largely for personal reasons and as a result of changes in their private lives, they have decided that they will stay in the Soviet Union after all; maybe they thought that they might still have to wait for years before getting permission and in the meantime what sort of life would that mean? They were also worried about the difficulty of working and performing in the West in the way that they could do in the Soviet Union. For my father, this would have been particularly difficult since there is really no market in the West for what he does, except for a sort of embryonic Estrada circuit in America for the various émigré colonies. His own situation in Russia has even improved; he was recently put onto the highest level of fees for an artist of his type. He has always been the sort of person who has fallen on his feet and knows how to make the most of things.

'With my mother it was different; quite apart from the personal bitterness she felt about the disappointment of all her hopes and ambitions for me, she was also someone deeply imbued with all sorts of irrational but passionately felt patriotic instincts, as indeed many Russians are, particularly those with relatively restricted horizons. She would automatically try to find excuses for any inadequacies in the Soviet Union and would say that all the wonderful things one can enjoy in the West were all rubbish, all show, and what does freedom of thought and freedom of expression mean? To her these things really did not matter; there are millions of people in Russia like that – just going on doggedly from day to day, making the best of the situation they find without thinking of what else there could be in life, just accepting things as they are. For her everything was coloured by her depression and frustration that I had abandoned her and had gone to live in the West; as a consequence, anything we liked or found good in the West and the general fact that we were happy and fulfilled there was quite unacceptable. The first time she came out, it was really very painful for us at times. Later she gradually began to open her eyes and the last visit was much easier because she began to admit occasionally that there might just be some things wrong with Russia which were better handled in the West.

'In order not to make things too difficult for my parents and sister, I was generally very careful about making public statements until after the Soviet invasion of Czechoslovakia and the whole *Guardian* affair. Even after that I avoided anti-Soviet statements in general. The most important objective, even more than that of trying to get my parents out to visit us, was to try to protect my sister who was a talented young pianist studying at that time in the Central Music School in Moscow. But the very fact that I stayed in the West in the first place had such a negative effect on her prospects that when she tried to enter the Moscow Conservatoire – and I have had independent confirmation that she was certainly gifted enough to be accepted – she was told officially and unofficially after two years of trying to get in that she should not bother again; she would never be admitted because of me. In the end she went instead to the Gnesin Institute, another high level music school, primarily concerned with the preparation of music teachers. She was also told that she would never be put forward for any international competitions – all because of me. I am sure that there are many other examples of the sort of discrimination she has suffered as a result of my defection – there have been plenty of hints of this in telephone conversations and in letters I have had from my father and from her, but only if she were finally to leave would we be able to find out in detail exactly what went on.'

It now appears certain that neither Ashkenazy's father nor sister will revive their plans to emigrate. Both have found new partners in their private lives and this raises further problems about how they would eventually get their emigration papers not to mention whether their respective partners would be eligible to accompany them. The prospect of more years of uncertainty, of living almost with suitcases packed, is hardly attractive.

Ashkenazy views this turn of events with mixed feelings; over the years he tried many different and ingenious gambits in his attempts to accelerate the reunification of his family, but the prospect of their arrival in the West was also daunting. He had never known his father sufficiently well to feel confident that a new, very close relationship in the West would succeed, given all the obvious uncertainties about employment and a different way of life. As for his sister, he has had little contact with her except as a child and now that she is a trained pianist and teacher with expectations of a continued career, there would be the heavy responsibility of trying to seek out opportunities that she would find fulfilling.

There has already been, alas, one unhappy example of how far apart members of a family can grow when separated for too long across the iron curtain. With the help of Ashkenazy, an aunt of whom he was and is very fond left Russia with her husband some two years ago. They had the choice of settling in Israel or of going on to America but they viewed both choices with some apprehension, especially since they had no strong contacts or job prospects in either country. The Ashkenazys then suggested as a third possibility that they might settle, at least temporarily, in Iceland where they could live free of charge in the Ashkenazys' house, and where, sheltered by their influential standing and with their financial aid, they could take their time to adjust to the West until the husband could find employment. This last part of the arrangement worked out very well, and the couple decided after a few months to stay permanently in Iceland. Regrettably, relationships with the Ashkenazys on a personal level deteriorated rapidly.

'People in Russia don't know what the basics of life are. They forget that in the end the main things they need to be able to count on are to find a roof over their heads, to be able to eat and sleep properly, and to have a job. In Russia, all this means nothing – somehow it's all provided for by the government. You will have some work, you will live somewhere, you'll never move very far from it but that's the way things are. Whether any of it bears any relation to what you as an individual want or to how you want to live your life is quite another matter, but in Russia you don't really ask such questions – they have no relevance.

'For a newcomer to the West these things are crucial. When my aunt and uncle left Russia, we thought in practical terms about what we could do for them since they had nothing, no resources, no friends. We explained to them the various alternatives – what America is like, also Israel, since we know both countries well. In the end, since we could offer them an empty house in Iceland and were willing to support them financially until the husband could find a job, they chose to go there.

'Later, when we found that they not only neglected our wishes about looking after our house, but even resented the fact that we made any such requests, relations began to get strained. They did not seem to be able to understand that we wanted to try to help them in a practical and realistic manner. Instead, they began to suggest that they had been somehow forced to go to Iceland to suit our purposes, which is both absurd and untrue. But Soviet people are very strange – they tend to think that if you offer them something, there must be a catch in the arrangement and that you are pushing them into something against their will and their best interests. That is how the authorities always treat people in the Soviet Union, of course, and so the scale of values in dealing with people in the West becomes completely distorted. It is very difficult, therefore, for a balanced relationship to be maintained with recent émigrés from the Soviet Union; either they feel that they are being exploited and cheated or, if they think that they have the upper hand, they want to try to do the exploiting themselves.

'In the end it became clear that it would be much better for our relations with my aunt and uncle if they stood on their own feet; and so we asked them to find their own place to live, now that they could afford to do so. I have very warm feelings towards my aunt despite these upsetting incidents, and it seems that our personal relationship could survive once the major source of friction had been removed. After all, I can still remember how difficult it is to adjust to an open society after being brought up in an environment where it becomes second nature to assume that nothing is what it appears or is described to be.

'There is an argument that there were long-established foundations for all of this in Russia, upon which the communists found it easy to build. It is certainly true that throughout their history, the Russians have never really had the experience of personal liberty but have always been under the domination of one type of authority or another. As a result, some of the characteristics which people have described as being typically Russian may have been influenced by an ambivalent attitude to authority; both resenting it and trying to find little ways of evading it so as to mark out a little area of freedom of action, and an almost slavish acceptance of the fact that such limitless despotism, with its paternalistic overtones in Tsarist times (and to an even greater degree under Stalin) effectively removed from the individual any duties as well as any freedoms.

'In the case of the Soviet system, it is altogether more difficult to find these little areas of evasion, of illicit freedoms. Before the Revolution it was much easier – the apparat of control over the population was really very rudimentary. The security services were just a joke compared with those of Soviet times – the Bolsheviks could almost do what they liked. When someone like Lenin or Stalin was sent in exile to Siberia, they could just get on a train and go back to Moscow and then leave for abroad. Now you can't take a step without somebody informing on you and your being stopped almost before you leave your apartment. And the idea of successful escape from a camp or from prison is simply laughable.

'So, this lack of concern for the individual, this atrophied sense of responsibility for one's own life, was always a feature of Russian society. Now, under the communist system, one of the cruellest imaginable, the effects are accelerated and concentrated so that people have, with very rare exceptions, lost the power to decide for themselves. It has effectively suppressed, perhaps even eradicated, an objective moral sense in the mass of the people and replaced it with a view of life based on how to get by, how to jump the queue, how to avoid trouble. Why, therefore, anyone should be an artist, musician or writer is very unclear, except possibly as a means of capitalizing on certain basic talents or skills which may make the most mundane objectives more readily accessible.

'Paradoxically, one could almost say that by now Soviet Man has become what he was designed to be: "the freest on earth", according to the old cliché, because he is free of any duties or responsibilities to himself as an individual. He does not have to decide anything for himself, nor to think for himself except about the most trivial matters. As such, Soviet Man is what he should be; an integrated element in a self-serving system with perpetuated total control over the individual.

'As for me, of course I left Russia when I was only twenty-six, at an age when perhaps the system had not yet become ineradicably part of my body and soul; to shed my Soviet skin may, therefore, have taken some years but at least it did not need to take up the rest of my life. By now I know for sure that my mentality is no longer that of a Soviet; I believe in free will, and know that I should and can shape my own life. Here in the West many people, perhaps even the majority, think the same.

'On the other hand, I see much too often that Soviet émigrés find it very difficult not to remain stuck with their Soviet mentality, attempting somehow to bend the Western way of life to fit in with their procrustean attitudes. This, alas, often leads them into difficulties in their relations with others and can seriously harm their prospects for a satisfying life in the West. I do not blame them, but rather feel a great sense of sympathy for them in their predicament. I try to do what I can to help friends and acquaintances from Russia to recognize their problems in this area and to be aware of their inevitable limitations when they first have to grapple with the responsibility for deciding things for themselves. I try to explain to them how people who have not grown up and reached maturity under the control of a totalitarian system feel and think; I am not often too successful.

'In my own case, it may be that the fact that I now feel increasingly free to reshape my life on rather more flexible lines has something to do with the successful shedding of the last traces of my Soviet skin. Perhaps, unlike many Soviets, I sensed right from the start the need for some sort of personal structure in my life – I think back to my instinctive feeling that Neuhaus was not right for me – and I was fortunate in that my mother never flinched from the task of instilling in me the habit of work and an appreciation of the value of self-discipline. As a result one could almost say that the way that the Soviet system rules one's life combined with the other influences around me were transformed into positive and useful attitudes; in many cases the progressive regimentation of Soviet life simply persuades people to reject or escape from any additional onus of self-discipline.

'Since living in the West, it has certainly been essential for me to maintain a high degree of personal discipline in my work and life. This has always seemed like second nature, and vital if I were to hold to my objectives in building up the quality of my work. It may also be that in the early days after my emigration I needed to find some solid structure in my life to replace what I had left behind; now, after all these years of relentless work, I find that I don't need quite so many props or supports – the structure can still be there to provide the points of reference but the spirit, the imagination can be a little freer to roam.

'As for the future, I have no idea. I shall continue to try to seek out the truth in music and if I succeed in finding a little more time to think about things, maybe I can significantly improve the quality of my music-making. That is certainly the most important objective. It is a very slow process but at least I never feel that I am marking time. I face each performance as another challenge to try to achieve what I have in mind. Inevitably, I may not feel that I am always progressing but a little more elasticity in my life might produce a different sort of spacing in my music-making. I don't think that I ever lose the umbilical cord to Mother Earth but there is a degree to which my life is a little artificial, everything being geared to travelling, going to rehearsals, practising, preparing for concerts. These things are partly just features of modern life, and thousands of people in other walks of life suffer from the tyranny of such things. In my case, I feel that it must be beneficial to have the time to respond to a much wider range of experiences, whether they are mundane, like going for a walk with my children and our dog, or going to the market to buy mushrooms, or elevated through contact with art or books or other people's ideas. Even a few hours without anything specific to do – at the moment this never happens – might at times prove to be of more value than weeks of hectic, concentrated activity as a performer.

'There must be, after all, a connection between truth in music, on the most exalted plane of experience, and truth in everyday things, a true relationship to oneself in one's normal environment. I don't anticipate any dramatic change in my way of life – I'll just see how it works. If things go well, maybe I'll change even more, who knows?'

APPENDIX

VLADIMIR ASHKENAZY

Discography
compiled by John Kehoe

Since 1962, Vladimir Ashkenazy has been an exclusive Decca recording artist. This discography lists both his Decca recordings available at the time of publication and those no longer currently available, as well as the small number of recordings made by agreement for other companies.

In North America, Decca recordings are issued on the London label; both Decca label and London label record numbers are included here.

CD = Compact Disc
LP = 12" stereo long-playing record
MC = Stereo Musicassette
'Digital' means that the CD, LP or MC concerned has been made from an original digital master recording.

BACH (not currently available)
CONCERTO IN D MINOR
London Symphony Orchestra
conducted by David Zinman
Decca SXL 6174 (LP)   KSXC 6174
  (MC)

BARTÓK
PIANO CONCERTO NO 1*
SONATA FOR TWO PIANOS AND
  PERCUSSION**
**London Philharmonic Orchestra*
conducted by Sir Georg Solti
***with Vovka Ashkenazy, piano and*
  David Corkhill and Andrew Smith,
  percussion
Decca 410 108-1 DH (LP)   410
  108-4 DH (MC)
London 410 108-1 LH (LP)   410
  108-4 LH (MC)

BARTÓK
PIANO CONCERTO NO 2
PIANO CONCERTO NO 3
London Philharmonic Orchestra
conducted by Sir Georg Solti
Decca SXL 6937 (LP)   KSXC 6937
  (MC)
London CS 7167 (LP)   CS5 7167
  (MC)

BEETHOVEN
THE FIVE PIANO CONCERTOS
Chicago Symphony Orchestra
conducted by Sir Georg Solti
Decca SXLG 6594 (4 LP set)   K44K
  43 (3 MC set)
London CSA 2404 (4 LP set)   CSA5
  2404 (MC)
Also available separately.

BEETHOVEN
PIANO CONCERTO NO I IN C MAJOR,
OP 15
PIANO SONATA NO 8 IN C MINOR, OP
13 (Pathétique)
Chicago Symphony Orchestra
conducted by Sir Georg Solti
Decca SXL 6651 (LP)   KSXC 6651
(MC)
London CS 6853 (LP)   CS5 6853
(MC)

BEETHOVEN
PIANO CONCERTO NO 2 IN B FLAT
MAJOR, OP 19
PIANO SONATA NO 21 IN C MAJOR, OP
53 (Waldstein)
Chicago Symphony Orchestra
conducted by Sir Georg Solti
Decca SXL 6652 (LP)   KSXC 6652
(MC)
London CS 6854 (LP)   CS5 6854
(MC)

BEETHOVEN
PIANO CONCERTO NO 3 IN C MINOR,
OP 37
PIANO SONATA NO 26 IN E FLAT
MAJOR, OP 81a (Les Adieux)
Chicago Symphony Orchestra
conducted by Sir Georg Solti
Decca SXL 6653 (LP)   KSXC 6653
(MC)
London CS 6855 (LP)   KC5 6855
(MC)

BEETHOVEN
PIANO CONCERTO NO 4 IN G MAJOR,
OP 58
OVERTURE LEONORA NO 3, OP 72b
Chicago Symphony Orchestra
conducted by Sir Georg Solti
Decca SXL 6654 (LP)   KSXC 6654
(MC)
London CS 6856 (LP) CS5 6856
(MC)

BEETHOVEN
PIANO CONCERTO NO 5 IN E FLAT
MAJOR (Emperor)
OVERTURE EGMONT, OP 84
Chicago Symphony Orchestra
conducted by Sir Georg Solti
Decca SXL 6655 (LP)   KSXC 6655
(MC)
London CS 6857 (LP)   CS5 6857
(MC)

BEETHOVEN
THE THIRTY-TWO PIANO SONATAS
Decca D258D 12 (12 LP set)
London CS 7223 (12 LP set)
Also available separately.

BEETHOVEN
THE TEN VIOLIN SONATAS
Itzhak Perlman, violin
Decca D92D 5 (5 LP set)   K92K 53
(3 MC set)
London OSA 2501 (5 LP set)   OSA5
2501 (MC)
Also available separately.

BEETHOVEN
PIANO TRIO NO 7 IN B FLAT MAJOR,
OP 97
PIANO TRIO NO 9 IN E FLAT MAJOR,
WO 039 (1812)
Vladimir Ashkenazy, piano, Itzhak
Perlman, violin, Lynn Harrell,
cello
EMI ASD 4315 (LP) (MC)
Angel DS-37818 (LP) (MC)

BEETHOVEN
QUINTET IN E FLAT MAJOR FOR PIANO
& WINDS, OP 16

MOZART
QUINTET FOR PIANO AND WINDS,
K452
The London Wind Soloists
Decca SXL 6252 (LP)
London CS 6464

BEETHOVEN
SYMPHONY NO 5 IN C MINOR, OP 67
OVERTURE LEONORA NO 3
Philharmonia Orchestra
conducted by Vladimir Ashkenazy
Decca Digital SXDL 7540
   (LP)   KSXDC 7540 (MC)   400
060-2 DH (CD)
London Digital LDR 71040
   (LP)   LDR5 71040 (MC)

BEETHOVEN
SYMPHONY NO 6 IN F MAJOR, OP 68
Philharmonia Orchestra
conducted by Vladimir Ashkenazy
Decca Digital SXDL 7578
   (LP)   KSXDC 7578 (MC)   410
003-2 DH (CD)
London Digital LDR 71078
   (LP)   LDR5 71078 (MC)

BRAHMS
PIANO CONCERTO NO 1 IN D MINOR,
  OP 15
Concertgebouw Orchestra,
  Amsterdam
conducted by Bernard Haitink
Decca Digital SXDL 7552
   (LP)   KSXDC 7552 (MC)
410 009-2DH(CD)
London Digital LDR 71052
   (LP)   LDR5 71052 (MC)

BRAHMS
PIANO CONCERTO NO 2 IN B FLAT
  MAJOR, OP 83
Vienna Philharmonic Orchestra
conducted by Bernard Haitink
Decca Digital 410 199-1 DH
   (LP)   410 199-4 DH (MC)   410
199-2 DH (CD)
London Digital 410 199-1 LH
   (LP)   410 199-4 LH (MC)   410
199-2 LH (CD)

BRAHMS
PIANO CONCERTO NO 2 IN B FLAT
  MAJOR, OP 83
London Symphony Orchestra

conducted by Zubin Mehta
Decca SXL 6309 (LP)
London CS 6539 (LP)

BRAHMS (not currently available)
CONCERTO NO 2 IN B FLAT MAJOR,
  OP 38
Berlin State Opera Orchestra
conducted by Leopold Ludwig
EMI 33CX 1637 (LP)

BRAHMS
CELLO SONATA NO 1 IN E MINOR,
  OP 38
CELLO SONATA NO 2 IN F MAJOR,
  OP 99
with Lynn Harrell, cello
Decca SXL 6979 (LP)   KSXC 6979
(MC)

CHOPIN
PIANO WORKS VOLUME I
ETUDES, OP 10; ETUDES, OP 25
Decca SXL 6710 (LP)   KSXC 6710
(MC)
London CS 6844 (LP)   CS5 6844
(MC)

CHOPIN
PIANO WORKS VOLUME II
WALTZES — NO 6 IN D FLAT MAJOR,
  OP 64/1; NO 7 IN C SHARP MINOR,
  OP 64/2; NO 8 IN A FLAT MAJOR, OP
  64/3; MAZURKAS — NO 39 IN B
  MAJOR, OP 63/1; NO 40 IN F
  MINOR, OP 63/2; NO 41 IN C SHARP
  MINOR, OP 63/3; POLONAISE NO 7
  IN A FLAT MAJOR, OP 61
  'POLONAISE FANTAISIE';
  MAZURKAS — NO 43 IN G MINOR,
  OP 67/2; NO 45 IN A MINOR, OP
  67/4 ; NO 49 IN F MINOR, OP 68/4;
  NOCTURNES — NO 17 IN B MAJOR,
  OP 61/2; NO 18 IN E MAJOR, OP
  62/2; BARCAROLLE IN F SHARP
  MAJOR, OP 60
Decca SXL 6801 (LP)   KSXC 6801
(MC)
London CS 7022 (LP)   CS5 7022
(MC)

CHOPIN

PIANO WORKS VOLUME III
SONATA NO 3 IN B MINOR, OP 58;
BERCEUSE IN D FLAT MAJOR, OP
57; MAZURKAS — NO 36 IN A
MINOR, OP 59/1; NO 37 IN A FLAT
MAJOR, OP 59/2; NO 38 IN F SHARP
MINOR, OP 59/3; NOCTURNES — NO
15 IN F MINOR, OP 55/1; NO 16 IN
E FLAT MAJOR, OP 55/2
Decca SXL 6810 (LP)   KSXC 6810
(MC)
London CS 7030 (LP)   CS5 7030
(MC)

CHOPIN

PIANO WORKS VOLUME V
FANTASIE IN F MINOR, OP 49;
NOCTURNES — NO 13 IN C MINOR,
OP 48/1; NO 14 IN F SHARP MINOR,
OP 48/2; BALLADE IN A FLAT
MAJOR, OP 47; MAZURKAS — NO 51
IN A MINOR 'à Emil Galliard'; NO
30 IN G MAJOR, OP 50/1; NO 31 IN
A FLAT MAJOR, OP 50/2; NO 32 IN F
SHARP MINOR, OP 50/3;
TARANTELLE, OP 43; PRELUDE IN C
SHARP MINOR, OP 45
Decca SXL 6922 (LP)   KSXC 6922
(MC)
London CS 7150 (LP)   CS5 7150
(MC)

CHOPIN

PIANO WORKS VOLUME VI
IMPROMPTU OP 36; WALTZ OP 42;
POLONAISE OP 44; NOCTURNES OP
37, NOS 1, 2; ALLEGRO DE
CONCERT, OP 46; MAZURKA IN A
MINOR; SOSTENUTO IN E FLAT
MAJOR; TROIS NOUVELLES ETUDES:
NOS 1, 2, 3
Decca Digital SXDL 7593
(LP)   KSXDC 7593 (MC)
London Digital LDR 71093
(LP)   LDR5 70193 (MC)

CHOPIN

PIANO WORKS VOLUME VII
SONATA NO 2 IN B FLAT MINOR, OP 35
(Funeral March); SCHERZO NO 3 IN
C SHARP MINOR, OP 39; MAZURKAS
OP 41, NOS 1, 2, 3, 4; POLONAISES
OP 40, NOS 1, 2
Decca SXL 6995 (LP)   KSXC 6995
(MC)
London CS 7235 (LP)   CS5 7235
(MC)

CHOPIN

PIANO WORKS VOLUME VIII
IMPROMPTU IN A FLAT MAJOR, OP 29;
MAZURKAS OP 30, NOS 1, 2, 3; OP
33, NOS 1, 2, 3, 4; SCHERZO IN B
FLAT MINOR, OP 31; LARGO IN E
FLAT MAJOR; NOCTURNES OP 32,
NOS 1, 5; NOCTURNE IN C MINOR;
GRANDE VALSE BRILLANTE IN F, OP
34 NO 3; VARIATIONS IN E
(Hexameron)
Decca Digital 410 122-1 DH
(LP)   410 122-4 DH (MC)
London Digital 410 122-1 LH
(LP)   410 122-4 LH (MC)

CHOPIN

PIANO WORKS VOLUME IX
BALLADE NO 2 IN F MAJOR, OP 38;
WALTZ IN A FLAT MAJOR, OP 34/1;
TWENTY-FOUR PRELUDES, OP 28
Decca SXL 6877 (LP)   KSXC 6877
(MC)
London CS 7101 (LP)   CS5 7101
(MC)

CHOPIN

PIANO WORKS VOLUME XIII
MAZURKAS OP 68, NOS 1, 3;
MAZURKA IN D MAJOR; WALTZES
OP 69/2; OP 70/3; WALTZ IN E
MAJOR (Posth); WALTZ IN E MINOR
(Posth); POLONAISES OP 71/3*;
POLONAISE IN G FLAT MAJOR
(Posth); NOCTURNE IN C MINOR;
NOCTURNES OP 9 NOS 1, 2, 3;
SOUVENIR DE PAGANINI;
VARIATIONS IN D MAJOR FOR

PIANO DUET*
*with Vovka Ashkenazy, piano
Decca Digital SXDL 7584
(LP)   KSXDC 7584 (MC)
London Digital LDR 71084
(LP)   LDR5 71084 (MC)

CHOPIN
PIANO WORKS VOLUME XIV
SONATA NO 1 IN C MINOR, OP 4;
MAZURKA IN A MINOR, OP 68/2;
NOCTURNE IN E MINOR, OP 72/1;
POLONAISE IN B FLAT MAJOR, OP
71/2; FUNERAL MARCH IN C
MINOR, OP 72/2; CONTREDANSE;
MAZURKA IN B FLAT MAJOR;
MAZURKA IN G MAJOR; WALTZ IN G
MAJOR; WALTZ IN E FLAT MAJOR;
WALTZ IN A FLAT MAJOR; RONDO
IN C MAJOR
Decca SXL 6911 (LP)   KSXC 6911
(MC)
London CS 7135 (LP)   CS5 7135
(MC)

CHOPIN
PIANO WORKS VOLUME XV
INTRODUCTION AND VARIATIONS ON
A GERMAN NATIONAL AIR, 'The
Swiss Boy', OP POSTH: POLONAISES
OP 71/1, NO 11 IN G MINOR
(POSTH), NO 13 IN A FLAT MAJOR
(POSTH), NO 12 IN B FLAT MAJOR,
NO 14 IN G SHARP MINOR, NO 15 IN
B FLAT MINOR; RONDO IN C MINOR
OP 1; 3 ECOSSAISES OP 72/3;
RONDO A LA MAZUR, OP 5
Decca SXL 6981 (LP)   KSXC 6981
(MC)
London CS 7210 (LP)   CS5 7210
(MC)

CHOPIN
PRELUDE IN C SHARP MINOR, OP 45;
SCHERZO NO 1 IN B MINOR, OP 20;
SCHERZO NO 2 IN B FLAT MINOR,
OP 31; SCHERZO NO 3 IN C SHARP
MINOR, OP 39; SCHERZO NO 4 IN E
MAJOR, OP 54; BARCAROLLE IN F
SHARP MINOR, OP 60

Decca SXL 6334 (LP)
London CS 6562 (LP)

CHOPIN
BALLADES – NO 1 IN G MINOR, OP 23;
NO 2 IN F MAJOR, OP 38; NO 3 IN A
FLAT MAJOR, OP 47; NO 4 IN F
MINOR, OP 52; TROIS NOUVELLES
ETUDES, OP POSTH – NO 1 IN F
MINOR; NO 2 IN D FLAT MAJOR; NO
3 IN A FLAT
Decca SXL 6143 (LP)   KSXC 6143
(MC)
London CS 6422 (LP)   CS5 6422
(MC)

CHOPIN
SONATA NO 2 IN B FLAT MINOR, OP
35; NOCTURNE IN F MAJOR, OP
15/1; NOCTURNE IN F SHARP
MAJOR, OP 15/2; MAZURKA IN A
FLAT, OP 59/2; GRANDE VALSE
BRILLANTE IN E FLAT, OP 18
Decca SXL 6575 (LP)
London CS 6794 (LP)   CS5 6794
(MC)

CHOPIN
PIANO CONCERTO NO 2 IN F MINOR,
OP 21*; BALLADE NO 3 IN A FLAT,
OP 47; NOCTURNE NO 17 IN B
MAJOR, OP 62/1; SCHERZO NO 3 IN
C SHARP MINOR, OP 39;
BARCAROLLE IN F SHARP MINOR,
OP 60
*London Symphony Orchestra
conducted by David Zinman
Decca SXL 6693 (LP)
London CS 6889 (LP)

CHOPIN (not currently available)
PIANO CONCERTO NO 2 IN F MINOR,
OP 21*; BALLADE NO 2 IN F
MAJOR, OP 38; ETUDE NO 1 IN C
MAJOR, OP 10/1; ETUDE NO 15 IN F
MAJOR, OP 25/3; MAZURKA NO 29
IN A FLAT MAJOR, OP 41/4;
MAZURKA OP 21 IN C SHARP
MINOR, OP 30/4; SCHERZO NO 4 IN
E MAJOR, OP 54

CHOPIN – *continued*
Warsaw Philharmonic Orchestra
conducted by Zdzislaw Gorzynski
EMI 33CX 1563 (LP)

CHOPIN (not currently available)
SONATA NO 3 IN B MINOR, OP 58
BARCAROLLE, OP 60; WALTZ NO 2 IN
    A FLAT MAJOR, OP 34/1; WALTZ NO
    6 IN D FLAT MAJOR, OP 64/1;
    MAZURKA NO 35 IN C MINOR, OP
    56/3; MAZURKA NO 36 IN A MINOR,
    OP 59/1
EMI 33CX 1621

CHOPIN
ETUDES, OP 10 and 25
Melodiya D 6035/6/7/8

DVOŘÁK
CELLO CONCERTO IN B MINOR, OP
    104

BRUCH
KOL NIDREI, OP 47
Lynn Harrell, cello
Philharmonia Orchestra
conducted by Vladimir Ashkenazy
Decca Digital SXDL 7608
    (LP)   KSXDC 7608 (MC)   410
    144-2 DH (CD)
London Digital LDR 71108
    (LP)   LDR5 71108 (MC)

GRIEG
PIANO CONCERTO IN A MINOR, OP 16
FRANCK
SYMPHONIC VARIATIONS FOR PIANO
    AND ORCHESTRA
LES DJINNS – SYMPHONIC POEM FOR
    PIANO AND ORCHESTRA
Cristina Ortiz, piano
Philharmonia Orchestra
conducted by Vladimir Ashkenazy
EMI ASD 3960 (LP)   (MC) TASD
    3960

MOZART
PIANO CONCERTO NO 6 IN B FLAT
    MAJOR, K238
PIANO CONCERTO NO 20 IN D MINOR,
    K466
London Symphony Orchestra
conducted by Hans
    Schmidt-Isserstedt
Decca SXL 6353 (LP)   KSXC 6353
    (MC)
London CS 6579 (LP)   CS5 6579
    (MC)

MOZART
PIANO CONCERTO NO 8 IN C MAJOR,
    K246
PIANO CONCERTO NO 9 IN E FLAT
    MAJOR, K271
RONDO IN A MAJOR, K386
London Symphony Orchestra
conducted by István Kertesz
Decca SXL 6259 (LP)   KSXC 6259
    (MC)
London CS 6501 (LP)   CS5 6501
    (MC)

MOZART
PIANO CONCERTO NO 12 IN A MAJOR,
    K414
PIANO CONCERTO NO 13 IN C MAJOR,
    K415
Philharmonia Orchestra
Vladimir Ashkenazy, soloist and
    conductor
Decca Digital SXDL 7556
    (LP)   KSXDC 7556 (MC)
London Digital LDR 71056
    (LP)   LDR5 71056 (MC)

MOZART
PIANO CONCERTO NO 15 IN B FLAT,
    K450
PIANO CONCERTO NO 16 IN D MAJOR,
    K451
Philharmonia Orchestra
Vladimir Ashkenazy, soloist and
    conductor
Decca SXL 7010 (LP)   KSXC 7010
    (MC)
London CS 7254 (LP)   CS5 7254
    (MC)

MOZART

PIANO CONCERTO NO 17 IN G MAJOR, K453
PIANO CONCERTO NO 21 IN C MAJOR, K467
Philharmonia Orchestra
Vladimir Ashkenazy, soloist and conductor
Decca SXL 6881 (LP)   KSXC 6881 (MC)
London CS 7104 (LP)   CS5 7104 (MC)

MOZART

PIANO CONCERTO NO 19 IN F MAJOR, K459
PIANO CONCERTO NO 24 IN C MINOR, K491
Philharmonia Orchestra
Vladimir Ashkenazy, soloist and conductor
Decca SXL 6947 (LP)   KSXC 6947 (MC)
London CS 7174 (LP)   CS5 7174 (MC)

MOZART

PIANO CONCERTO NO 22 IN E FLAT MAJOR, K482
CONCERT RONDO IN D MAJOR, K382
Philharmonia Orchestra
Vladimir Ashkenazy, soloist and conductor
Decca SXL 6982 (LP)   KSXC 6982 (MC)
London CS 7211 (LP)   CS5 7211 (MC)

MOZART

PIANO CONCERTO NO 23 IN A MAJOR, K488
PIANO CONCERTO NO 27 IN B FLAT MAJOR, K595
Philharmonia Orchestra
Vladimir Ashkenazy, soloist and conductor
Decca Digital SXDL 7530

(LP)   KSXDC 7530 (MC)
London Digital LDR 71007
(LP)   LDR5 71007 (MC)

MOZART

CONCERTO FOR 2 PIANOS AND ORCHESTRA, K365
CONCERTO FOR 3 PIANOS AND ORCHESTRA, K242*
*with Daniel Barenboim and *Fou Ts'ong*
English Chamber Orchestra
conducted by Daniel Barenboim
Decca SXL 6716 (LP)
London CS 6937 (LP)

MOZART

PIANO SONATA IN A MINOR, K310
PIANO SONATA IN D MAJOR, K576
RONDO IN A MINOR, K511
Decca SXL 6439 (LP)
London CS 6659 (LP)

MUSSORGSKY

PICTURES AT AN EXHIBITION
   (original solo piano version)
TANEYEV
PRELUDE AND FUGUE IN G SHARP MINOR
LIADOV
THE MUSICAL SNUFF-BOX, OP 32
BORODIN
SCHERZO IN A FLAT MAJOR
TCHAIKOVSKY
DUMKA, OP 59
Decca Digital SXDL 7624
   (LP)   KSXDC 7624 (MC)
London Digital LDR 71124
   (LP)   LDR5 71124 (MC)

MUSSORGSKY

PICTURES AT AN EXHIBITION
   (orchestrated by Ashkenazy)
BORODIN
POLOVTSIAN DANCES
Philharmonia Orchestra
conducted by Vladimir Ashkenazy

Decca Digital 410 121-1 DH
(LP)   410 121-4 DH (MC)
London Digital 410 121-1 LH
(LP)   410 121-4 LH (MC)

MUSSORGSKY
PICTURES AT AN EXHIBITION
(orchestrated by Ravel)*
PICTURES AT AN EXHIBITION
(original solo piano version)
*Los Angeles Philharmonic
Orchestra
conducted by Zubin Mehta
Decca SXL 6328 (LP)
London CS 6559 (LP)   CS5 6559
(MC)

MUSSORGSKY
THE NURSERY – Song Cycle
PROKOFIEV
THE UGLY DUCKLING, OP 18
GRECHANINOV
THE LANE, OP 89
Elisabeth Söderström, soprano
Decca SXL 6900 (LP)
London OS 26579 (LP)

PROKOFIEV
THE FIVE PIANO CONCERTOS
SYMPHONY NO 1 IN D MAJOR, OP 25
(Classical)*
AUTUMNAL, OP 8*
OVERTURE ON HEBREW THEMES**
**with Keith Puddy, clarinet,
Gabrieli String Quartet
London Symphony Orchestra
conducted by André Previn and
*Vladimir Ashkenazy
Decca 15BB 218 (3 LP set)
London CSA 2314 (3 LP set)   CSA5
2314 (3 MC set)
Also available separately.

PROKOFIEV
CINDERELLA, OP 87 (complete ballet)
Cleveland Orchestra
conducted by Vladimir Ashkenazy
Decca Digital 410 162-1 DH2 (2 LP
set)   410 162-4 DH2 (2 MC set)
London Digital 410 162-1 LH2 (2 LP
set)   410 162-4 LH2 (2 MC set)

PROKOFIEV
SONATA FOR VIOLIN AND PIANO NO 1
IN F MINOR, OP 80
SONATA NO 2 IN D MAJOR, OP 94A
Itzhak Perlman, violin
RCA VICS 2008 (LP)   VK 2008 (MC)

PROKOFIEV
THE UGLY DUCKLING, OP 18
See under Mussorgsky: The Nursery

RACHMANINOV
SYMPHONY NO 1 IN D MINOR, OP 13
Concertgebouw Orchestra,
Amsterdam
conducted by Vladimir Ashkenazy
Decca Digital SXDL 7603
(LP)   KSXDC 7603 (MC)
London Digital LDR 71103
(LP)   LDR5 71103 (MC)

RACHMANINOV
SYMPHONY NO 2 IN E MINOR, OP 27
Concertgebouw Orchestra,
Amsterdam
conducted by Vladimir Ashkenazy
Decca Digital SXDL 7563
(LP)   KSXDC 7563 (MC)
London Digital LDR 71063
(LP)   LDR5 71063 (MC)

RACHMANINOV
SYMPHONY NO 3 IN A MINOR, OP 44
YOUTH SYMPHONY
Concertgebouw Orchestra,
Amsterdam
conducted by Vladimir Ashkenazy
Decca Digital SXDL 7531
(LP)   KSXDC 7531 (MC)   410
231-2 DH (CD)
London Digital LDR 71031
(LP)   LDR5 71031 (MC)

RACHMANINOV
THE FOUR PIANO CONCERTOS
RHAPSODY ON A THEME OF PAGANINI
London Symphony Orchestra
conducted by André Previn
Decca SXLF 6565 (3 LP set)   K43K

33 (3 MC set)
London CSA 2311 (3 LP set)
Also available separately.

RACHMANINOV
PIANO CONCERTO NO 2 IN C MINOR,
OP 18
ETUDES-TABLEAUX, OP 39 NOS 1, 2, 5
Moscow Philharmonic Orchestra
conducted by Kiril Kondrashin
Decca JB 52 (LP)   KJBC 52 (MC)

RACHMANINOV
PIANO CONCERTO NO 3 IN D MINOR,
OP 30
London Symphony Orchestra
conducted by Anatole Fistoulari
Decca JB 53 (LP)   KJBC 53 (MC)

RACHMANINOV
PIANO CONCERTO NO 3 IN D MINOR,
OP 30
Philadelphia Orchestra
conducted by Eugene Ormandy
RCA ARL1 1324

RACHMANINOV
PIANO SONATA NO 2 IN B FLAT
MAJOR, OP 36 (original version)
ETUDES-TABLEAUX, OP 33
Decca SXL 6996 (LP)   KSXC 6996
(MC)
London CS 7236 (LP)   CS5 7236
(MC)

RACHMANINOV
ETUDES-TABLEAUX, OP 39, NOS 1, 2,
3–9
VARIATIONS ON A THEME BY CORELLI,
OP 42
Decca SXL 6604 (LP)
London CS 6822 (LP)

RACHMANINOV
PRELUDES, OP 3 NO 2; OP 23, NOS
1–10; OP 32, NOS 1–13
Decca 5BB 221 (2 LP set)   KSXC2

7038 (2 MC set)
London CSA 2241 (2 LP set)   CSA5
2241 (2 MC set)

RACHMANINOV
SYMPHONIC DANCES (orchestral
version)
FROM THE ISLE OF THE DEAD
Concertgebouw Orchestra,
Amsterdam
conducted by Vladimir Ashkenazy
Decca Digital 410 124-1 (LP)   410
124-4 (MC)
London Digital 410 124-1 (LP)   410
124-4 (MC)

RACHMANINOV
SYMPHONIC DANCES, OP 45 (2 piano
version)
RUSSIAN RHAPSODY
with André Previn, piano
Decca SXL 6926 (LP)   KSXC 6926
(MC)
London CS 7159 (LP)

RACHMANINOV
SUITE NO 1, OP 5 (Fantaisie)
SUITE NO 2, OP 17
with André Previn, piano
Decca SXL 6697 (LP)
London CS 6893 (LP)   CS5 6893
(MC)

RACHMANINOV
SONGS VOLUME I (sung in Russian)
with Elisabeth Söderström, soprano
Decca SXL 6718 (LP)
London OS 26428 (LP)

**RACHMANINOV (not currently
available)**
SONGS VOLUME II (sung in Russian)
Elisabeth Söderström, soprano
Decca SXL 6772 (LP)

**RACHMANINOV (not currently
available)**
SONGS VOLUME III (sung in Russian)
Elisabeth Söderström, soprano
Decca SXL 6832 (LP)

RACHMANINOV
SONGS VOLUME IV (sung in Russian)
*with Elisabeth Söderström, soprano
and John Shirley-Quirk, baritone*
Decca SXL 6869 (LP)
London OS 26559 (LP)

RACHMANINOV
SONGS VOLUME V (sung in Russian)
with Elisabeth Söderström, soprano
Decca SXL 6940 (LP)
London OS 26615 (LP)

SCHOENBERG
VERKLÄRTE NACHT, OP 4
WAGNER
SIEGFRIED IDYLL
*English Chamber Orchestra
conducted by Vladimir Ashkenazy*
Decca Digital 410 111-1 DH
(LP)   410 111-4 DH (MC)   410
111-2 DH (CD)
London Digital 410 111-1 LH
(LP)   410 111-4 LH (MC)

SCHUBERT
SONATA IN G MAJOR, D894
Decca SXL 6602 (LP)
London CS 6820 (LP)

SCHUMANN
PIANO CONCERTO IN A MINOR, OP 54
INTRODUCTION AND ALLEGRO
    APPASSIONATA IN D MINOR, OP
    134*
*London Symphony Orchestra
conducted by Uri Segal and
Vladimir Ashkenazy
Decca SXL 6861 (LP)   KSXC 6861
(MC)
London CS 7082 (LP)

SCHUMANN
FANTASIA IN C MAJOR, OP 17
ETUDES SYMPHONIQUES, OP 13
Decca SXL 6214 (LP)
London CS 6471 (LP)

SCHUMANN
KREISLERIANA, OP 16
HUMORESKE, OP 20
Decca SXL 6642 (LP)
London CS 6859 (LP)

SCRIABIN
PIANO CONCERTO IN F SHARP MINOR,
    OP 20
PROMETHEUS — THE POEM OF FIRE,
    OP 60*
*The Ambrosian Singers
London Philharmonic Orchestra
conducted by Lorin Maazel*
Decca SXL 6527 (LP)   KSXC 6527
(MC)
London CS 6732 (LP)   CS5 6732
(MC)

SCRIABIN
SONATA NO 2 IN G SHARP MINOR, OP
    19 (Sonata Fantasy)
SONATA NO 7 IN F SHARP MAJOR, OP
    64 (White Mass)
SONATA NO 10 IN C MAJOR, OP 70
QUATRE MORCEAUX, OP 56
DEUX POÈMES, OP 32
2 DANCES, OP 73
Decca SXL 6868 (LP)
London CS 7087 (LP)   CS5 7087
(MC)

SCRIABIN
PIANO SONATA NO 3 IN F SHARP
    MINOR, OP 23
PIANO SONATA NO 4 IN F SHARP
    MAJOR, OP 30
PIANO SONATA NO 5 IN F SHARP
    MAJOR, OP 53
PIANO SONATA NO 9 IN F MAJOR, OP
    68 (Black Mass)
Decca SXL 6705 (LP)
London CS 6920 (LP)   CS5 6920
(MC)

SIBELIUS
SYMPHONY NO 2 IN D MAJOR, OP 43
*Philharmonia Orchestra
conducted by Vladimir Ashkenazy*
Decca Digital SXDL 7513

(LP)   KSXDC 7513 (MC)   410
206-2 DH (CD)
London Digital LDR 10014 (LP)

SIBELIUS
SYMPHONY NO 4 IN A MINOR, OP 63
FINLANDIA, OP 26
LUONNOTAR, OP 70*
*with Elisabeth Söderström, soprano
Philharmonia Orchestra
conducted by Vladimir Ashkenazy
Decca Digital SXDL 7517
(LP)   KSXDC 7517 (MC)
London Digital LDR 71019 (LP)

SIBELIUS
SYMPHONY NO 5 IN E FLAT MAJOR,
OP 82
EN SAGA, OP 9
Philharmonia Orchestra
conducted by Vladimir Ashkenazy
Decca Digital SXDL 7541
(LP)   KSXDC 7541 (MC)
London Digital LDR 71041

SIBELIUS
SYMPHONY NO 7 IN C MAJOR, OP 105
TAPIOLA, OP 112
Philharmonia Orchestra
conducted by Vladimir Ashkenazy
Decca Digital SXDL 7580
(LP)   KSXDC 7580 (MC)
London Digital LDR 71080
(LP)   LDR5 71080 (MC)

SIBELIUS
VIOLIN CONCERTO IN D MINOR,
OP 47
2 SERIOUS MELODIES, OP 77
2 SERENADES, OP 69
Boris Belkin, violin
Philharmonia Orchestra
conducted by Vladimir Ashkenazy
Decca SXL 6953 (LP)   KSXC 6953
(MC)
London CS 7181 (LP)

TCHAIKOVSKY
SYMPHONY NO 4 IN F MINOR, OP 36
SYMPHONY NO 5 IN E MINOR, OP 64

SYMPHONY NO 6 IN B MINOR, OP 74
(Pathétique)
MANFRED SYMPHONY, OP 58*
Philharmonia Orchestra
*New Philharmonia Orchestra
conducted by Vladimir Ashkenazy
Decca D249D 4 (4 LP set)
Also available separately.

TCHAIKOVSKY
PIANO CONCERTO NO 1 IN B FLAT
MINOR, OP 23
MUSSORGSKY
PICTURES AT AN EXHIBITION
(original solo piano version)
London Symphony Orchestra
conducted by Lorin Maazel
Decca SXL 6840 (LP)   KSXC 6840
(MC)

TCHAIKOVSKY
PIANO CONCERTO NO 1 IN B FLAT
MINOR, OP 23
USSR State Symphony Orchestra
conducted by Konstantin Ivanov
Melodiya D 10005/6

TCHAIKOVSKY
PIANO TRIO IN A MINOR, OP 50
with Itzhak Perlman, violin and
Lynn Harrell, cello
EMI ASD 4036 (LP)   TSD 4036
(MC)

TCHAIKOVSKY
VIOLIN CONCERTO IN D, OP 35
WALTZ SCHERZO, OP 34
New Philharmonia Orchestra
conducted by Vladimir Ashkenazy
Soloist Boris Belkin
Decca SXL 6854 (LP)

TCHAIKOVSKY
PIANO TRIO IN A MINOR, OP 50
with Itzhak Perlman, violin and
Lynn Harrell, cello
EMI ASD 4036 (LP)

231

TCHAIKOVSKY
SONGS, VOLUME I (sung in Russian)
Elisabeth Söderström, soprano
Decca SXL 6972 (LP)
London OS 26653 (LP)

TCHAIKOVSKY
SONGS, VOLUME II (sung in Russian)
Elisabeth Söderström, soprano
Decca Digital SXDL 7606 (LP)
London Digital LDR 71106 (LP)

VILLA-LOBOS
BACHIANAS BRASILEIRAS NO 3
MÔMO PRECÓCE – FANTASY FOR
  PIANO AND ORCHESTRA
Cristina Ortiz, piano
New Philharmonia Orchestra
conducted by Vladimir Ashkenazy
EMI ASD 3429 (LP)

COLLECTIONS AND RECITALS

BEETHOVEN
PIANO CONCERTO NO 5 (Emperor)
Chicago Symphony Orchestra
  conducted by Sir Georg
  Solti
CHOPIN
PIANO CONCERTO NO 2
London Symphony Orchestra
  conducted by David Zinman
RACHMANINOV
PIANO CONCERTO NO 2
London Symphony Orchestra
  conducted by André Previn
SCHUMANN
PIANO CONCERTO
London Symphony Orchestra
  conducted by Uri Segal
Decca D271D 3 (3 LP set)   K271K
  33 (3 MC set)
London CSP 12 (3 LP set)   CSP5 12
  (3 MC set)

FRANCK
SONATA IN A MAJOR FOR VIOLIN AND
  PIANO
BRAHMS
TRIO IN E FLAT FOR VIOLIN, HORN
  AND PIANO, OP 40
Itzhak Perlman, violin; Barry
  Tuckwell, horn
Decca SXL 6408 (LP)   KSXC 6408
  (MC)
London CS 6628 (LP)

CHOPIN
SCHERZO NO 4 IN E MAJOR, OP 54
NOCTURNE NO 17 IN B MAJOR, OP
  62/1
DEBUSSY
L'ISLE JOYEUSE
RAVEL
GASPARD DE LA NUIT
Decca SXL 6215 (LP)
London CS 6472 (LP)

BEETHOVEN
SONATA FOR HORN AND PIANO IN F
  MAJOR, OP 17
SCHUMANN
ADAGIO AND ALLEGRO FOR HORN
  AND PIANO IN A FLAT MAJOR,
  OP 70
DANZI
SONATA FOR HORN AND PIANO IN E
  FLAT MAJOR, OP 28
SAINT-SAENS
ROMANCE FOR HORN AND PIANO,
  OP 67
Barry Tuckwell, horn
Decca SXL 6717 (LP)
London CS 6938 (LP)

MOZART (not currently available)
SONATA FOR TWO PIANOS IN D, K448
SCHUMANN
ANDANTE AND VARIATIONS FOR TWO
  PIANOS*, TWO CELLOS AND HORN

SCHUMANN (arr. Debussy)
ETUDE IN THE FORM OF A CANON, OP
56, NO 4
with Malcolm Frager, piano and
*Amaryllis Fleming, Terence Weil,
cellos, and Barry Tuckwell, horn
Decca SXL 6130 (LP)

RACHMANINOV (not currently
available)
VARIATIONS ON A THEME OF
CORELLI, OP 42
LISZT
MEPHISTO WALTZ
FEUX FOLLETS

PROKOFIEV
SONATA NO 7 IN B FLAT MAJOR,
OP 83
EMI 33 CX 1813

BARTOK
SONATA FOR TWO PIANOS AND
PERCUSSION
SCHUMANN
ANDANTE AND VARIATIONS*
with Malcolm Frager, piano,
*Shakhovskaya and Natalya
Gutman, cellos, Boris Afanassiev,
horn
Melodiya D 12631/2

FUTURE RECORDINGS

The following works are among the recordings which Vladimir Ashkenazy had in preparation at the time of publication.

BEETHOVEN
THE FIVE PIANO CONCERTOS
Wiener Philharmoniker
conducted by Zubin Mehta
Decca

BEETHOVEN
SYMPHONY NO 7
EGMONT OVERTURE
CORIOLAN OVERTURE
Philharmonia Orchestra
conducted by Vladimir Ashkenazy
Decca

BEETHOVEN
THE PIANO TRIOS (COMPLETE)
with Vladimir Ashkenazy, Itzhak
Perlman, violin, and Lynn
Harrell, cello
EMI

BRAHMS
THE SONATAS FOR VIOLIN AND PIANO
with Itzhak Perlman, violin
EMI

CHOPIN
PIANO WORKS (completion of series)
Decca

MOZART
PIANO CONCERTOS (continuation of
series)

Philharmonia Orchestra
Vladimir Ashkenazy, soloist and
conductor
Decca

RAVEL
GASPARD DE LA NUIT
PAVANE POUR UNE INFANTE DEFUNTE
VALSES NOBLES ET SENTIMENTALES
Decca

SCRIABIN
SONATAS NOS 1, 6, 8
Decca

SHOSTAKOVICH
PIANO QUINTET
Fitzwilliam String Quartet
Decca

SIBELIUS
SYMPHONIES (completion of cycle)
Philharmonia Orchestra
conducted by Vladimir Ashkenazy
Decca

STRAUSS
EIN HELDENLEBEN
Cleveland Orchestra
conducted by Vladimir Ashkenazy
Decca

INDEX

237